Memoirs of an
American Prima Donna

Da Capo Press Music Reprint Series

MUSIC EDITOR

BEA FRIEDLAND
Ph.D., City University of New York

This title was recommended for Da Capo reprint by

Dr. Léonie Rosenstiel
Associate Producer
Caribbean Network System

Memoirs of an American Prima Donna

By

Clara Louise Kellogg
(Mme. Strakosch)

DA CAPO PRESS • NEW YORK • 1978

Library of Congress Cataloging in Publication Data

Kellogg, Clara Louise, 1842-1916.
    Memoirs of an American prima donna.

    (Da Capo Press music reprint series)
    Reprint of the 1913 ed. published by Putnam, New York.
    1. Kellogg, Clara Louise, 1842-1916. 2. Singers—
United States—Biography. I. Title.
ML420.K27A3 1978   782.1'092'4 [B]   77-16534
ISBN 0-306-77527-1

This Da Capo Press edition of *Memoirs of an American Prima Donna*
is an unabridged republication of the first edition
published in New York and London in 1913.

Published by Da Capo Press, Inc.
A Subsidiary of Plenum Publishing Corporation
227 West 17th Street, New York, N.Y. 10011

Memoirs of an
American Prima Donna

By

Clara Louise Kellogg
(Mme. Strakosch)

With 40 Illustrations

G. P. Putnam's Sons
New York and London
The Knickerbocker Press
1913

The Knickerbocker Press, New York

WITH AFFECTION AND DEEPEST APPRECIATION OF HER WORTH

AS BOTH A RARE WOMAN AND A RARER FRIEND

I INSCRIBE THIS RECORD OF MY

PUBLIC LIFE TO

JEANNETTE L. GILDER

FOREWORD

THE name of Clara Louise Kellogg is known to the immediate generation chiefly as an echo of the past. Yet only thirty years ago it was written of her, enthusiastically but truthfully, that "no living singer needs a biography less than Miss Clara Louise Kellogg; and nowhere in the world would a biography of her be so superfluous as in America, where her name is a household word and her illustrious career is familiar in all its triumphant details to the whole people."

The past to which she belongs is therefore recent; it is the past of yesterday only, thought of tenderly by our fathers and mothers, spoken of reverently as a poignant phase of their own ephemeral youth, one of their sweet lavender memories. The pity is (although this is itself part of the evanescent charm), that the singer's best creations can live but in the hearts of a people, and the fame of sound is as fugitive as life itself.

A record of such creations is, however, possible and also enduring; while it is also necessary for a just estimate of the development of civilisations. As such, this record of her musical past—presented by Clara Louise Kellogg herself—will have a place in the annals of the evolution of musical art on the North American continent long after every vestige of fluttering personal reminiscence has vanished down the ages. A word of appreciation with regard to the preparation of this record is due to John Jay Whitehead, Jr., whose diligent chronological labours have materially assisted the editor.

Clara Louise Kellogg came from New England stock of English heritage. She was named after Clara Novello. Her father, George Kellogg, was an inventor of various machines and instruments and, at the time of her birth, was principal of Sumter Academy, Sumterville, S. C. Thus the famous singer was acclaimed in later years not only as the Star of the North (the *rôle* of Catherine in Meyerbeer's opera of that name being one of her achievements) but also as "the lone star of the South in the operatic world." She first sang publicly in New York in 1861 at an evening party given by Mr. Edward Cooper, the brother of Mrs. Abram Hewitt. This was the year of her *début* as Gilda in Verdi's opera of *Rigoletto* at the Academy of Music in New York City. When she came before her countrymen as a singer, she was several decades ahead of her musical public, for she was a lyric artist as well as a singer. America was not then producing either singers or lyric artists; and in fact we were, as a nation, but just getting over the notion that America could not produce great voices. We held a very firm contempt for our own facilities, our knowledge, and our taste in musical matters. If we did discover a rough diamond, we had to send it to Italy to find out if it were of the first water and to have it polished and set. Nothing was so absolutely necessary for our self-respect as that some American woman should arise with sufficient American talent and bravery to prove beyond all cavil that the country was able to produce both singers and artists.

For rather more than twenty-five years, from her appearance as Gilda until she quietly withdrew from public life, when it seemed to her that the appropriate moment for so doing had come, Clara Louise Kellogg filled this need and maintained her contention. She was educated in America, and her career, both in America and abroad, was remarkable in its consistent triumphs. When Gounod's *Faust* was a musical and an operatic innovation, she broke through the Italian traditions of her training and created the *rôle* of Marguerite according to her own beliefs; and throughout her later characterisations in Italian opera, she sustained a wonderfully poised attitude of independence and of observance with regard to these same traditions. In London, in St. Petersburg, in Vienna, as well as in the length and breadth of the United States, she gained a recognition and an appreciation in opera, oratorio, and concert, second to none: and when, later, she organised an English Opera Company and successfully piloted it on a course of unprecedented popularity, her personal laurels were equally supreme.

In 1887, Miss Kellogg married Carl Strakosch, who had for some time been her manager. Mr. Strakosch is the nephew of the two well-known impresarios, Maurice and Max Strakosch. After her marriage, the public career of Clara Louise Kellogg virtually ended. The Strakosch home is in New Hartford, Connecticut, and Mrs. Strakosch gave to it the name of "Elpstone" because of a large rock shaped like an elephant that is the most conspicuous feature, as one enters the grounds through the poplar-guarded gate. Mr. and Mrs. Strakosch are very fond of their New Hartford home, but, the Litchfield County climate in winter being severe, they usually spend their winters in Rome. They have also travelled largely in Oriental countries.

In 1912, Mr. and Mrs. Strakosch celebrated their Silver Wedding at Elpstone. On this occasion, the whole village of New Hartford was given up to festivities, and friends came from miles away to offer their·

congratulations.   Perhaps the most pleasant incident of the celebration was the presentation of a silver loving cup to Mr. and Mrs. Strakosch by the people of New Hartford in token of the affectionate esteem in which they are both held.

The woman, Clara Louise Kellogg, is quite as distinct a personality as was the *prima donna*.   So thoroughly, indeed, so fundamentally, is she a musician that her knowledge of life itself is as much a matter of harmony as is her music.   She lives her melody; applying the basic principle that Carlyle has expressed so admirably when he says: "See deeply enough and you see musically."

ISABEL MOORE.

WOODSTOCK, N. Y.
August, 1913

CONTENTS

ILLUSTRATIONS

Illustrations

Memoirs of
An American Prima Donna

CHAPTER I

MY FIRST NOTES

I WAS born in Sumterville, South Carolina, and had a negro mammy to take care of me, one of the real old-fashioned kind, of a type now almost gone. She used to hold me in her arms and rock me back and forth, and as she rocked she sang. I don't know the name of the song she crooned; but I still know the melody, and have an impression that the words were:

> "Hey, Jim along,—Jim along Josy;
> Hey, Jim along,—Jim along Joe!"

She used to sing these two lines over and over, so that I slept and waked to them. And my first musical efforts, when I was just ten months old, were to try to sing this ditty in imitation of my negro mammy.

When my mother first heard me she became apprehensive. Yet I kept at it; and by the time I was a year old I could sing it so that it was quite recognisable. I do not remember this period, of course, but my mother

I

often told me about it later, and I am sure she was not telling a fairy story.

There is, after all, nothing incredible or miraculous about the fact, extraordinary as it certainly is. We are not surprised when the young thrush practises a trill. And in some people the need for music and the power to make it are just as instinctive as they are in the birds. What effects I have achieved and what success I have found must be laid to this big, living fact: music was in me, and it had to find expression.

My music was honestly come by, from both sides of the house. When the family moved north to New England and settled in Birmingham, Connecticut,—it is called Derby now—my father and mother played in the little town choir, he a flute and she the organ. They were both thoroughly musical people, and always kept up with musical affairs, making a great many sacrifices all their lives to hear good singers whenever any sort of opportunity offered. As for my maternal grandmother—she was a woman with a man's brain. A widow at twenty-three, with no money and three children, she chose, of all ways to support them, the business of cotton weaving; going about Connecticut and Massachusetts, setting up looms—cotton gins they were called—and being very successful. She was a good musician also, and, in later years, after she had married my grandfather and was comfortably off, people begged her to give lessons; so she taught *thorough-base*, in that day and generation! Pause for a moment to consider what that meant, in a time when the activity of women was very limited and unrecognised. Is it any wonder that the granddaughter of a woman who could master and teach the science of *thorough-base* at such a period should be born with music in her blood?

Lydia Atwood
Maternal Grandmother of Clara Louise Kellogg

My other grandmother, my father's mother, was musical, too. She had a sweet voice, and was the soprano of the church choir.

Everyone knew I was naturally musical from my constant attempts to sing, and from my deep attention when anyone performed on any instrument, even when I was so little that I could not reach the key-board of the piano on tip-toe. That particular piano, I remember, was very old-fashioned—one of the square box-shaped sort—and stood extremely high.

One day my grandmother said to my mother:

"I do believe, Jane, if we lifted that baby up to the piano, she could play!"

Mother said: "Oh, pshaw!"

But they did lift me up, and I did play. I played not only with my right hand but also with my left hand; and I made harmonies. Probably they were not in any way elaborate chords, but they *were* chords, and they harmonised. I have known some grown-up musicians whose chords did n't!

I was three then, and a persistent baby, already detesting failure. I never liked to try to do anything, even at that age, in which I might be unsuccessful, and so learned to do what I wanted to do as soon as possible.

My mother was gifted in many ways. She used to paint charmingly; and has told me that when she was a young girl and could not get paint brushes, she made her own of hairs pulled from their old horse's tail.

My maternal grandfather was not at all musical. He used to say that to him the sweetest note on the piano was when the cover went down! Yet it was he who accidentally discovered a fortunate possession of mine—something that has remained in my keeping ever since, and, like many fortunate gifts, has at times troubled as much as it has consoled me.

One day he was standing by the piano in one room and I was playing on the floor in another. He idly struck a note and asked my mother:

"What note is that I am striking? Guess!"

"How can I tell?" said my mother. "No one could tell that."

"Why, mother!" I cried from the next room, "don't you know what note that is?"

"I do not," said my mother, "and neither do you."

"I do, too," I declared. "It 's the first of the three black keys going up!"

It was, in fact, F sharp, and in this manner it was discovered that I had what we musicians call "absolute pitch"; the ability to place and name a note the moment it is heard. As I have said, this has often proved to be a very trying gift, for it is, and always has been impossible for me to decipher a song in a different key from that in which it is written. If it is written in C, I hear it in C; and conceive the hideous discord in my brain while the orchestra or the pianist renders it in D flat! When I see a "Do," I want to sing it as a "Do," and not as a "Re."

This episode must have been when I was about five years old, and soon afterward I began taking regular piano lessons. I remember my teacher quite well. He used to come out from New Haven by the Naugatuck railway—that had just been completed and was a great curiosity—for the purpose of instructing a class of which I was a member.

I had the most absurd difficulty in learning my notes. I could play anything by ear, but to read a piece of

Charles Atwood
Maternal Grandfather of Clara Louise
Kellogg
From a daguerreotype

music and find the notes on the piano was another matter. My teacher struggled with this odd incapacity; but I used to cheat him shockingly.

"*Do* play this for me!" I would beg. "Just once, so I can tell how it goes."

In spite of this early slowness in music reading, or, perhaps because of it, when I *did* learn to read, I learned to read thoroughly. I could really play; and I cannot over-estimate the help this has been to me all my life. It is so essential—and so rare—for a *prima donna* to be not only a fine singer but also a good musician.

There was then no idea of my becoming a singer. All my time was given to the piano and to perfecting myself in playing it. But my parents made every effort to have me hear fine singing, for the better cultivation of my musical taste, and I am grateful to them for doing so, as I believe that singing is largely imitative and that, while singers need not begin to train their voices very early, they should as soon as possible familiarise themselves with good singing and with good music generally. The wise artist learns from many sources, some of them quite unexpected ones. Patti once told me that she had caught the trick of her best "turn" from listening to Faure, the baritone.

My father and mother went to New York during the Jenny Lind *furore* and carried me in their arms to hear her big concert. I remember it clearly, and just the way in which she tripped on to the stage that night with her hair, as she always wore it, drawn down close over her ears—a custom that gave rise to the popular report that she had no ears.

That concert is my first musical recollection. I was much amused by the baritone who sang *Figaro là*

Figaro quà from *The Barber*. I thought him and
his song immensely funny; and everyone around us was
in a great state over me because I insisted that the
drum was out of tune. I was really dreadfully annoyed
by that drum, for it *was* out of tune! I remember
Jenny Lind sang:

> " Birdling, why sing'st thou in the forest wild?
> Say why,—say why,—say why!"

and one part of it sounded exactly like the call of a
bird. Sir Jules Benedict, who was always her accompanist, once told me many years later in London that
she had a "hole" in her voice. He said that he had
been obliged to play her accompaniments in such a way
as to cover up certain notes in her middle register.
A curious admission to come from him, I thought, for
few people knew of the "hole."

Only once during my childhood did I sing in public,
and that was in a little school concert, a song *Come
Buy My Flowers*, dressed up daintily for the part and
carrying a small basketful of posies of all kinds. When
I had finished singing, a man in the audience stepped
down to the footlights and held up a five-dollar bill.

"To buy your flowers!" said he.

That might be called my first professional performance! The local paper said I had talent. As a matter
of fact, I don't remember much about the occasion;
but I do remember only too well a dreadful incident that
occurred immediately afterward between me and the
editor of the aforesaid local paper,—Mr. Newson by
name.

I had a pet kitten, and it went to sleep in a rolled
up rug beside the kitchen door one day, and the cook

stepped on it. The kitten was killed, of course, and the affair nearly killed me. I was crying my eyes out over my poor little pet when that editor chanced along. And he made fun of me!

I turned on him in the wildest fury. I really would have killed him if I could.

"Laugh, will you!" I shrieked, beside myself. "Laugh! laugh! laugh!"

He said afterwards that I absolutely frightened him, I was so small and so tragic.

"I knew then," he declared, "that that child had great emotional and dramatic possibilities in her. Why, she nearly burned me up!"

Years later, when I was singing in St. Paul, the *Dispatch* printed this story in an interview with Mr. Newson himself. He made a heartless jest of the alliteration—"Kellogg's Kitten Killed"—and referred to my "inexpressible expression of sorrow and disgust" as I cried, "Laugh, will you!" Said Mr. Newson in summing up:

"It was a real tragedic act!"

Mr. Newson's description of me as a child is: "A black-eyed little girl, somewhat wayward—as she was an only child—kind-hearted, affectionate, self-reliant, and very independent!"

Well—sight-reading became so easy to me, presently, that I could not realise any difficulty about it. To see a note was to be able to sing it; and I was often puzzled when people expressed surprise at my ability. When I was about eleven, someone took me to Hartford to "show me off" to William Babcock, a teacher and a thorough musician. He got out some of his most difficult German songs; songs far more intricate than anything I had ever before seen, of course, and was frankly amazed to find that I read them just about as readily as the simple airs to which I was accustomed.

My childhood was very quiet and peaceful, rather commonplace in fact, except for music. Reading was a pleasure, too, and, as my father was a student and had a wonderful library, I had all the books I wanted. I was literally brought up on Carlyle and Chaucer. I must have been a rather queer child, in some ways. Even as a little thing I liked clothes. When only nine years old I conceived a wild desire for a pair of kid gloves. Kid gloves were a sign of great elegance in those days. At last my clamours were successful and I was given a pair at Christmas. They were a source of great pride, and I wore them to church, where I did my little singing in the choir with the others. By this time I could read any music at sight and would sit up and chirp and peep away quite happily. As I spread my kid-gloved hands out most conspicuously, what I had not noticed became very noticeable to everyone else: the fingers were nearly two inches too long. And the choir laughed at me. I was dreadfully mortified and sat there crying, until the kind contralto comforted me.

In my young days the negro minstrels were a great diversion. They were amusing because they were so typical. There are none left, but in the old times they were delightful, and it is a thousand pities that they have passed away. All the essence of slavery, and the efforts of the slaves to amuse themselves, were in their quaint performances. The banjo was almost unknown to us in the North, and when it found its way to New England it was a genuine novelty. I was simply fascinated by it as a little girl and used to go to all the minstrel shows, and sit and watch the men play. Their banjos had five strings only and were played with the back of the nail,—not like a guitar. This was the only way to get the real negro twang. There was no refinement about such playing, but I loved it. I said:

"I believe I could play that if I had one!"

My father, the dignified scholar, was horrified.

"When a banjo comes in, I go out," said he.

At last a friend gave me one, and I watched and studied the darkies until I had picked up the trick of playing it, and soon acquired a real negro touch. And I also acquired some genuine darky songs. One, of which I was particularly fond, was called: *Hottes' co'n y' ever eat.*

I really believe I was the first American girl who ever played a banjo! In a few years along came Lotta, and made the banjo a great feature.

Banjo music has natural syncopation, and its peculiarities undoubtedly originated the "rag-time" of our present-day imitations. There was one song that I learned from hearing a man sing it who had, in turn, caught it from a darky, that has never to my knowledge been published and is not to be found in any collection.

It began:

It'll set this dar - key cra - zy, I don't know what I'll do,

and remains with me in my *répertoire* unto this day. I have been known to sing it with certain effect—for when I am asked, now, to sing it, my husband leaves the room! The last time I sang it was only a couple of years ago in Norfolk. Herbert Witherspoon said:

"Listen to that high C!"

"Ah," said I, "that is the last remnant—the very last!"

But this chapter is to be about my first notes, **not** my last ones.

In 1857, my father failed, the beautiful books were sold and we went to New York to live. Almost directly afterward occurred one of the most important events of my career. Although I was not being trained for a singer, but as a musician in general, I could no more help singing than I could held breathing, or sleeping, or eating; and, one day, Colonel Henry G. Stebbins, a well-known musical amateur, one of the directors of the Academy of Music, was calling on my father and heard me singing to myself in an adjoining room. Then and there he asked to be allowed to have my voice cultivated; and so, when I was fourteen, I began to study singing. The succeeding four years were the hardest worked years of my life.

To young girls who are contemplating vocal study, I always say that it is mostly a question of what one is willing to give up.

If you really are prepared to sacrifice all the fun that your youth is entitled to; to work, and to deny yourself; to eat and sleep, not because you are hungry or sleepy, but because your strength must be conserved for your art; to make your music the whole interest of your existence;—if you are willing to do all this, you may have your reward.

But music will have no half service. It has to be all or nothing.

In Rostand's play, they ask Chanticleer:

"What is your life?"

And he answers:

"My song."

"What is your song?"

"My life."

George Kellogg
Father of Clara Louise Kellogg
Photograph by Gurney & Son

CHAPTER II

IN taking up vocal study, however, I had no fixed intention of going on the stage. All I decided was to make as much as I could of myself and of my voice. Many girls I knew studied singing merely as an accomplishment. In fact, the girl who aspired professionally was almost unknown.

I first studied under a Frenchman named Millet, a graduate of the Conservatory of Paris, who was teaching the daughters of Colonel Stebbins and, also, the daughter of the Baron de Trobriand. Later, I worked with Manzocchi, Rivarde, Errani and Muzio, who was a great friend of Verdi.

Most of my fellow-students were charming society girls. Ella Porter and President Arthur's wife were with me under Rivarde, and Anna Palmer who married the scientist, Dr. Draper. The idea of my going on the stage would have appalled the families of these girls. In those days the life of the theatre was regarded as altogether outside the pale. One did n't know stage people; one could n't speak to them, nor shake hands with them, nor even look at them except from a safe distance across the footlights. There were no "decent people on the stage"; how often did I hear that foolish thing said!

11

It is odd that in that most musical and artistic country, Italy, much the same prejudice exists to this day. I should never think of telling a really great Italian lady that I had been on the stage; she would immediately think that there was something queer about me. Of course in America all that was changed some time ago, after England had established the precedent. People are now pleased not only to meet artists socially, but to lionise them as well. But when I was a girl there was a gulf as deep as the Bottomless Pit between society and people of the theatre; and it was this gulf that I knew would open between myself and the friends of whom I was really fond as, in time, I realised that I was improving sufficiently to justify some definite ambitions. My work was steady and unremitting, and by the time I began study with Muzio my mind was pretty nearly made up.

A queer, nervous, brusque, red-headed man was Muzio, from the north of Italy, where the type always seems so curiously German. Besides being one of the conductors of the Opera, he organised concert tours, and promised to see that I should have my chance. It was said that he had fled from political disturbances in Italy, but this I never heard verified. Certainly he was quite a big man in the New York operatic world of his day, and was a most cultivated musician, with the "Italian traditions" of opera at his fingers' ends. It is to Muzio, incidentally, that I owe my trill.

Oddly enough, I had great difficulty with that trill for three years; but in four weeks' study he taught me the trick,—for it is a trick, like so many other big effects. I believe I got it finally by using my sub-

Clara Louise Kellogg. Aged Three

From a photograph by Black & Case

conscious mind. Don't you know how, after striving and straining for something, you at last relax and let some inner part of your brain carry on the battle? And how, often and often, it is then that victory comes? So it was with my trill; and so it has been with many difficult things that I have succeeded in since then.

No account of my education would be complete without a mention of the great singers whom I heard during that receptive period; that is, the years between fourteen and eighteen, before my professional *début*. The first artist I heard when I was old enough really to appreciate good singing was Louisa Pine, who sang in New York in second-rate English Opera with Harrison, of whom she was deeply enamoured and who usually sang out of tune. We did not then fully understand how well-schooled and well-trained she was; and her really fine qualities were only revealed to me much later in a concert.

Then there was D'Angri, a contralto who sang Rossini to perfection. *Italiani in Algeria* was produced especially for her. About that same time Mme. de la Grange was appearing, together with Mme. de la Borde, a light and colorature soprano, something very new in America. Mme. de la Borde sang the Queen to Mme. de la Grange's Valentine in *Les Huguenots*, and had a French voice—if I may so express it—light, and of a strange quality. The French claimed that she sang a scale of *commas*, that is, a note between each of our chromatic intervals. She may have; but it merely sounded to the listener as if she was n't singing the scale clearly. Mme. de la Grange was a sort of goddess to me, I remember. I heard her first in *Trovatore* with Brignoli and Amodio.

Piccolomini arrived here a couple of years later and I heard her, too. She was of a distinguished Italian family, and, considering Italy's aristocratic prejudices, it is strange that she should have been an opera singer. She made *Traviata*, in which she had already captured the British public, first known to us: yet she was an indifferent singer and had a very limited *répertoire*. She received her adulation partly because people did n't know much then about music. Adulation it was, too. She made $5000 a month, and America had never before imagined such an operatic salary. She looked a little like Lucca; was small and dark, and decidedly clever in comedy. I was fortunate enough to see her in Pergolese's delightful, if archaic, opera, *La Serva Padrona*—"The Maid as Mistress"—and she proved herself to be an exceptional *comédienne*. She was excellent in tragedy, too.

Brignoli was the first great tenor I ever heard; and Amodio the first famous baritone. Brignoli—but all the world knows what Brignoli was! As for Amodio; he had a great and beautiful voice; but, poor man, what a disadvantage he suffered under in his appearance. He was so fat that he was grotesque, he was absurdly short, and had absolutely no saving grace as to physique. He played Mazetto to Piccolomini's Zerlina, and the whole house roared when they came on dancing.

I heard nearly all the great singers of my youth; all that were to be heard in New York, at any rate, except Grisi. I missed Grisi, I am sorry to say, because on the one occasion when I was asked to hear her sing, with Mario, I chose to go to a children's party instead. I am much ashamed of this levity, although I was, to be sure, only ten years old at the time.

Clara Louise Kellogg.   Aged Seven
Photograph by Black & Case

Adelina Patti I heard the year before my own *début*. She was a slip of a girl then, when she appeared over here in *Lucia*, and carried the town by storm. What a voice! I had never dreamed of anything like it. But, for that matter, neither had anyone else.

What histrionic skill I ever developed I attribute to the splendid acting that I saw so constantly during my girlhood. And what actors and actresses we had! As I look back, I wonder if we half appreciated them. It is certainly true that, viewed comparatively, we must cry "there were giants in those days!" Think of Mrs. John Wood and Jefferson at the Winter Garden; of Dion Boucicault and his wife, Agnes Robertson; of Laura Keene—a revelation to us all—and of the French Theatre, which was but a little hole in the wall, but the home of some exquisite art (I was brought up on the Raouls in French pantomime); and all the wonderful old Wallack Stock Company! Think of the elder Sothern, and of John Brougham, and of Charles Walcot, and of Mrs. John Hoey, Mrs. Vernon, and Mary Gannon,—that most beautiful and perfect of all *in-génues!* Those people would be world-famous stars if they were playing to-day; we have no actors or companies like them left. Not even the Comédie Française ever had such a gathering.

It may be imagined what an education it was for a young girl with stage aspirations to see such work week after week. For I was taken to see everyone in everything, and some of the impressions I received then were permanent. For instance, Matilda Heron in *Camille* gave me a picture of poor Marguerite Gautier so deep and so vivid that I found it invaluable, years later, when I myself came to play Violetta in *Traviata*.

I saw both Ristori and Rachel too. The latter I heard recite on her last appearance in America. It was the *Marseillaise*, and deeply impressive. Personally, I loved best her *Moineau de Lesbie*. Shall I ever forget her enchanting reading of the little scene with the jewels?—*Suis-je belle?*

The father of one of my fellow students was, as I have said before, Baron de Trobriand, a very charming man of the old French aristocracy. He came often to the home of Colonel Stebbins and always showed a great deal of interest in my development. He knew Rachel very well; had known her ever since her girl-hood indeed, and always declared that I was the image of her. As I look at my early portraits, I can see it myself a little. In all of them I have a desperately serious expression as though life were a tragedy. How well I remember the Baron and his wonderful stories of France! He had some illustrious kindred, among them the Duchesse de Berri, and we were never tired of his tales concerning her.

I find, to-day, as I look through some of my old press notices, that nice things were always said of me as an actress. Once, John Wallack, Lester's father, came to hear me in *Fra Diavolo*, and exclaimed:

"I wish to God that girl would lose her voice!"

He wanted me to give up singing and go on the dramatic stage; and so did Edwin Booth. I have a letter from Edwin Booth that I am more proud of than almost anything I possess. But these incidents happened, of course, later.

From all I saw and all I heard I tried to learn and to keep on learning. And so I prepared for the time of my own initial bow before the public. As I gradually studied and developed, I began to feel more and more

sure that I was destined to be a singer. I felt that it
was my life and my heritage; that I was made for it,
and that nothing else could ever satisfy me. And
Muzio told me that I was right. In another six
months I would be ready to make my *début*. It was
a serious time, when I faced the future as a public
singer, but I was very happy in the contemplation of
it.

That summer I took a rest, preparatory to my first
season,—how thrillingly professional that sounded, to
be sure!—and it was during that summer that I had
one of the most pleasant experiences of my girlhood,—
one really delightful and *young* experience, such as
other girls have,—a wonderful change from the hard-
working, serious months of study. I went to West
Point for a visit. In spite of my sober bringing-up, I
was full of the joy of life, and loved the days spent in
a place filled with the military glamour that every
girl adores.

West Point was more primitive then than it is now.
But it was just as much fun. I danced, and watched
the drill, and walked about, and made friends with the
cadets,—to whom the fact that they were entertaining
a budding *prima donna* was both exciting and interesting—and had about the best time I ever had in my
life.

Looking back now, however, I can feel a shadow of
sadness lying over the memory of all that happy visit.
We were just on the eve of war, little as we young
people thought of it, and many of the merry, good-
looking boys I danced with that summer fell at the
front within the year. Some of them entered the
Union Army the following spring when war was declared, and some went South to serve under the Stars

2

and Bars. Among the former was Alec McCook—
"Fighting McCook," as he was called. Lieutenant
McCreary was Southern, and was killed early in the
war. So, also, was the son of General Huger—the
General Huger who was then Postmaster General
and later became a member of the Cabinet of the
Confederacy.

It is interesting to consider that West Point, at
the time of which I write, was a veritable hotbed of
conspiracy. The Southerners were preparing hard and
fast for action; the atmosphere teemed with plotting,
so that even I was vaguely conscious that something
exceedingly serious was going on. The Commandant
of the Post, General Delafield, was an officer of strong
Southern sympathies and later went to fight in Dixie
land. When the war did finally break out, nearly all
the ammunition was down South; and this had been
managed from West Point.

Of course, all was done with great circumspection.
Buchanan was a Democratic president; and the Demo-
crats of the South sent a delegation to West Point to
try to get the commanding officers to use their influence
in reducing the military course from four to three
years. This at least was their ostensible mission, and
it made an excellent excuse as well as offered great
opportunities for what we Federal sympathisers would
call treason, but which they probably considered was
justified by patriotism. Indeed, James Buchanan was
allotted a very difficult part in the political affairs of
the day; and the censure he received for what is called
his "vacillation" was somewhat unjust. He held that
the question of slavery and its abolition was not a
national, but a local problem; and he never took any
firm stand about it. But the conditions were bewilder-

ingly new and complex, and statesmen often suffer from their very ability to look on both sides of a question.

Jefferson Davis was then at West Point; and, as for "Mrs. Jeff"—I always believed she was a spy. She had her niece and son with her at the Point, the latter, "Jeff, Jr.," then a child of five or six years old. He had the worst temper I ever imagined in a boy; and I am ashamed to relate that the officers took a wicked delight in arousing and exhibiting it. He used to sit several steps up on the one narrow stairway of the hotel and swear the most horrible, hot oaths ever heard, getting red in the face with fury. Alec McCook, assistant instructor and a charming fellow of about thirty, would put him on a bucking donkey that was there and say:

"Now then, lad, don't you let him put you off!"

And the "lad" would sit on the donkey, turning the air blue with profanity. But one thing can be said for him: he did stick on!

Lieutenant Horace Porter, who was among my friends of that early summer, was destined to serve with distinction on the Northern side. I met him not long ago, a dignified, distinguished General; and it was difficult to see in him the high-spirited, young lieutenant of the old Point days.

"Do you know," he said, "Mrs. Jeff Davis sent for me to come and see her when she was in New York! *Of course* I did n't go!"

He had not forgotten. One does not forget the things that happened just before the war. The great struggle burned them too deeply into our memories.

Nothing would satisfy the cadets, who were aware that I was preparing to go on the stage as a profes-

sional singer, but that I should sing for them. I
was only too delighted to do so, but I did n't want to
sing in the hotel. So they turned their "hop-room"
into a concert-hall for the occasion and invited the
officers and their friends, in spite of Mrs. Jeff Davis,
who tried her best to prevent the ball-room from being
given to us for our musicale. She did not attend;
but the affair made her exceedingly uncomfortable,
for she disliked me and was jealous of the kindness
and attention I received from everyone. She always
referred to me as "that singing girl!"

As I have said, many of those attractive West Point
boys and officers were killed in the war so soon to break
upon us. Others, like General Porter, have remained
my friends. A few I have kept in touch with only by
hearsay. But throughout the Civil War I always felt
a keener and more personal interest in the battles
because, for a brief space, I had come so close to the
men who were engaged in them; and the sentiment
never passed.

Ever and ever so many years after that visit to West
Point, a note came behind the scenes to me during one
of my performances, and with it was a mass of exquisite
flowers. "Please wear one of these flowers to-night!"
the note begged me. It was from one of the cadets to
whom I had sung so long before, but whom I had never
seen since.

I wore the flower: and I put my whole soul into my
singing that night. For that little episode of my girlhood, the meeting with those eager and plucky young
spirits just before our great national crisis, has always
been close to my heart. As for the three dark years
that followed—ah, well,—I never want to read about
the war now.

Clara Louise Kellogg as a Girl
From a photograph by Sarony

It was almost time for my *début*, and there was still something I had to do. To my sheltered, puritanically brought up consciousness, there could be no two views among conventional people as to the life I was about to enter upon. I knew all about it. So, a few weeks before I was to make my professional bow to the public, I called my girl friends together, the companions of four years' study, and I said to them:

"Girls, I 've made up my mind to go on the stage! I know just how your people feel about it, and I want to tell you now that you need n't know me any more. You need n't speak to me, nor bow to me if you meet me in the street. I shall quite understand, and I shan't feel a bit badly. *Because I think the day will come when you will be proud to know me!*"

CHAPTER III

"LIKE A PICKED CHICKEN"

BEFORE my *début* in opera, Muzio took me out on a concert tour for a few weeks. Colson was the *prima donna*, Brignoli the tenor, Ferri the baritone, and Susini the basso. Susini had, I believe, distinguished himself in the Italian Revolution. His name means *plums* in Italian, and his voice as well as his name was rich and luscious.

I was a general utility member of the company, and sang to fill in the chinks. We sang four times a week, and I received twenty-five dollars each time—that is, one hundred dollars a week—not bad for inexperienced seventeen, although Muzio regarded the tour for me as merely educational and part of my training.

My mother travelled with me, for she never let me out of her sight. Yet, even with her along, the experience was very strange and new and rather terrifying. I had no knowledge of stage life, and that first *tournée* was comprised of a series of shocks and surprises, most of them disillusioning.

We opened in Pittsburg, and it was there, at the old Monongahela House, that I had my first exhibition of Italian temperament, or, rather, temper!

When we arrived, we found that the dining-room was officially closed. We were tired out after a long hard trip of twenty-four hours, and, of course, almost starved. We got as far as the door, where we could look in hungrily, but it was empty and dark. There were no waiters; there was nothing, indeed, except the rows of neatly set tables for the next meal.

Brignoli demanded food. He was very fond of eating, I recall. And, in those days, he was a sort of little god in New York, where he lived in much luxury. When affairs went well with him, he was not an un-amiable man; but he was a selfish egotist, with the devil's own temper on occasion.

The landlord approached and told us that the dinner hour was past, and that we could not get anything to eat until the next meal, which would be supper. And oh! if you only knew what supper was like in the provincial hotel of that day!

Brignoli was wild with wrath. He would start to storm and shout in his rage, and would then suddenly remember his voice and subside, only to begin again as his anger rose in spite of himself. It was really amusing, though I doubt if anyone appreciated the joke at the moment.

At last, as the landlord remained quite unmoved, Brignoli dashed into the room, grabbed the cloth on one of the tables near the door and pulled it off—dishes, silver, and all! The crash was terrific, and naturally the china was smashed to bits.

"You 'll have to pay for that!" cried the landlord, indignantly.

"Pay for it!" gasped Brignoli, waving his arms and fairly dancing with rage, "of course I 'll pay for it— just as I 'll pay for the dinner, if——"

"What!" exclaimed the landlord, in a new tone, "you will pay *extra* for the dinner, if we are willing to serve it for you now?"

"*Dio mio*, yes!" cried Brignoli.

The landlord stood and gaped at him.

"Why did n't you say so in the first place?" he asked with a sort of contemptuous pity, and went off to order the dinner.

When will the American and the Italian temperaments begin to understand each other!

Brignoli was not only a fine singer but a really good musician. He told me that he had given piano lessons in Paris before he began to sing at all. But of his absolute origin he would never speak. He was a handsome man, with ears that had been pierced for ear-rings. This led me to infer that he had at some time been a sailor, although he would never let anyone mention the subject. Anyhow, I always thought of Naples when I looked at him.

Most stage people have their pet superstitions. There seems to be something in their make-up that lends itself to an interest in signs. But Brignoli had a greater number of singular ones than any person I ever met. He had, among other things, a mascot that he carried all over the country. This was a stuffed deer's head, and it was always installed in his dressing-room wherever he might be singing. When he sang well, he would come back to the room and pat the deer's head approvingly. When he was not in voice, he would pound it and swear at it in Italian.

Brignoli lived for his voice. He adored it as if it were some phenomenon for which he was in no sense responsible. And I am not at all sure that this is not the right point of view for a singer. He always took tremendous pains with his voice and the greatest possible care of himself in every way, always eating huge quantities of raw oysters each night before he

sang. The story is told of him that one day he fell
off a train. People rushed to pick him up, solicitous
lest the great tenor's bones were broken. But Brignoli
had only one fear. Without waiting even to rise to
his feet, he sat up, on the ground where he had fallen,
and solemnly sang a bar or two. Finding his voice
uninjured, he burst into heartfelt prayers of thanks-
giving, and climbed back into the car.

Brignoli only just missed being very great. But
he had the indolence of the Neapolitan sailor, and he
was, of course, sadly spoiled. Women were always
crazy about him, and he posed as an *élégante*. Years
afterward, when I heard of his death, I never felt the
loss of any beautiful thing as I did the loss of his voice.
The thought came to me:—"and he has n't been able
to leave it to anyone as a legacy——"

But to return to our concert tour.

I remember that the concert room in Pittsburg was
over the town market. That was what we had to
contend with in those primitive days! Imagine our
little company of devoted and ambitious artists trying
to create a musical atmosphere one flight up, while
they sold cabbages and fish downstairs!

The first evening was an important event for me,
my initial public appearance, and I recall quite distinctly that I sang the Cavatina from *Linda di Chamounix*—which I was soon to sing operatically—and
that I wore a green dress. Green was an unusual
colour in gowns then. Our young singers generally
chose white or blue or pink or something insipid;
but I had a very definite taste in clothes, and liked
effects that were not only pretty but also individual
and becoming.

Speaking of clothes, I learned on that first experimental tour the horrors of travel when it comes to keeping one's gowns fresh. I speedily acquired the habit, practised ever since, of carrying a big crash cloth about with me to spread on stages where I was to sing. This was not entirely to keep my clothes clean, important as that was. It was also for the sake of my voice and its effect. Few people know that the floor-covering on which a singer stands makes a very great difference. On carpets, for instance, one simply cannot get a good tone.

Just before I went on for that first concert, Madame Colson stopped me to put a rose in my hair, and said to me:

"Smile much, and show your teeth!"

After the concert she supplemented this counsel with the words:

"Always dress your best, and always smile, and always be gracious!"

I never forgot the advice.

The idea of pretty clothes and a pretty smile is not merely a pose nor an artificiality. It is likewise carrying out a spirit of courtesy. Just as a hostess greets a guest cordially and tries to make her feel at ease, so the tactful singer tries to show the people who have come to hear her that she is glad to see them.

Pauline Colson was a charming artist, a French soprano of distinction in her own country and always delightful in her work. She had first come to America to sing in the French Opera in New Orleans where, for many years, there had been a splendid opera season each winter. She had just finished her winter's work there when some northern impresario engaged her for a brief season of opera in New York; and it was at the termination of this that Muzio engaged her for our

concert tour. She was one of the few artists who
rebelled against the bad costuming then prevalent;
and it was said that for more than one of her *rôles* she
made her gowns herself, to be sure that they were
correct. It was her example that fired me in the
revolutionary steps I was to take later with regard
to my own costumes.

Our next stop was Cincinnati—*Cincinnata*, as it was
called! I had there one of the shocks of my life.
The leading newspaper of the city, in commenting on
our concert, said of me that "this young girl's parents
ought to remove her from public view, do her up in
cotton wool, nourish her well, and not allow her to
appear again until she looks less like a picked chicken"!

No one said anything about my voice! Indeed, I
got almost no encouragement before we reached Detroit,
and I recall that I cried a good part of the way between
the two cities over my failure in Cincinnati. But in
Detroit Colson was taken ill, so I had a chance to do
the *prima donna* work of the occasion. And I profited
by the chance, for it was in Detroit that an audience
first discovered that I had some nascent ability.

I *must* have been an odd, young creature—just five
feet and four inches tall, and weighing only one hundred
and four pounds. I was frail and big-eyed, and
wrapped up in music (not cotton wool), and exceedingly childlike for my age. I knew nothing of life, for
my puritanical surroundings and the way in which I
had been brought up were developing my personality
very slowly.

That was a hard tour. Indeed, all tours were hard
in those days. Travelling accommodations were limited
and uncomfortable, and most of the hotels were very
bad. Trains were slow, and connections uncertain,

and of course there was no such thing as a Pullman or, much less, a dining-car. Sometimes we had to sit up all night and were not able to get anything to eat, not infrequently arriving too late for the meal hour of the hotel where we were to stop. The journeys were so long and so difficult that they used to say Pauline Lucca always travelled in her nightgown and a black velvet wrapper.

All through that tour, as during every period of my life, I was working and studying and practising and learning: trying to improve my voice, trying to develop my artistic consciousness, trying to fit myself in a hundred ways for my career. Work never frightened me; there was always in me the desire to express myself —and to express that self as fully and as variously as I might have opportunity for doing.

It sometimes seems to me that one of the strangest things in this world is the realisation that there is never time to perfect everything in us; that we carry seeds in our souls that cannot flower in one short life. Perhaps Paradise will be a place where we can develop every possibility and become our complete selves.

In one's brain and one's soul lies the power to do almost anything. I believe that the psychological phenomena we hear so much about are nothing but un-discovered forces in ourselves. I am not a spiritualist. I do not care for so-called supernatural manifestations. Many of my friends have been interested in such matters, and I was taken to the celebrated "Stratford Knockings" and other mediumistic demonstrations when I was a mere child; but it has never seemed to me that the marvels I encountered came from an outside spiritual agency. I believe, profoundly, that, one and all, they are the workings of forces in *us* that

Clara Louise Kellogg as a Young Lady
From a photograph by Black & Case

we have not yet learned to develop fully nor to use wisely.

I never did anything in my life without study. The ancient axiom that "what is worth doing at all is worth doing well" is more of a truth than most people understand. The thing that one has chosen for one's life work in the world:—what labour could be too great for it, or what too minute?

When I knew that I was to make my *début* as Gilda, in Verdi's opera of *Rigoletto*, I settled down to put myself into that part. I studied for nine months, until I was not certain whether I was really Gilda—or only myself!

I was taking lessons in acting with Scola then, in addition to my musical study. And, besides Scola's regular course, I closely observed the methods of individuals, actors, and singers. I remember seeing Brignoli in *I Puritani*, during that "incubating period" before my first appearance in opera. I was studying gesture then,—the free, simple, *inevitable* gesture that is so necessary to a natural effect in dramatic singing; and during the beautiful melody, *A te, o cara*, which he sang in the first act, Brignoli stood still in one spot and thrust first one arm out, and then the other, at right angles from his body, twenty-three consecutive times. I counted them, and I don't know how many times he had done it before I began to count!

"Heavens!" I said, "that's one thing not to do, anyway!"

Languages were a very important part of my training. I had studied French when I was nine years old, in the country, and as soon as I began taking singing lessons I began Italian also. Much later, when I sang in *Les Noces de Jeannette*, people would speak of my

French and ask where I had studied. But it was all learned at home.

I never studied German. There was less demand for it in music than there is now. America practically had no "German opera;" and Italian was the accepted tongue of dramatic and tragic music, as French was the language of lighter and more popular operas. Besides, German always confused me; and I never liked it.

Many years later than the time of which I am now writing, I was charmed to be confirmed in my anti-German prejudices when I went to Paris. After the Franco-Prussian War the signs and warnings in that city were put up in every language in the world except German! The German way of putting things was too long; and, furthermore, the French people did n't care if Germans did break their legs or get run over.

Of course, all this is changed—and in music most of all. For example, there could be no greater convert to Wagnerism than I!

My mother hated the atmosphere of the theatre even though she had wished me to become a singer, and always gloried in my successes. To her rigid and delicate instinct there was something dreadful in the free and easy artistic attitude, and she always stood between me and any possible intimacy with my fellow-singers. I believe this to have been a mistake. Many traditions of the stage come to one naturally and easily through others; but I had to wait and learn them all by experience. I was always working as an outsider, and, naturally, this attitude of ours antagonised singers with whom we appeared.

Not only that. My brain would have developed much more rapidly if I had been allowed—no, if I had

been *obliged* to be more self-reliant. To profit by one's
own mistakes;—all the world's history goes to show
that is the only way to learn. By protecting me, my
mother really robbed me of much precious experience.
For how many years after I had made my *début* would
she wait for me in the *coulisses*, ready to whisk me off
to my dressing-room before any horrible opera singer
had a chance to talk with me!

Yet she grieved for my forfeited youth—did my
dear mother. She always felt that I was being sacrificed to my work, and just at the time when I would
have most delighted in my girlhood. Of course, I was
obliged to live a life of labour and self-denial, but it was
not quite so difficult for me as she felt it to be, or as
other people sometimes thought it was. Not only did
I adore my music, and look forward to my work as an
artist, but I literally never had any other life. I
knew nothing of what I had given up; and so was happy
in what I had undertaken, as no girl could have been
happy who had lived a less restricted, hard-working
and yet dream-filled existence.

My mother was very strait-laced and puritanical,
as I have said, and, naturally, by reflection and association, I was the same. I lay stress on this because
I want one little act of mine to be appreciated as a
sign of my ineradicable girlishness and love of beauty.
When I earned my first money, I went to Mme. Perci-
val's, the smart lingerie shop of New York, and bought
the three most exquisite chemises I could find, imported
and trimmed with real lace!

I daresay this harmless ebullition of youthful daintiness would have proved the last straw to some of my
Psalm-singing New England relatives. There was one
uncle of mine who vastly disapproved of my going on

the stage at all, saying that it would have been much
better if I had been a good, honest milliner. He used
to sing:

"Broad   is   the   road   That   leads   to   Hell!"

in a minor key, with the true, God-fearing, nasal
twang in it.

How I detested that old man! And I had to bury
him, too, at the last. I wonder whether I should have
been able to do so if I had gone into the millinery
business!

CHAPTER IV

A YOUTHFUL REALIST

AS I have said, I studied Gilda for nine months.
At the end of that time I was so imbued with the
part as to be thoroughly at ease. Present-day actors
call this condition "getting inside the skin" of a *rôle*.
I simply could not make a mistake, and could do
everything connected with the characterisation with
entire unconsciousness. Yet I want to add that I had
little idea of what the opera really meant.

My *début* was in New York at the old Academy
of Music, and Rigoletto was the famous Ferri. He
was blind in one eye and I had always to be on his
seeing side,—else he could n't act. Stigelli was the
tenor. Stiegel was his real name. He was a German
and a really fine artist. But I had then had no experience with stage heroes and thought they were all
going to be exactly as they appeared in my romantic
dreams, and—poor man, he is dead now, so I can say
this!—it was a dreadful blow to me to be obliged to
sing a love duet with a man smelling of lager beer and
cheese!

Charlotte Cushman—who was a great friend of
Miss Emma Stebbins, the sister of Colonel Stebbins—
had always been interested in me; so when she knew
that I was to make my *début* on February 26 (1861),

she put on *Meg Merrilies* for that night because she
could get through with it early enough for her to see
part of my first performance. She reached the Academy in time for the last act of *Rigoletto;* and I felt that
I had been highly praised when, as I came out and
began to sing, she cried:
"The girl does n't seem to know that she has any
arms!"

My freedom of gesture and action came from nothing
but the most complete familiarity with the part and
with the detail of everything I had to do. In opera
one cannot be too temperamental in one's acting.
One cannot make pauses when one thinks it effective,
nor alter the stage business to fit one's mood, nor work
oneself up to an emotional crescendo one night and not
do it the next. Everything has to be timed to a second
and a fraction of a second. One cannot wait for unusual effects. The orchestra does not consider one's
temperament, and this fact cannot be lost sight of for
a moment. This is why I believe in rehearsing and
studying and working over a *rôle* so exhaustively—
and exhaustingly. For it is only in that most rigidly
studied accuracy of action that any freedom can be
attained. When one becomes so trained that one
cannot conceivably retard a bar, and cannot undertime
a stage cross nor fail to come in promptly in an
ensemble, then, and only then, can one reach some
emotional liberty and inspiration.

If I had not worked so hard at Gilda I should
never have got through that first performance. I was
not consciously nervous, but my throat—it is quite
impossible to tell in words how my throat felt. I have
heard singers describe the first-night sensation variously,
—a tongue that felt stiff, a palate like a hot griddle,

and so on. My throat and my tongue were dry and thick and woolly, like an Oriental rug with a "pile" so deep and heavy that, if water is spilled on it, the water does not soak in, but lies about the surface in globules,—just a dry and unabsorbing carpet.

My mother was with me behind the scenes; and my grandmother was in front to see me in all my stage grandeur. I am afraid I did not care particularly where either of them were. Certainly I had no thought for anyone who might be seated out in the Great Beyond on the far side of the footlights. I sang the second act in a dream, unconscious of any audience:— hardly conscious of the music or of myself—going through it all mechanically. But the sub-conscious mind had been at work all the time. As I was changing my costume after the second act, my mother said to me:

"I cannot find your grandmother anywhere. I have been looking and peeping through the hole in the curtain and from the wings, but I cannot seem to discover where she is sitting."

Hardly thinking of the words, I answered at once: "She is over there to the left, about three rows back, near a pillar."

The criticisms of the press next day said that my most marked specialty was my ability to strike a tone with energy. I liked better, however, one kindly reviewer who observed that my voice was "cordial to the heart!" The newspapers found my stage appearance peculiar. There was about it "a marked development of the intellectual at the expense of the physical to which her New England birth may afford a key." The man who wrote this was quite correct. He had discovered the Puritan maid behind the stage trappings of Gilda.

If omens count for anything I ought to have had a disastrous first season, for everything went wrong during that opening week. I lost a bracelet of which I was particularly fond; I fell over a stick in making an entrance and nearly went on my head; and at the end of the third act of the second performance of *Rigoletto* the curtain failed to come down, and I was obliged to stay in a crouching attitude until it could be put into working order again. But these trying experiences were not auguries of failure or of disaster. In fact my public grew steadily kinder to me, although it hung back a little until after Marguerite. Audiences were not very cordial to new singers. They distrusted their own judgment; and I don't altogether wonder that they did.

The week after my *début* we went to Boston to sing. Boston would not have *Rigoletto*. It was considered objectionable, particularly the ending. For some inexplicable reason *Linda di Chamounix* was expected to be more acceptable to the Bostonian public, and so I was to sing the part of Linda instead of that of Gilda. I had been working on Linda during a part of the year in which I studied Gilda, and was quite equal to it. The others of the company went to Boston ahead of me, and I played Linda at a *matinée* in New York before following them. This was the first time I sang in opera with Brignoli. I went on in the part with only one rehearsal. Opera-goers do not hear *Linda* any more, but it is a graceful little opera with some pretty music and a really charmingly poetic story. It was taken from the French play, *La Grâce de Dieu*, and *Rigoletto* was taken from Victor Hugo's *Le Roi S'Amuse*. The story of *Linda* is that of a Swiss peasant girl of Chamounix who falls in love with a French noble whom she has met as a strolling painter in her village. He returns to Paris and she follows him there, walking all the way and accompanied by a faithful rustic, Pierotto, who loves her humbly. He plays a hurdy-gurdy and Linda sings, and so the poor young vagrants pay their way. In Paris the nobleman finds her and lavishes all manner of jewels and luxuries upon little Linda, but at last abandons her to make a rich marriage. On the same day that she hears the news of her lover's wedding her father comes to her house in Paris and denounces her. She goes mad, of course. Most operatic heroines did go mad in those days. And, in the last act, the peasant lover with the hurdy-gurdy takes her back to Chamounix among the hills. On the lengthy journey he can lure her along only by playing a melody that she knows and loves. It is a dear little story; but I never could comprehend how Boston was induced to accept the second act since they drew the line at *Rigoletto!*

I liked Linda and wanted to give a truthful and appealing impersonation of her. But the handicaps of those days of crude and primitive theatre conditions were really almost insurmountable. Now, with every assistance of wonderful staging, exquisite costuming, and magical lighting, the artist may rest upon his or her surroundings and accessories and know that everything possible to art has been brought together to enhance the convincing effect. In the old days at the Academy, however, we had no system of lighting except glaring footlights and perhaps a single, unimaginative calcium. We had no scenery worthy the name; and as for costumes, there were just three sets called by the theatre *costumier* "Paysannes" (peasant dress); "Norma" (they did not know enough even to call it "classic"); and "Rich!" The last were more or less of the Louis XIV period and could be slightly modified for various operas. These three sets were combined and altered as required. Yet, of course, the audiences were correspondingly unexacting. They were so accustomed to nothing but primitive effects that the simplest touch of true realism surprised and delighted them. Once during a performance of *Il Barbiere* the man who was playing the part of Don Basilio sent his hat out of doors to be snowed on. It was one of those Spanish shovel hats, long and square-edged, like a plank. When he wore it in the next act, all white with snowflakes from the blizzard outside, the audience was so simple and childlike that it roared with pleasure, "Why, it 's *real* snow!"

It was also the time when hoop skirts were universally fashionable, so we all wore hoops, no matter what the period we were supposed to be representing. Scola first showed me how to fall gracefully in a hoop skirt, not in the least an easy feat to accomplish; and I shall always remember seeing Mme. de la Grange go to bed in one, in her sleep-walking scene in *Sonnambula*. Indeed, there was no illusion nor enchantment to help one in those elementary days. One had to conquer one's public alone and unaided.

I confided myself at first to the hands of the *costumier* with characteristic truthfulness. I had considered the musical and dramatic aspects of the part; it did not occur to me that the clothes would become my responsibility as well. That theatre *costumier* at the Academy, I found, could not even cut a skirt. Linda's was a strange affair, very long on the sides, and startlingly short in front. But this was the least of my troubles on the afternoon of that first *matinée* in New York. When it came to the last act—there having been no rehearsals, and my experience being next to nothing—I asked innocently for my costume, and was told that I would have to wear the same dress I had worn in the first act.

"But, I can't!" I gasped. "That fresh new gown, after months are supposed to have gone by!—when Linda has walked and slept in it during the whole journey!"

"No one will think of that," I was assured.

But *I* thought of it and simply could not put on that clean dress for poor Linda's travel-worn last act. I sent for an old shawl from the chorus and ripped my costume into rags. By this time the orchestra was almost at the opening bars of the third act and there was not a moment to lose. Suddenly I looked at my shoes and nearly collapsed with despair. One always provided one's own foot-gear and the shoes I had on were absolutely the only pair of the sort required that I possessed; neat little slippers, painfully new and clean. We had not gone to any extra expense, in case I did not happen to make a success that would justify it, and that was the reason I had only the one pair. Well—there was a moment's struggle before I attacked my pretty shoes—but my passion for realism triumphed. I sent a man out into Fourteenth Street at the stage door of the Academy and had him rub those immaculate slippers in the gutter until they were thoroughly dirty, so that when I wore them onto the stage three minutes later they looked as if I had really walked to Paris and back in them.

The next day the newspapers said that the part of Linda had never before been sung with so much pathos.

"Aha!" said I, "that 's my old clothes! That 's my dirt!"

I had learned that the more you look your part the less you have to act. The observance of this truth was always Henry Irving's great strength. The more completely you get inside a character the less, also, are you obliged to depend on brilliant vocalism. Mary Garden is a case in point. She is not a great singer, although she sings better than she is credited with doing or her voice could not endure as much as it does, but above all she is intelligent and an artistic realist, taking care never to lose the spirit of her *rôle*. Renaud is one of the few men I have ever seen in opera who was willing to wear dirty clothes if they chanced to be in character. I shall never forget Jean de Reszke in *L'Africaine*. In the Madagascar scene, just after the rescue from the foundered vessel, he appeared in the most beautiful fresh tights imaginable and a pair of superb light leather boots. Indeed, the most distinguished performance becomes weak and valueless if the note of truth is lacking.

Theodore Thomas was the first violin in the Academy at the time of which I am writing, and not a very good one either. The director was Maretzek—"Maretzek the Magnificent" as he was always called, for he was very handsome and had a vivid and compelling personality—on whom be benisons, for it was he who, later, suggested the giving of *Faust*, and me for the leading *rôle*.

I was not popular with my fellow-artists and did not have a very pleasant time preparing and rehearsing for my first parts. The chorus was made up of Italians who never studied their music, merely learned it at rehearsal, and the rehearsals themselves were often farcical. The Italians of the chorus were always bitter against me for, up to that time, Italians had had the monopoly of music. It was not generally conceded that Americans could appreciate, much less interpret opera; and I, as the first American *prima donna*, was in the position of a foreigner in my own country. The chorus, indeed, could sometimes hardly contain themselves. "Who is she," they would demand indignantly, "to come and take the bread out of our mouths?"

One other person in the company who never gave me a kind word (although she was not an Italian) was Adelaide Phillips, the contralto. She was a fine artist and had been singing for many years, so, perhaps, it galled her to have to "support" a younger countrywoman. When it came to dividing the honours she was not at all pleased. As Maddalena in *Rigoletto* she was very plain; but when she did Pierotto, the boyish, rustic lover in *Linda*, she looked well. She had the most perfectly formed pair of legs—ankles, feet and all—that I ever saw on a woman.

In singing with Brignoli there developed a difficulty to which Ferri's blindness was nothing. Brignoli seriously objected to being touched during his scene! Imagine playing love scenes with a tenor who did not want to be touched, no matter what might be the emotional exigencies of the moment or situation. The bass part in *Linda* is that of the Baron, and when I first sang the opera it was taken by Susini, who had been with us on our preparatory *tournée*. His wife was Isabella Hinckley, a good and sweet woman, also a singer with an excellent soprano voice. I found that the big basso (he was a very large man with a buoyant sense of humour) was a fine actor and had a genuine dramatic gift in singing. His sense of humour was always bubbling up, in and out of performances. I once lost a diamond from one of my rings during the first act. My dressing-room and the stage were searched, but with no result. We went on for the last act and, in the scene when I was supposed to be unconscious, Susini caught sight of the stone glittering on the floor and picked it up. As he needed his hands for gesticulations, he popped the diamond into his mouth and when I "came to" he stuck out his tongue at me with the stone on the end of it!

While I was working on the part of Linda myself, I heard Mme. Medori sing it. She gave a fine emotional interpretation, getting great tragic effects in the Paris act, but she did not catch the *naïve* and ingenuous quality of poor, young Linda. It could hardly have been otherwise, for she was at the time a mature woman. There are some parts,—Marguerite is one of them, also,—that can be made too complicated, too subtle, too dramatic. I was criticised for my immaturity and lack of emotional power until I was tired of hearing such criticism; and once had a quaint little argument about my abilities and powers with "Nym Crinkle," the musical critic of *The World*, A. C. Wheeler. (Later he made a success in literature under the name of "J. P. Mowbray.")

"What do you expect," I demanded, in my old-fashioned yet childish way, being at the time eighteen, "what do you expect of a person of my age?"

Brignoli, 1865
From a photograph by C. Silvy

CHAPTER V

MY friends in New York had given me letters to people in Boston, so I went there with every opportunity for an enjoyable visit. But, naturally, I was much more absorbed in my own *début* and in what the public would think of me than I was in meeting new acquaintances and receiving invitations. Now I wish that I had then more clearly realised possibilities, for Boston was at the height of its literary reputation. All my impressions of that Boston season, however, sink into insignificance compared to that of my first public appearance. I sang Linda; and there were only three hundred people in the house!

If anything in the world could have discouraged me that would have, but, as a matter of fact, I do not believe anything could. At any rate, I worked all the harder just because the conditions were so adverse; and I won my public (such as it was) that night. I may add that I kept it for the remainder of my stay in Boston.

At that period of my life I was very fragile and one big performance would wear me out. Literally, I used myself up in singing, for I put into it every ounce of my strength. I could not save myself when I was actually working, but my way of economising my vitality was to sing only twice a week.

43

It was after that first performance of *Linda*, some time about midnight, and my mother and I had just returned to our apartment in the Tremont House and had hardly taken off our wraps, when a knock came at the door. Our sitting-room was near a side entrance for the sake of quietness and privacy, but we paid a penalty in the ease with which we could be reached by anyone who knew the way. My mother opened the door; and there stood two ladies who overwhelmed us with gracious speeches. "They had heard my Linda! They had come because they simply could not help it; because I had moved them so deeply! Now, *would* we both come the following evening to a little *musicale;* and they would ask that delightful Signor Brignoli too! It would be *such* a pleasure! etc."

Although I was not singing the following night, I objected to going to the *musicale* because certain experiences in New York had already bred caution. I said, however, with perfect frankness, that I would go on one condition.

"On *any* condition, dear Miss Kellogg!"

"You would n't expect me to sing?"

"Oh no; no, no!"

Accordingly, the next night my mother and I presented ourselves at the house of the older of the two ladies. The first words our hostess uttered when I entered the room were:

"Why! where's your music?"

"I thought it was understood that I was not to sing," said I.

But, in spite of their previous earnest disclaimers on this point, they became so insistent that, after resisting their importunities for a few moments, I finally consented to satisfy them. I asked Brignoli to play for me, and I sang the Cavatina from *Linda*. Then I turned on my heel and went back to my hotel; and I never again entered that woman's house. After so many years there is no harm in saying that the hostess who was guilty of this breach of tact, good taste, and consideration, was Mrs. Paran Stevens, and the other lady was her sister, Miss Fanny Reed, one of the talented amateurs of the day. They were struggling hard for social recognition in Boston and every drawing card was of value, even a new, young singer who might become famous. Later, of course, Mrs. Stevens did "arrive" in New York; but she travelled some difficult roads first.

This was by no means the first time that I had contended with a lack of consideration in the American hostess, especially toward artists. Her sisters across the Atlantic have better taste and breeding, never subjecting an artist who is their guest to the annoyance and indignity of having to "sing for her supper." But whenever I was invited anywhere by an American woman, I always knew that I would be expected to bring my music and to contribute toward the entertainment of the other guests. An Englishwoman I once met when travelling on the Continent hit the nail on the head, although in quite another connection.

"You Americans are so queer," she remarked. "I heard a woman from the States ask a perfectly strange man recently to stop in at a shop and match her some silk while he was out! I imagine it is because you don't mind putting yourselves under obligations, is n't it?"

Literary Boston of that day revolved around Mr. and Mrs. James T. Fields, at whose house often assembled such distinguished men and women as Emerson, Longfellow, Oliver Wendell Holmes, Lowell, Anthony Trollope, Harriet Beecher Stowe, and Julia Ward Howe. Mr. Fields was the editor of *The Atlantic Monthly*, and his sense of humour was always a delight.

"A lady came in from the suburbs to see me this morning," he once remarked to me. "'Well, Mr. Fields,' she said, with great impressiveness, 'what have you new in literature to-day? I'm just *thusty* for knowledge!'"

Your true New Englander always says "thust" and "fust" and "wust," and Mr. Fields had just the intonation—which reminds me somehow—in a round-about fashion—of a strange woman who battered on my door once after I had appeared in *Faust*, in Boston, to tell me that "that man Mephisto-fleas was just great!"

It was a wonderful privilege to meet Longfellow. He was never gay, never effusive, leaving these attributes to his talkative brother-in-law, Tom Appleton, who was a wit and a humourist. Indeed, Longfellow was rather noted for his cold exterior, and it took a little time and trouble to break the ice, but, though so unexpressive outwardly, his nature was most winning when one was once in touch with it. His first wife was burned to death and the tragedy affected him permanently, although he made a second and a very successful marriage with Tom Appleton's sister. The brothers-in-law were often together and formed the oddest possible contrast to each other.

Longfellow and I became good friends. I saw him many times and often went to his house to sing to him. He greatly enjoyed my singing of his own *Beware*. It was always one of my successful *encore* songs, although it certainly is not Longfellow at his best. But he

James Russell Lowell in 1861
From a photograph by Brady

liked me to sit at the piano and wander from one song to another. The older the melodies, the sweeter he found them. Longfellow's verses have much in common with simple, old-fashioned songs. They always touched the common people, particularly the common people of England. They were so simple and so true that those folk who lived and laboured close to the earth found much that moved them in the American writer's unaffected and elemental poetry. Yet it seems a bit strange that his poems are more loved and appreciated in England than in America, much as Tennyson's are more familiar to us than to his own people. Some years later, when I was singing in London, I heard that Longfellow was in town and sent him a box. He and Tom Appleton, who was with him, came behind the scenes between the acts to see me and, my mother being with me, both were invited into my dressing-room. In the London theatres there are women, generally advanced in years, who assist the *prima donna* or actress to dress. These do not exist in American theatres. I had a maid, of course, but there was this woman of the theatre, also, a particularly ordinary creature who contributed nothing to the gaiety of nations and who, indeed, rarely showed feeling of any sort. I happened to say to her:

"Perkins, I am going to see Mr. Longfellow."

Her face became absolutely transfigured.

"Oh, Miss," she cried in a tone of awe and curtseying to his name, "you don't mean 'im that wrote *Tell me not in mournful numbers?* Oh, Miss! *'im!*"

Lowell I knew only slightly, yet his distinguished and distinctive personality made a great impression on me. Thomas Bailey Aldrich, a blond, curly-headed young man, whose later prosperity greatly interfered with his ability, I first met about this same time. He was too successful too young, and it stultified his gifts, as being successful too young usually does stultify the natural gifts of anybody. On one occasion I met Anthony Trollope at the Fields', the English novelist whose works were then more or less in vogue. He had just come from England and was filled with conceit. English people of that time were incredibly insular and uninformed about us, and Mr. Trollope knew nothing of America, and did not seem to want to know anything. Certainly, English people when they are not thoroughbred can be very common! Trollope was full of himself and wrote only for what he could get out of it. I never, before or since, met a literary person who was so frankly "on the make." The discussion that afternoon was about the recompense of authors, and Trollope said that he had reduced his literary efforts to a working basis and wrote so many words to a page and so many pages to a chapter. He refrained from using the actual word "money"—the English shrink from the word "money"—but he managed to convey to his hearers the fact that a considerable consideration was the main incentive to his literary labour, and put the matter more specifically later, to my mother, by telling her that he always *chose the words that would fill up the pages quickest.*

Nathaniel Hawthorne, though he was one of the Fields' circle, I never met at all. He was tragically shy, and more than once escaped from the house when we went in rather than meet two strange women.

"Hawthorne has just gone out the other way," Mrs. Fields would whisper, smiling. "He's too frightened to meet you!"

I met his boy Julian, however, who was about twelve years old. He was a nice lad and I kissed him— to his great annoyance, for he was shy too, although not so much so as his father. Not so very long ago Julian Hawthorne reminded me of this episode.

"Do you remember," he said, laughing, "how embarrassed I was when you kissed me? 'Never you mind' you said to me then, 'the time will come, my boy, when you'll be glad to remember that I kissed you!' And it certainly did come!"

All Boston that winter was stirred by the approaching agitations of war; and those two remarkable women, Mrs. Stowe and Mrs. Howe were using their pens to excite the community into a species of splendid rage. I first met them both at the Fields' and always admired Julia Ward Howe as a representative type of the highest Boston culture. Harriet Beecher Stowe had just finished *Uncle Tom's Cabin*. Many people believed that it and the disturbance it made were partly responsible for the war itself. Mr. Fields told me that her "copy" was the most remarkable "stuff" that the publishers had ever encountered. It was written quite roughly and disconnectedly on whatever scraps of paper she had at hand. I suppose she wrote it when the spirit moved her. At any rate, Mr. Fields said it was the most difficult task imaginable to fit it into any form that the printers could understand. Mrs. Stowe was a quiet, elderly woman, and talked very little. I had an odd sort of feeling that she had put so much of herself into her book that she had nothing left to offer socially.

I did not realise until years afterwards what a precious privilege it was to meet in such a charming *intime* way the men and women who really "made"

4

American literature. The Fields literally kept open house. They were the most hospitable of people, and I loved them and spent some happy hours with them. I cannot begin to enumerate or even to remember all the literary lights I met in their drawing-room. Of that number there were James Freeman Clarke, Harriet Prescott Spofford, whom I knew later in Washington, and Gail Hamilton who was just budding into literary prominence; and Sidney Lanier. But, as I look back on that first. Boston engagement, I see plainly that the most striking impression made upon my youthful mind during the entire season was the opening night of *Linda di Chamounix* and the three hundred auditors!

It was long, long after that first season that I had some of my pleasantest times in Boston with Sidney Lanier. This may not be the right place to mention them, but they certainly belong under the heading of this chapter.

The evening that stands out most clearly in my memory was one, in the 'seventies, that I spent at the house of dear Charlotte Cushman who was then very ill and who died almost immediately after. Sidney Lanier was there with his flute, which he played charmingly. Indeed, he was as much musician as poet, as anyone who knows his verse must realise. He was poor then, and Miss Cushman was interested in him and anxious to help him in every way she could. There were two dried-up, little, Boston old maids there too—queer creatures—who were much impressed with High Art without knowing anything about it. One composition that Lanier played somewhat puzzled me —my impertinent absolute pitch was, as usual, hard at work—and at the end I exclaimed:

"That piece does n't end in the same key in which it begins!"

Lanier looked surprised and said:

"No, it does n't. It is one of my own compositions."

He thought it remarkable that I could catch the change of key in such a long and intricately modulated piece of music. The little old maids of Boston were somewhat scandalised by my effrontery; but there was even more to come. After another lovely thing which he played for us, I was so impressed by the rare tone of his instrument that I asked:

"Is that a Böhm flute?"

He, being a musician, was delighted with the implied compliment; but the old ladies saw in my question only a shocking slight upon his execution. Turning to one another they ejaculated with one voice, and that one filled with scorn and pity:

"She thinks it 's the *flute!*"

This difference between professionals and the laity is odd. The more enchanted a professional is with another artist's performance, the more technical interest and curiosity he feels. The amateur only knows how to rhapsodise. This seems to be so in everything. When someone rides in an automobile for the first time he only thinks how exciting it is and how fast he is going. The experienced motorist immediately wants to know what sort of engine the machine has, and how many cylinders.

I have always loved a flute. It is a difficult instrument to play with colour and variety. It is not like the violin, on which one can get thirds, and sixths, and sevenths, by using the arpeggio: it is a single, thin tone and can easily become monotonous if not played skilfully. Furthermore, there are only certain pieces of music that ever ought to be played on it. Wagner uses the flute wonderfully. He never lets it bore his audience. The Orientals have brought flute playing and flute music to a fine art, and it is one of the oldest of instruments, but, unlike the violin and other instruments, it is more perfectly manufactured to-day than it was in the past. The modern flutes have a far more mellow and sympathetic tone than the old ones.

That whole evening at Miss Cushman's was complete in its fulness of experience, as I recall it, looking back across the years. How many people know that Miss Cushman had studied singing and had a very fine *baritone* contralto voice? Two of her songs were *The Sands o' Dee* and *Low I Breathe my Passion*. That night, the last time I ever heard her sing, I recalled how often before I had seen her seating herself at the piano to play her own accompaniments, always a difficult thing to do. Again I can see her, at this late day, turning on the stool to talk to us between songs, emphasising her points with that odd, inevitable gesture of the forefinger that was so characteristic of her, and then wheeling back to the instrument to let that deep voice of hers roll through the room in

" Will she wake and say good night ?"   . . .

During that first Boston season of mine, my mother and I used to give breakfasts at the Parker House. We were somewhat noted characters there as we were the first women to stop at it, the Parker House being originally a man's restaurant exclusively; and breakfast was a meal of ceremony. The *chef* of the Parker House used to surpass himself at our breakfast entertainments for he knew that such an epicure as Oliver

Charlotte Cushman, 1861

From a photograph by Silsbee, Case & Co.

Wendell Holmes might be there at any time. This *chef*, by the way, was the first man to put up soups in cans and, after he left the Parker House kitchens, he made name and money for himself in establishing the canned goods trade.

Dear Dr. Holmes! What a delightful, warm spontaneous nature was his, and what a fine mind! We were always good friends and I am proud of the fact. Shall I ever forget the dignity and impressiveness of his bearing as, after the fourth course of one of my breakfasts, he glanced up, saw the waiter approaching, arose solemnly as if he were about to make a speech, went behind his chair,—we all thought he was about to give us one of his brilliant addresses—shook out one leg and then the other, all most seriously and without a word, so as to make room for the next course!

Years later Dr. Holmes and I crossed from England on the same steamer. He had been fêted and made much of in England and we discussed the relative brilliancy of American and English women. I contended that Americans were the brighter and more sparkling, while English women had twice as much real education and mental training. Dr. Holmes agreed, but with reservations. He professed himself to be still dazzled with British feminine wit.

"I'm tired to death," he declared. "At every dinner party I went to they had picked out the cleverest women in London to sit on each side of me. I'm utterly exhausted trying to keep up with them!"

This was the voyage when the benefit for the sailors was given—for the English sailors, that is. It was well arranged so that the American seamen could get nothing out of it. Dr. Holmes was asked to speak and I was asked to sing; but we declined to perform.

We did write our names on the programmes, however, and as these sold for a considerable price, we added to the fund in spite of our intentions.

My first season in Boston—from which I have strayed so far so many times—was destined to be a brief one, but also very strenuous, due to the fact that in the beginning I had only two operas in my *répertoire*, one of which Boston did not approve. After *Linda*, I was rushed on in Bellini's *I Puritani* and had to "get up in it" in three days. It went very well, and was followed with *La Sonnambula* by the same composer and after only one week's rehearsal. I was a busy girl in those weeks; and I should have been still busier if opera in America had not received a sudden and tragic blow.

The "vacillating" Buchanan's reign was over. On March 4th Lincoln was inaugurated. A hush of suspense was in the air:—a hush broken on April 12th by the shot fired by South Carolina upon Fort Sumter. On April 14th Sumter capitulated and Abraham Lincoln called for volunteers. The Civil War had begun.

CHAPTER VI

A T first the tremendous crisis filled everyone with a
purely impersonal excitement and concern; but
one fine morning we awoke to the fact that our opera
season was paralysed.

The American people found the actual dramas of
Bull Run, Big Bethel and Harpers Ferry more absorbing than any play or opera ever put upon the boards,
and the airs of *Yankee Doodle* and *The Girl I Left Behind
Me* more inspiring than the finest operatic *arias* in the
world. They did not want to go to the theatres in
the evening. They wanted to read the bulletin boards.
Every move in the big game of war that was being
played by the ruling powers of our country was of
thrilling interest, and as fast as things happened they
were "posted."

Maretzek "the Magnificent," so obstinate that he
simply did not know how to give up a project merely
because it was impossible, packed a few of us off to
Philadelphia to produce the *Ballo in Maschera*. We
hoped against hope that it would be light enough to
divert the public, at even that tragic moment. But
the public refused to be diverted. Why I ever sang
in it I cannot imagine. I weighed barely one hundred
and four pounds and was about as well suited to the
part of Amelia as a sparrow would have been. I

never liked the *rôle*; it is heavy and uncongenial and altogether out of my line. I should never have been permitted to do it, and I have always suspected that there might have been something of a plot against me on the part of the Italians. But all this made no difference, for we abandoned the idea of taking the opera out on a short tour. We could plainly see that opera was doomed for the time being in America.

Then Maretzek bethought himself of *La Figlia del Reggimento*, a military opera, very light and infectious, that might easily catch the wave of public sentiment at the moment. We put it on in a rush. I played the Daughter and we crowded into the performance every bit of martial feeling we could muster. I learned to play the drum, and we introduced all sorts of military business and bugle calls, and altogether contrived to create a warlike atmosphere. We were determined to make a success of it; but we were also genuinely moved by the contagious glow that pervaded the country and the times, and to this combined mood of patriotism and expediency we sacrificed many artistic details. For example, we were barbarous enough to put in sundry American national airs and we had the assistance of real Zouaves to lend colour; and this reminds me that about the same period Isabella Hinckley even sang *The Star Spangled Banner* in the middle of a performance of *Il Barbiere*.

Our attempt was a great success. We played Donizetti's little opera to houses of frantic enthusiasm, first in Baltimore, then in Washington on May the third, where naturally the war fever was at its highest heat. The audiences cheered and cried and let themselves go in the hysterical manner of people wrought up by great national excitements. Even on the stage we

Clara Louise Kellogg as Figlia
From a photograph by Black & Case

caught the feeling. I sang the Figlia better than I had ever sung anything yet, and I found myself wondering, as I sang, how many of my cadet friends of a few months earlier were already at the front.

I felt very proud of these friends when I read the despatches from the front. They all distinguished themselves, some on one side and some on the other. Alec McCook was Colonel of the 1st Ohio Volunteers, being an Ohio man by birth, and did splendid service in the first big battle of the war, Bull Run. He was made Major-General of Volunteers later, I believe, and always held a prominent position in American military affairs. From Fort Pulaski came word of Lieutenant Horace Porter who, though only recently graduated, was in command of the battlements there. He was speedily brevetted Captain for "distinguished gallantry under fire," and after Antietam he was sent to join the Army of the Ohio. He was everywhere and did everything imaginable during the war—Chattanooga, Chickamauga, the Battle of the Wilderness— and was General Grant's *aide-de-camp* in some of the big conflicts. McCreary and young Huger I heard less of because they were on the other side; but they were both brave fellows and did finely according to their convictions. It is odd to recall that Huger's father, General Isaac Huger, had fought for the Union in the early wars and yet turned against her in the civil struggle between the blues and the greys. The Hugers were South Carolinians though, and therefore rabid Confederates.

With the war and its many memories, ghosts will always rise up in my recollection of Custer, the "Golden Haired Laddie,"—as his friends called him. He was a good friend of mine, and after the war was over he used to come frequently to see me and tell me the most wonderful, thrilling stories about it, and of his earliest fights with the Indians. He was a most vivid creature; one felt a sense of vigour and energy and eagerness about him; and he was so brave and zealous as to make one know that he would always come up to the mark. I never saw more magnificent enthusiasm. He was not thirty at that time and when on horseback, riding hard, with his long yellow hair blowing back in the wind, he was a marvellously striking figure. He was not really a tall man, but looked so, being a soldier. Oh, if I could only remember those stories of his—stories of pluck and of danger and of excitement!

It has always been a matter of secret pride with me that, in my small way, I did something for the Union too. I heard that our patriotic and inartistic *Daughter of the Regiment* caused several lads to enlist. I do not know if this were true, but I hoped so at the time, and it might well have been so.

I had a dresser, Ellen Conklin, who had some strange and rather ghastly tales to tell of the slave trade in the days before the war. She had been in other opera companies, small troupes, that sang their way from the far South, and the primitive and casual manner of their travel had offered many opportunities for her to visit any number of slave markets. She frequently had been harrowed to the breaking point by the sight of mothers separated from their children, and men and women who loved each other being parted for life. The worst horror of it all had been to her the examining of the female slaves as to their physical equipment, in which the buyers were more often brutal than not. Ellen was Irish and emotional; and it tore her heart

General Horace Porter
From a photograph by Pach Bros.

out to see such things; but she kept on going to the slave sales just the same.

"They nearly killed me, Miss," she declared to me with tears in her eyes, "but I could never resist one!"

Though I quite understood Ellen's emotions, I found it a little difficult to understand why she invited them so persistently. But I have learned that this is a very common human weakness—luckily for managers who put on harrowing plays. Many people go to the theatre to cry. When I sang Mignon the audience always cried and wiped its eyes; and I felt convinced that many had come for exactly that purpose. Two women I know once went to see Helena Modjeska in *Adrienne Lecouvreur* and, when the curtain fell, one of them turned to the other with streaming eyes and gasped between her choking sobs:

"L — l — let 's come — (sob) — again — (sob)—t— t—to-morrow night! (sob, sob)."

Personally, I think there are occasions enough for tears in this life, bitter or consoling, without having somebody on the stage draw them out over fictitious joys and sorrows.

In the beginning of the war the feeling against the negroes was really more bitter in the North than in the South. The riots in New York were a scandal and a disgrace, although very few people have any idea how bad they actually were. The Irish Catholics were particularly rabid and asserted openly, right and left, that the freeing of the slaves would mean an influx of cheap labour that would become a drug on the market. It was an Irish mob that burned a coloured orphan asylum, after which taste of blood the most innocent black was not safe. Perfectly harmless coloured people were hanged to lamp-posts with impunity. No one ever seemed to be punished for such outrages. The time was one of open lawlessness in New York City. The Irish seem sometimes to be peculiarly possessed by this unreasoning and hysterical mob spirit which, as Ruskin once pointed out, they always manage to justify to themselves by some high abstract principle or sentiment. A story that has always seemed to me illustrative of this is that of the Hibernian contingent that hanged an unfortunate Jew because his people had killed Jesus Christ and, when reminded that it had all happened some time before, replied that "that might be, but they had only just heard of it!" It is a singularly significant story, with much more truth than jest in it. Years later, I recollect that those Irish riots in New York over the negro question served as the basis for some exceedingly heated arguments between an English friend of mine at Aix-les-Bains and a Catholic priest living there. The priest sought to justify them, but his reasonings have escaped me.

At the time of these riots our New York home was on Twenty-second Street where Stern's shop now stands. We rented it from the Bryces, Southerners, who had a coloured coachman, a fact that made our residence a target for the animosity of our more ignorant neighbours who lived in the rear. The house was built with a foreign porte-cochère; and, time and again, small mobs would throng under that porte-cochère, battering on the door and trying to break in to get the coachman. The hanging of a negro near St. John's Chapel was an occasion for rejoicing and festivity, and the lower class Irish considered it a time for their best clothes. One hears of bear-baiting and bull-fights. But think of the barbarity of all this!

Once, when we went away for a day or two, we left

Irish servants in the house and, on returning, I found
that the maids had been wearing my smartest gowns to
view the riots and lynchings. A common lace collar
was pinned to one of my French dresses and I had little
difficulty in getting the waitress to admit that she had
worn it. She explained *naïvely* that the riots were
gala occasions, "a great time for the Irish." She
added that she had met my father on the stairs and had
been afraid that he would recognise the dress; but,
although she was penitent enough about "borrowing"
the finery, she did not in the least see anything odd in
her desire to dress up for the tormenting of an unfortunate fellow-creature.

Everybody went about singing Mrs. Howe's *Battle
Hymn of the Republic* and it was then that I first
learned that the air—the simple but rousing little
melody of *John Brown's Body*—was in reality a melody
by Felix Mendelssohn. Martial songs of all kinds
were the order of the day and all more classic music
was relegated to the background for the time being.
It was not until the following winter that public sentiment subsided sufficiently for us to really consider
another musical season.

CHAPTER VII

IN the three years between my *début* and my appearance in *Faust* I sang, in all, a dozen operas:—*Rigoletto, Linda, I Puritani, Sonnambula, Ballo in Maschera, Figlia del Reggimento, Les Noces de Jeannette, Lucia, Don Giovanni, Poliuto, Marta,* and *Traviata.* Besides these, I sang a good deal in concert, but I never cared for either concert or oratorio work as much as for opera. My real growth and development came from big parts in which both musical and dramatic accomplishment were necessary.

Like all artists, I look back upon many fluctuations in my artistic achievements. Sometimes I was good, and often not so good; and, curiously enough, I was usually best, according to my friends and critics, when most dissatisfied with myself. But of one thing I am fairly confident:—I never really went backward, never seriously retrograded artistically. Each *rôle* was a step further and higher. To each I brought a clearer vision, a surer touch, a more flexible method, a finer (how shall I say it in English?) *attaque* is nearest what I mean. This I say without vanity, for the artist who does not grow and improve with each succeeding part is deteriorating. There is no standing still in any life work; or, if there is, it is the standing still of successful effort, the hard-won tenure of a difficult place from which most people slip back. The Red Queen in *Through the Looking Glass* expressed it rightly when she told Alice that "you have to run just as hard as you can to stay where you are."

As Gilda I was laying only the groundwork. My performance was, I believe, on the right lines. It rang true. But it was far from what it became in later years when the English critics found me "the most beautiful and convincing of all Gildas!" As Linda I do not think that I showed any great intellectual improvement over Gilda, but I had acquired a certain confidence and authority. I sang and acted with more ease; and for the first time I had gained a sense of *personal responsibility* toward, and for, an audience. When I beheld only three hundred people in my first-night Boston audience and determined to win them, and did win them, I came into possession of new and important factors in my work. This consciousness and earnest will-power to move one's public by the force of one's art is one of the first steps toward being a true *prima donna*.

I Puritani never taught me very much, simply as an opera. The part was too heavy as my voice was then, and our production of it was so hurried that I had not time to spend on it the study which I liked to give a new *rôle*. But in this very fact lay its lesson for me. The necessity for losing timidity and self-consciousness, the power to fling oneself into a new part without time to coddle one's vanity or one's habits of mind, the impersonal courage needed to attack fresh difficulties:—these points are of quite as much importance to a young opera singer as are fine breath control and a gift for phrasing. *Sonnambula*, too, had to be "jumped into" in the same fashion and was even more of an undertaking, though the *rôle* suited me better and is, in fact, a rarely grateful one. Yet think of being Amina with only one week's rehearsing! *Sonnambula* was first given by us as a benefit performance for Brignoli. It was generally understood to be in the nature of a farewell. Indeed, I think he said so himself. But, of course, he never had the slightest idea of really leaving America. He stayed here until he died. But to his credit be it said that he never had any more "farewell" appearances. He did not form the habit.

I have spoken of how hopeless it is for an opera singer to try to work emotionally or purely on impulse; of how futile the merely temperamental artist becomes on the operatic stage. Yet too much stress cannot be laid on the importance of feeling what one does and sings. It is in just this seeming paradox that the truly professional artist's point of view may be found. The amateur acts and sings temperamentally. The trained student gives a finished and correct performance. It is only a genius—or something very near it— who can do both. There is something balanced and restrained in a genuine *prima donna's* brain that keeps her emotions from running away with her, just as there is at the same time something equally warm and inspired in her heart that animates the most clear-cut of her intellectual work and makes it living and lovely. Sometimes it is difficult for an experienced artist to say just where instinct stops and art begins. When I sang Amina I was greatly complimented on my walk and my intonation, both most characteristic of a somnambulist. I made a point of keeping a strange, rhythmical, dreamy step like that of a sleep-walker and sang as if I were talking in my sleep. I breathed in a hard, laboured way, and walked with the headlong yet dragging gait of someone who neither sees, knows, nor cares where she is going. Now, this effect came not entirely from calculation nor yet from intuition, but from a combination of the two. I was in the *mood* of somnambulism and acted accordingly. But I deliberately placed myself in that mood. This only partly expresses what I wish to say on the subject; but it is the root of dramatic work as I know it.

The opera of *Sonnambula*, incidentally, taught me one or two things not generally included in stage essentials. Among others, I had to learn not to be afraid, physically afraid, or at any rate not to mind being afraid. In the sleep-walking scene Amina, carrying her candle and robed in white, glides across the narrow bridge at a perilous height while the watchers below momentarily expect her to be dashed to pieces on the rocks underneath. Our bridge used to be set very high indeed (it was especially lofty in the Philadelphia Opera House where we gave the opera a little later), and I had quite a climb to get up to it at all. There was a wire strung along the side of the bridge, but it was not a bit of good to lean on—merely a moral support. I had to carry the candle in one hand and could n't even hold the other outstretched to balance myself, for sleep-walkers do not fall! This was the point that I had to keep in mind; I could not walk carefully, but I had to walk with certainty. In a sense it was suggestive of a hypnotic condition and I had to get pretty nearly into one myself before I could do it. At all events, I had to compose myself very summarily first. Just in the middle of the crossing the bridge is supposed to crack. Of course the edges were only broken; but I had to give a sort of "jog"

5

to carry out the illusion and I used to wonder, the
while I jogged, if I were going over the side *that* time!
In the wings they used to be quite anxious about me
and would draw a general breath of relief when I was
safely across.   Every night I would be asked if I were
sure I wanted to undertake it that night, and every
time I would answer:

"I don't know whether I *can!*"

But, of course, I always did it.   Somehow, one
always does do one's work on the stage, even if it is
trying to the nerves or a bit dangerous.   I have heard
that when Maud Adams put on her big production of
Joan of Arc, her managers objected seriously to having
her lead the mounted battle charge herself.   A "double"
was costumed exactly like her and was ready to mount
Miss Adams's horse at the last moment.   But did she
ever give a double a chance to lead her battle charge?
Not she: and no more would any true artist.

Sonnambula also helped fix in my mentality the
traditions of Italian opera; those traditions that my
teachers—Muzio particularly—had been striving so
hard to impress upon and make real to me.   The
school of the older operas, while the greatest school for
singers in the world, is one in which tradition is, and
must be, pre-eminent.   In the modern growths, spring-
ing up among us every year, the singer has a chance to
create, to trace new paths, to take venturesome flights.
The new operas not only permit this, they require it.
But it is a pity to hear a young, imaginative artist try
to interpret some old and classic opera by the light of
his or her modern perceptions.   They do not improve
on the material.   They only make a combination that
is bizarre and inartistic.   This struck me forcibly not
long ago when I heard a young, talented American sing

Muzio
From a photograph by Gurney & Son

A non giunge, the lovely old *aria* from the last act of *Sonnambula*. The girl had a charming voice and she sang with musical feeling and taste. But she had not one "tradition" as we understood the term, and, in consequence, almost any worn-out, old-school singer could have rendered the *aria* more acceptably to trained ears. Traditions are as necessary to the Bellini operas as costumes are to Shakespeare's plays. To dispense with them may be original, but it is bad art. And yet, while I became duly impressed with the necessity of the "traditions," during those early performances, I always tried to avoid following them too servilely or too artificially. I tried to interpret for myself, within certain well-defined limits, according to my personal conception of the characters I was personating. The traditions of Italian opera combined with my own ideals of the lyric heroines,—this became my object and ambition.

The summer after my *début*, I went on a concert tour under Grau's management, but my throat was tired after the strain and nervous effort of my first season, and I finally went up to the country for a long rest. In New Hartford, Connecticut, my mother, father, and I renewed many old friendships, and it was a genuine pleasure to sing again in a small choir, to attend sewing circles, and to live the every-day life from which I had been so far removed during my studies and professional work. People everywhere were charming to me. Though only nineteen, I was an acknowledged *prima donna*, and so received all sorts of kindly attentions. This was the summer, I believe, (although it may have been a later one) when Herbert Witherspoon, then only a boy, determined to become a professional singer. He has always insisted that it was my presence and the glamour that surrounded the stage because of me that finally decided him.

I did not sing again in New York until the January of 1862. Before that we had a short season on the road, Philadelphia, Baltimore, and other places. As there were then but nine opera houses in America our itinerary was necessarily somewhat limited. In November of that year I sang in *Les Noces de Jeannette*, in Philadelphia, a charming part although not a very important one. It is a simple little operetta in one act by Victor Macci. The *libretto* was in French and I sang it in that language. Pleasing speeches were made about my French and people wanted to know where I had studied it—I, who had never studied it at all except at home! The opera was not long enough for a full evening's entertainment, so Miss Hinckley was put on in the same bill in Donizetti's *Betly*. The two went very well together.

The critics found *Jeannette* a great many surprising things, "broad," "risqué," "typically French," and so on. In reality it was innocent enough; but it must be remembered that this was a day and generation which found *Faust* frightfully daring, and *Traviata* so improper that a year's hard effort was required before it could be sung in Brooklyn. I sympathised with one critic, however, who railed against the translated *libretto* as sold in the lobby. After stating that it was utter nonsense, he added with excellent reason:

"But this was to have been expected. That anyone connected with an opera house should know enough about English to make a decent translation into it is, of course, quite out of the question."

It was really funny about *Traviata*. In 1861 President Chittenden, of the Board of Directors of the

Brooklyn Academy of Music, made a sensational speech arraigning the plot of *Traviata*,[1] and protesting against its production in Brooklyn on the grounds of propriety, or, rather, impropriety. Meetings were held and it was finally resolved that the opera was objectionable. The feeling against it grew into a series of almost religious ceremonies of protest and, as I have said, it took Grau a year of hard effort to overcome the opposition. When, at last, in '62, the opera was given, I took part; and the audience was all on edge with excitement. There had been so much talk about it that the whole town turned out to see *why* the Directors had withstood it for a year. Every clergyman within travelling distance was in the house.

Its dramatic sister *Camille* was also opposed violently when Mme. Modjeska played it in Brooklyn in later years. These facts are amusing in the light of present-day productions and their morals, or dearth of them. *Salome* is, I think, about the only grand opera of recent times that has been suppressed by a Directors' Meeting. But in my youth Directors were very tender of their public's virtuous feelings. When *The Black Crook* and the Lydia Thompson troupe first appeared in New York, people spoke of those comparatively harmless shows with bated breath and no one dared admit having actually seen them. The "Lydia Thompson Blonds" the troupe was called. They did a burlesque song and dance affair, and wore yellow wigs. Mr. Brander Matthews married one of the most popular and charming of them. I wonder what would have happened to an audience of that time if a modern, up-to-date, Broadway musical farce had been presented to their consideration!

[1] The book is founded upon Dumas's *La Dame aux Camélias*.

At any rate, the much-advertised *Traviata* was finally given, being a huge and sensational success. Probably I did not really understand the character of Violetta down in the bottom of my heart. Modjeska once said that a woman was only capable of playing Juliet when she was old enough to be a grandmother; and if that be true of the young Verona girl, how much more must it be true of poor Camille. My interpretation of the Lady of the Camellias must have been a curiously impersonal one. I know that when Emma Abbott appeared in it later, the critics said that she was so afraid of allowing it to be suggestive that she made it so, whereas I apparently never thought of that side of it and consequently never forced my audiences to think of it either.

There are some things accessible to genius that are beyond the reach of character [wrote one reviewer]. Abbott expects to make *Traviata* acceptable very much as she would make a capon acceptable. She is always afraid of the words. So she substitutes her own. Kellogg sang this opera and nobody ever thought of the bad there is in it. Why? *Because Kellogg never thought of it.* Abbott reminds me of a girl of four who weeps for pantalettes on account of the wickedness of the world!

Violetta's gowns greatly interested me. I liked surprising the public with new and startling effects. I argued that Violetta would probably love curious and exotic combinations, so I dressed her first act in a gown of rose pink and pale primrose yellow. Odd? Yes; of course it was odd. But the colour scheme, bizarre as it was, always looked to my mind and the minds of other persons altogether enchanting.

A propos of the Violetta gowns, I sang the part during one season with a tenor whose hands were always dirty. I found the back of my pretty frocks becoming grimier and grimier, and greasier and greasier, and, as I provided my own gowns and had to be economical, I finally came to the conclusion that I could not and would not afford such wholesale and continual ruin. So I sent my compliments to Monsieur and asked him please to be extra careful and particular about washing his hands before the performance as my dress was very light and delicate, etc.,—quite a polite message considering the subject. Politeness, however, was entirely wasted on him. Back came the cheery and nonchalant reply:

"All right! Tell her to send me some soap!"

I sent it: and I supplied him with soap for the rest of the season. This was cheaper than buying new clothes.

Tenors are queer creatures. Most of them have their eccentricities and the soprano is lucky if these are innocuous peculiarities. I used to find it in my heart, for instance, to wish that they did not have such queer theories as to what sort of food was good for the voice. Many of them affected garlic. Stigelli usually exhaled an aroma of lager beer; while the good Mazzoleni invariably ate from one to two pounds of cheese the day he was to sing. He said it strengthened his voice. Brignoli had been long enough in this country to become partly Americanised, so he never smelled of anything in particular.

Poliuto by Donizetti was never as brilliant a success as other operas by the same composer. It is never given now. The scene of it is laid in Rome, in the days of the Christian martyrs, and it has some very effective moments, but for some reason those classic days did not appeal to the public of our presentation. I do not believe *Quo Vadis* would ever have gone then as it did later. The music of *Poliuto* was easy and showed off the voice, like all of Donizetti's music: and the part of Paulina was exceptionally fine, with splendid opportunities for dramatic work. The scene where she is thrown into the Colosseum was particularly effective. But the American audiences did not seem to be deeply interested in the fate of Paulina nor in that of Septimus Severus. The year before my *début* in *Rigoletto* I had rehearsed Paulina and had made something tragically near to a failure of it as I had not then the physical nor vocal strength for the part. Indeed, I should never then have been allowed to try it, and I have always had a suspicion that I was put in it for the express purpose of proving me a failure. That was when Muzio decided to "try me out" in the concert *tournée* as a sort of preliminary education. Therefore, one of the most comforting elements of the final *Poliuto* production to me was the realisation that I was appearing, and appearing well, in a part in which I had rehearsed so very discouragingly such a short time before. It was a small triumph, perhaps, but it combined with many other small matters to establish that sure yet humble confidence which is so essential to a singer. So far as personal success went, Brignoli made the hit of *Poliuto*.

Lucia was never one of my favourite parts, but it is a singularly grateful one. It has very few bad moments, and one can attack it without the dread one sometimes feels for a *rôle* containing difficult passages. Of course Lucia, with her hopeless, weak-minded love for Edgardo, and her spectacular mad scene,

Clara Louise Kellogg as Lucia
From a photograph by Elliott & Fry

reminded me of my beloved Linda, and there were many points of similarity in the two operas. I found, therefore, that Lucia involved much less original and interpretive work than most of my new parts; and it was never fatiguing. Being beautifully high, I liked singing it. My voice, though flexible and of wide range, always slipped most easily into the far upper registers. I can recall the positive ache it was to sing certain parts of Carmen that took me down far too low for comfort. Sometimes too, I must admit, I used to "cheat" it. We nearly always opened in *Lucia* when we began an opera season. Its success was never sensational, but invariably safe and sure. Sometimes managers would be dubious and suggest some production more startling as a commencement, but I always had a deep and well-founded faith in *Lucia*.

"It never draws a capacity house," I would be told.

"But it never fails to get a fair one."

"It never makes a sensation."

"But it never gets a bad notice." I would say.

Martha was a light and pleasing part to play. Vocally it taught me very little—little, that is to say, that I can now recognise, although I am loath to make such a statement of any *rôle*. There are so many slight and obscure ways in which a part can help one, almost unconsciously. The point that stands out most strikingly in my recollection of *Martha* is the rather rueful triumph I had in it with regard to realistic acting. Everyone who knows the story of Flotow's opera will recall that the heroine is horribly bored in the first act. She is utterly uninterested, utterly blasée, utterly listless. Accordingly, so I played the first act. Later in the opera, when she is in the midst of interesting happenings and no longer bored, she becomes animated and eager, quite a different person from the languid great lady in the beginning. So, also, I played that part. Here came my triumph, although it was a left-handed compliment aimed with the intention only to criticise and to criticise severely. One reviewer said, the morning after I had first given my careful and logical interpretation, that "it was a pity Miss Kellogg had taken so little pains with the first act. She had played it dully, stupidly, without interest or animation. Later, however, she brightened up a little and somewhat redeemed our impression of her work as we had seen it in the early part of the evening." I felt angry and hurt about this at the time, yet it pleased me too, for it was a huge tribute even if the critic did not intend it to be so.

Although I did sing in *Don Giovanni* under Grau that year in Boston, I never really considered it as belonging to that period. I did so much with this opera in after years—singing both Donna Anna and Zerlina at various times and winning some of the most notable praise of my career—that I always instinctively think of it as one of my later and more mature achievements. I always loved the opera and feel that it is an invaluable part of every singer's education to have appeared in it. *The Magic Flute* never seemed to me to be half so genuinely big or so inspired. In *Don Giovanni* Mozart gave us his richest and most complete flower of operatic work. In our cast were Amodio, whom I had heard with Piccolomini, and Mme. Medori, my old rival in *Linda*, who had recently joined the Grau Company.

All this time the war was going on and our opera ventures, even at their best, were nothing to what they

Clara Louise Kellogg as Martha

From a photograph by Turner

had been in the days of peace. It seemed quite clear for a while that the old favourites would not draw audiences from among the anxious and sorrowing people. For a big success we needed something novel, sensational, exceptional.

On the other side of the world people were all talking of Gounod's new opera—the one he had sold for only twelve hundred dollars, but which had made a wonderful hit both in Paris and London. It was said to be startlingly new; and Max Maretzek, in despair over the many lukewarm successes we had all had, decided to have a look at the score. The opera was *Faust*.

With all my pride, I was terrified and appalled when "the Magnificent" came to me and abruptly told me that I was to create the part of Marguerite in America. This was a "large order" for a girl of twenty; but I took my courage in both hands and resolved to make America proud of me. I was a pioneer when I undertook Gounod's music and I had no notion of what to do with it, but my will and my ambition arose to meet the situation.

Just here, because of its general bearing on the point, I feel that it is desirable to quote a paragraph which was written by my old friend—or was he enemy? —many years later when I had won my measure of success, "Nym Crinkle" (A. C. Wheeler), and which I have always highly valued:

There is n't a bit of snobbishness about Kellogg's opinions [he wrote]. For a woman who has sung everywhere, she retains a very wholesome opinion of her own country. She always seems to me to be trying to win two imperishable chaplets, one of which is for her country. So you see we have got to take our little flags and wave them whether it is the correct thing or not. And, so far as I am concerned,

I think it is the correct thing. . . . She has this tremendous advantage that, when she declares in print that America can produce its own singers, she is quite capable of going afterwards upon the stage and proving it!

CHAPTER VIII

MME. Miolan-Carvalho created Marguerite in Paris, at the Théâtre Lyrique. In London Patti and Titjiens had both sung it before we put it on in America,—Adelina at Covent Garden and Titjiens at Her Majesty's Opera House, where I was destined to sing it later. Except for these productions of *Faust* across the sea, that opera was still an unexplored field. I had absolutely nothing to guide me, nothing to help me, when I began work on it. I, who had been schooled and trained in "traditions" and their observances since I had first begun to study, found myself confronted with conditions that had as yet no traditions. I had to make them for myself.

Maretzek secured the score during the winter of '62–'63 and then spoke to me about the music. I worked at the part off and on for nine months, even while I was singing other parts and taking my summer vacation. But when the season opened in the autumn of 1863, the performance was postponed because a certain reaction had set in on the part of the public. People were beginning to want some sort of distraction and relaxation from the horrors and anxieties of war, and now began to come again to hear the old favourites. So Maretzek wanted to wait and put off his new sensation until he really needed it as a drawing card.

77

Then came the news that Anschutz, the German manager, was about to bring a German company to the Terrace Garden in New York with a fine *répertoire* of grand opera, including *Faust*. Of course this settled the question. Maretzek hurried the new opera into final rehearsal and it was produced at The Academy of Music on November 25, 1863, when I was very little more than twenty years old.

Before I myself say anything abouﾩ *Faust*, in which I was soon to appear, I want to quote the views of a leading newspaper of New York after I had appeared.

A brilliant audience assembled last night. The opera was *Faust*. Such an audience ought, in figurative language, "to raise the roof off" with applause. But with the clumsily written, uninspired melodies that the solo singers have to declaim there was the least possible applause. And this is not the fault of the vocalists, for they tried their best We except to this charge of dullness the dramatic love scene where the tolerably broad business concludes the act. With these facts plain to everyone present we cannot comprehend the announcement of the success of *Faust!*

Who was it said "the world goes round with revolutions"? It is a great truth, whoever said it. Every new step in art, in progress along any line, has cost something and has been fought for. Nothing fresh or good has ever come into existence without a convulsion of the old, dried-up forms. Beethoven was a revolutionist when he threw aside established musical forms with the *Ninth Symphony*; Wagner was a revolutionist when he contrived impossible intervals of the eleventh and the thirteenth, and called them for the first time dissonant harmonies; so, also, was Gounod when he departed from all accepted operatic forms and institutions in *Faust*.

You who have heard *Cari fior* upon the hand-organs in the street, and have whistled the *Soldiers' Chorus* while you were in school; who have even grown to regard the opera of *Faust* as old-fashioned and of light weight, must re-focus your glass a bit and look at Gounod's masterpiece from the point of view of nearly fifty years ago! It was just as startling, just as strange, just as antagonistic to our established musical habit as Strauss and Debussy and Dukas are to some persons to-day. What is new must always be strange, and what is strange must, except to a few adventurous souls, prove to be disturbing and, hence, disagreeable. People say "it is different, therefore it must be wrong." Even as battle, murder, and sudden death are upsetting to our lives, so Gounod's bold harmonies, sweeping airs, and curious orchestration were upsetting to the public ears.

Not the public alone, either. Though from the first I was attracted and fascinated by the "new music," it puzzled me vastly. Also, I found it very difficult to sing. I, who had been accustomed to Linda and Gilda and Martha, felt utterly at sea when I tried to sing what at that time seemed to me the remarkable intervals of this strange, new, operatic heroine, Marguerite. In the simple Italian school one knew approximately what was ahead. A *recitative* was a fairly elementary affair. An *aria* had no unexpected cadences, led to no striking nor unusual effects. But in *Faust* the musical intelligence had an entirely new task and was exercised quite differently from in anything that had gone before. This sequence of notes was a new and unlearned language to me, which I had to master before I could find freedom or ease. But when once mastered, how the music enchanted me; how it satisfied a thirst that had never been satisfied by Donizetti or Bellini! Musically, I loved the part of Marguerite—and I still love it. Dramatically, I confess to some impatience over the imbecility of the girl. From the first I summarily apostrophised her to myself as "a little fool!"

Stupidity is really the keynote of Marguerite's character. She was not quite a peasant—she and her brother owned their house, showing that they belonged to the stolid, sound, sheltered burgher class. On the other hand, she explicitly states to Faust that she is "not a lady and needs no escort." In short, she was the ideal victim and was selected as such by Mephistopheles who, whatever else he may have been, was a judge of character. Marguerite was an easy dupe. She was entirely without resisting power. She was dull, and sweet, and open to flattery. She liked pretty things, with no more discrimination or taste than other girls. She was a well-brought-up but uneducated young person of an ignorant age and of a stupid class, and innocent to the verge of idiocy.

I used to try and suggest the peasant blood in Marguerite by little shynesses and awkwardnesses. After the first meeting with Faust I would slyly stop and glance back at him with girlish curiosity to see what he looked like. People found this "business" very pretty and convincing, but I understand that I did not give the typically Teutonic bourgeois impression as well as Federici, a German soprano who was heard in America after me. She was of the class of Gretchen, and doubtless found it easier to act like a peasant unused to having fine gentlemen speak to her, than I did.

There was very little general enthusiasm before the

production of *Faust*. There were so few American musicians then that no one knew nor cared about the music. Neither was the poem so well read as it was later. The public went to the opera houses to hear popular singers and familiar airs. They had not the slightest interest in a new opera from an artistic standpoint.

I had never been allowed to read Goethe's poem until I began to study Marguerite. But even my careful mother was obliged to admit that I would have to familiarise myself with the character before I interpreted it. It is doubtful, even then, if I entered fully into the emotional and psychological grasp of the *rôle*. All that part of it was with me entirely mental. I could seize the complete mental possibilities of a character and work them out intelligently long before I had any emotional comprehension of them. As a case in point, when I sang Gilda I gave a perfectly logical presentation of the character, but I am very sure that I had not the least notion of what the latter part of *Rigoletto* meant. Fear, grief, love, courage,— these were emotions that I could accept and with which I could work; but I was still too immature to have much conception of the great sex complications that underlay the opera that I sang so peacefully. And I dare say that one reason why I played Marguerite so well was because I was so ridiculously innocent myself.

Most of the Marguerites whom I have seen make her too sophisticated, too complicated. The moment they get off the beaten path, they go to extremes like Calvé and Farrar. It is very pleasant to be original and daring in a part, but anything original or daring in connection with Marguerite is a little like mixing

6

red pepper with vanilla *blanc mange.* Nilsson, even, was too—shall I say, *knowing?* It seems the only word that fits my meaning. Nilsson was much the most attractive of all the Marguerites I have ever seen, yet she was altogether too sophisticated for the character and for the period, although to-day I suppose she would be considered quite mild. Lucca was an absolute little devil in the part. She was, also, one of the Marguerites who wore black hair. As for Patti—I have a picture of Adelina as Marguerite in which she looks like Satan's own daughter, a young and feminine Mephistopheles to the life. Once I heard *Faust* in the Segundo Teatro of Naples with Alice Neilson, and thought she gave a charming performance. She was greatly helped by not having to wear a wig. A wig, however becoming, and no matter how well put on, does certainly do something strange to the expression of a woman's face. This was what I had to have— a wig—and it was one of the most dreadful difficulties in my preparations for the great new part.

A wig may sound like a simple requirement. But I wonder if anybody has any idea how difficult it was to get a good wig in those days. Nobody in America knew how to make one. There was no blond hair over here and none could be procured, none being for sale. The poor affair worn by Mme. Carvalho as Marguerite, illustrates what was then considered a sufficient wig equipment. It is hardly necessary to add that to my truth-loving soul no effort was too great to obtain an effect that should be an improvement on this sort of thing. My own hair was so dark as to look almost black behind the footlights, and in my mind there was no doubt that Marguerite must be a blond. To-day *prime donne* besides Lucca justify the use of

Clara Louise Kellogg as Marguerite, 1865
From a photograph by Sarony

their own dark locks—notably Mme. Eames and Miss Farrar—but I cannot help suspecting that this comes chiefly from a wish to be original, to be *different* at all costs. There is no real question but that the young German peasant was fair to the flaxen point. Yet, though I knew how she should be, I found it was simpler as a theory than as a fact. I tried powders— light brown powder, yellow powder, finally, gold powder. The latter was little, I imagine, but brass filings, and it gave the best effect of all my early experiments, looking, so long as it stayed on my hair, very burnished and sunny. But—it turned my scalp green! This was probably the verdigris from the brass filings in the stuff. I was frightened enough to dispense entirely with the whole gold and green effect; after which I experimented with all the available wigs, in spite of a popular prejudice against them as immovable. They were in general composed of hemp rope with about as much look about them of real hair as—Mme. Carvalho's! I had, finally, to wait until I could get a wig made in Europe and have it imported. When it came at last, it was a beauty—although my hair troubles were not entirely over even then. I had so much hair of my own that all the braiding and pinning in the world would not eliminate it entirely, and it had a tendency to stick out in lumps over my head even under the wig, giving me some remarkable bumps of phrenological development. I will say that we put it on pretty well in spite of all difficulties, my mother at last achieving a way of brushing the hair of the wig into my own hair and combining the two in such a way as to let the real hair act as a padding and lining to the artificial braids. The result was very good, but it was, I am inclined to believe, more trouble than it was worth. Wigs were so rare and, as a rule, so ugly in those days that my big, blond perruque, that cost nearly $200 (the hair was sold by weight), caused the greatest sensation. People not infrequently came behind the scenes and begged to be allowed to examine it. Artists were not nearly so sacred nor so safe from the public then. Now, it would be impossible for a stranger to penetrate to a *prima donna's* dressing-room or hotel apartment; but we were constantly assailed by the admiring, the critical and, above all, the curious.

Of course I did not know what to wear. My old friend Ella Porter was in Paris at the time and went to see Carvalho in Marguerite, especially on my account, and sent me rough drawings of her costumes. I did not like them very well. I next studied von Kaulbach's pictures and those of other German illustrators, and finally decided on the dress. First, I chose for the opening act a simple blue and brown frock, such as an upper-class peasant might wear. Everyone said it ought to be white, which struck me as singularly out of place. German girls don't wear frocks that have to be constantly washed. Not even now do they, and I am certain they had even less laundry work in the period of the story. It was said that a white gown in the first act would symbolise innocence. In the face of all comment and suggestion, however, I wore the blue dress trimmed with brown and it looked very well. Another one of my points was that I did not try to make Marguerite angelically beautiful. There is no reason to suppose that she was even particularly pretty. "Henceforth," says Mephisto to the rejuvenated Faustus, "you will greet a Helen in every wench you meet!"

In the church scene I wore grey and, at first, a

different shade of grey in the last act; but I changed this eventually to white because white looked better when the angels were carrying me up to heaven.

As for the cut of the dresses, I seem to have been the first person to wear a bodice that fitted below the waist line like a corset. No living mortal in America had ever seen such a thing and it became almost as much of a curiosity as my wonderful golden wig. The theatre costumier was horrified. She had never cared for my innovations in the way of costuming, and her tradition-loving Latin soul was shocked to the core by the new and dreadful make-up I proposed to wear as Marguerite.

"I make for Grisi," she declared indignantly, "and I *nevair* see like dat!"

Well, I worked and struggled and slaved over every detail. No one else did. There was no great effort made to have good scenic effects. The lighting was absurd, and I had to fight for my pot of daisies in the garden scene. The jewel box I provided myself, and the jewels. I felt—O, how deeply I felt—that everything in my life, every note I had sung, every day I had worked, had been merely preparation for this great and lovely opera.

Colonel Stebbins, who was anxious, said to Maretzek:

"Don't you think she had better have a German coach in the part?"

Maretzek, who had been watching me closely all along, shook his head.

"Let her alone," he said. "Let her do it her own way."

So the great night came around.

There was no public excitement before the production. People knew nothing about the new opera. On

the first night of *Faust* there was a good house because,
frankly, the public liked me! Nevertheless, in spite of
"me," the house was a little inanimate. The audience
felt doubtful. It was one thing to warm up an old and
popular piece; but something untried was very different!
The public had none of the present-day chivalry toward
the first "try-out" of an opera.

Mazzoleni of the cheese addiction was Faust, and
on that first night he had eaten even more than usual.
In fact, he was still eating cheese when the curtain
went up and munched cheese at intervals all through
the laboratory scene. He was a big Italian with a
voice as big as himself and was, in a measure, one of
Max Maretzek's "finds." "The Magnificent" had
taken an opera company to Havana when first the war
slump came in operatic affairs, and had made with it a
huge success and a wide reputation. Mazzoleni was
one of the leading tenors of that company. He
sang Faust admirably, but dressed it in an atrocious
fashion, looking like a cross between a Jewish rabbi
and a Prussian *gene d'arme*. Of course, he gave no
idea of the true age of Faust—the experienced,
mature point of view showing through the outward
bloom of his artificial youth. Very few Fausts do
give this; and Mazzoleni suggested it rather less than
most of them. But the public was not enlightened
enough to realise the lack.

Biachi was Mephistopheles. He was very good
and sang the *Calf of Gold* splendidly. Yet that solo,
oddly enough, never "caught on" with our houses.
Biachi was one of the few artists of my day who gave
real thought and attention to the question of costuming. He took his general scheme of dress from *Robert
le Diable* and improved on it, and looked very well

indeed. The woman he afterwards married was our contralto, a Miss Sulzer, an American, who made an excellent Siebel and considered her work seriously.

At first everyone was stunned by the new treatment. In ordinary, accepted operatic form there were certain things to be expected;—*recitatives, andantes, arias,* choruses—all neatly laid out according to rule. In this everything was new, startling, overthrowing all traditions. About the middle of the evening some of my friends came behind the scenes to my dressing-room with blank faces.

"Heavens, Louise," they exclaimed, "what do you do in this opera anyway? Everyone in the front of the house is asking 'where 's the *prima donna?'*"

Indeed, an opera in which the heroine has nothing to do until the third act might well have startled a public accustomed to the old Italian forms. However, I assured everyone:

"Don't worry. You 'll get more than enough of me before the end of the evening!"

The house was not much stirred until the love scene. That was breathless. We felt more and more that we were beginning to "get them."

There were no modern effects of lighting; but a calcium was thrown on me as I stood by the window, and I sang my very, very best. As Mazzoleni came up to the window and the curtain went down there was a dead silence.

Not a hand for ten seconds. Ten seconds is a long time when one is waiting on the stage. Time and the clock itself seemed to stop as we stood there motionless and breathless. Maretzek had time to get through the little orchestra door and up on the stage before the applause came. We were standing as though paralysed,

waiting. We saw Maretzek's pale, anxious face. The silence held a second longer; then—
The house came down. The thunders echoed and beat about our wondering ears.
"Success!" gasped Maretzek, "success—success—success!"
Yet read what the critics said about it. The musicians picked it to pieces, of course, and so did the critics, much as the German reviewers did Wagner's music dramas. The public came, however, packing the houses to more than their capacity. People paid seven and eight dollars a seat to hear that opera, an unheard-of thing in those days when two and three dollars were considered a very fair price for any entertainment. Furthermore, only the women occupied the seats on the *Faust* nights. I speak in a general way, for there were exceptions. As a rule, however, this was so, while the men stood up in regiments at the back of the house. We gave twenty-seven performances of *Faust* in one season; seven performances in Boston in four weeks; and I could not help the welcome knowledge that, in addition to the success of the opera itself, I had scored a big, personal triumph.

As I have mentioned, we took wicked liberties with the operas, such as introducing the *Star Spangled Banner* and similar patriotic songs into the middle of Italian scores. I have even seen a highly tragic act of *Poliuto* put in between the light and cheery scenes of *Martha;* and I have myself sung the *Venzano* waltz at the end of this same *Martha*, although the real quartette that is supposed to close the opera is much more beautiful, and the *Clara Louise Polka* as a finish for *Linda di Chamounix!* The *Clara Louise Polka* was written for me by my old master, Muzio, and I never

Clara Louise Kellogg as Marguerite, 1864

From a silhouette by Ida Waugh

thought much of it. Nothing could give anyone so clear an idea of the universal acceptance of this custom of interpolation as the following criticism, printed during our second season:

"The production of *Faust* last evening by the Maretzek troupe was excellent indeed. But why, O why, the eternal *Soldiers' Chorus?* Why this everlasting, tedious march, *when there are so many excellent band pieces on the market that would fit the occasion better?*"

As a rule the public were quite satisfied with this chorus. It was whistled and sung all over the country and never failed to get eager applause. But no part of the opera ever went so well as the *Salve dimora* and the love scene. All the latter part of the garden act went splendidly although nearly everyone was, or professed to be, shocked by the frankness of the window episode that closes it. It is a pity those simple-souled audiences could not have lived to see Miss Geraldine Farrar draw Faust with her into the house at the fall of the curtain! There is, indeed, a place for all things. *Faust* is not the place for that sort of suggestiveness. It is a question, incidentally, whether any stage production is; but the argument of that is outside our present point.

Dear Longfellow came to see the first performance of *Faust;* and the next day he wrote a charming letter about it to Mr. James T. Fields of Boston. Said he:

"The Margaret was beautiful. She reminded me of Dryden's lines:

"'So pois'd, so gently she descends from high,
It seems a soft dismission from the sky.'"

CHAPTER IX

OPÉRA COMIQUE

TO most persons "opéra comique" means simply comic opera. If they make any distinction at all it is to call it "high-class comic opera." As a matter of fact, tragedy and comedy are hardly farther apart in spirit than are the rough and farcical stuff that we look upon as comic opera nowadays and the charming old pieces that formed the true "opéra comique" some fifty years ago. "Opéra bouffe" even is many degrees below "opéra comique." Yet "opéra bouffe" is, to my mind, something infinitely superior and many steps higher than modern comic opera. So we have some delicate differentiations to make when we go investigating in the fields of light dramatic music.

In Paris at the Comique they try to keep the older distinction in mind when selecting their operas for production. There are exceptions to this rule, as to others, for play-houses that specialise; but for the most part these Paris managers choose operas that are light. I use the word advisedly. By *light* I mean, literally, *not heavy*. Light music, light drama, does not necessarily mean humorous. It may, on the contrary, be highly pathetic and charged with sentiment. The only restriction is that it shall not be expressed in the stentorian orchestration of a Meyerbeer, nor in the heart-rending tragedy of a Wagner. In theme and in treatment, in melodies and in text, it must be of delicate fibre, something easily seized and swiftly assimilated, something intimate, perfumed, and agreeable, with no more harshness of emotion than of harmony.

Judged by this standard such operas as *Martha, La Bohème,* even *Carmen*—possibly, even *Werther*—are not entirely foreign to the requirements of "opera comique." *Le Donne Curiose* may be considered as an almost perfect revival and exemplification of the form. A careful differentiation discovers that humour, a happy ending, and many rollicking melodies do not at all make an "opéra comique." These qualities all belong abundantly to *Die Meistersinger* and to Verdi's *Falstaff*, yet these great operas are no nearer being examples of genuine "comique" than *Les Huguenots* is or *Götterdämmerung*.

It was my good fortune to sing in the space of a year three delightful *rôles* in "opéra comique," each of which I enjoyed hugely. They were Zerlina in *Fra Diavolo;* Rosina in *Il Barbiere;* and Annetta in *Crispino e la Comare.* *Fra Diavolo* was first produced in Italian in America during the autumn of 1864, the year after I appeared in Marguerite, and it remained one of our most popular operas throughout the season of '65–'66. I loved it and always had a good time the nights it was given. We put it on for my "benefit" at the end of the regular winter season at the Academy. The season closed with the old year and the "benefit" took place on the 28th of December. The "benefit" custom was very general in those days. Everybody had one a year and so I had to have mine, or, at least, Maretzek thought I had to have it. *Fra Diavolo* was his choice for this occasion as I had made one of my best successes in the part of Zerlina, and the opera had been the most liked in our whole *répertoire* with the exception of *Faust*. *Faust* had remained from the beginning our most unconditional success, our *cheval de bataille*, and never failed to pack the house.

I don't know quite why that *Fra Diavolo* night stands out so happily and vividly in my memory. I have had other and more spectacular "benefits"; but that evening there seemed to be the warmest and most personal of atmospheres in the old Academy. The audience was full of friends and, what with the glimpses I had of these familiar faces and my loads of lovely flowers and the kindly, intimate enthusiasm that greeted my appearance, I felt as if I were at a party and not playing a performance at all. I had to come out again and again; and finally became so wrought up that I was nearly in tears.

As a climax I was entirely overcome when I suddenly turned to find Maretzek standing beside me in the middle of the stage, smiling at me in a friendly and encouraging manner. I had not the slightest idea what his presence there at that moment meant. The applause stopped instantly. Whereupon "Max the Magnificent" made a little speech in the quick hush, saying charming and overwhelming things about the young girl whose musical beginning he had watched and who in a few years had reached "a high pinnacle in the world of art. The young girl"—he went on to say—"who at twenty-one was the foremost *prima donna* of America."

"And now, my dear Miss Kellogg," he wound up with, holding out to me a velvet case, "I am instructed by the stockholders of the Opera Company to hand you this, to remind you of their admiration and their pride in you!"

I took the case; and the house cheered and cheered as I lifted out of it a wonderful flashing diamond bracelet and diamond ring. Of course I could n't speak. I could hardly say "thank you." I just ran off with eyes and heart overflowing to the wings where my mother was waiting for me.

The bracelet and the ring are among the dearest things I possess. Their value to me is much greater than any money could be, for they symbolise my young girl's sudden comprehension of the fact that I had made my countrymen proud of me! That seemed like the high-water mark; the finest thing that could happen.

Annetta was my second creation. There could hardly be imagined a greater contrast than she presented to the part of Marguerite. Gretchen was all the virtues in spite of her somewhat spectacular career; gentleness and sweetness itself. Annetta, the ballad singer, was quite the opposite. I must say that I really enjoyed making myself shrewish, sparkling, and audacious. Perhaps I thus took out in the lighter *rôles* I sang many of my own suppressed tendencies. Although I lived such an essentially ungirlish life, I was, nevertheless, full of youthful feeling and high spirits, so, when I was Annetta or Zerlina or Rosina, I had a flying chance to "bubble" just a little bit. Merriment is one of the finest and most helpful emotions in the world and I dare say we all have the possibilities of it in us, one way or another. But it is a shy sprite and does not readily come to one's call. I often think that the art, or the ability,—on the stage or off it—which makes people truly and innocently gay, is very high in the scale of human importance. Personally, I have never been happier than when I was frolicking through some entirely light-weight opera, full of whims and quirks and laughing music. I used to feel intimately in touch with the whole audience then, as though they and I were shar-ing some exquisite secret or delicious joke; and I would reach a point of ease and spontaneity which I have never achieved in more serious work.

Crispino had made a tremendous hit in Paris the year before when Malibran had sung Annetta with brilliant success. It has been sometimes said that Grisi created the *rôle* of Annetta in America; but I still cling to the claim of that distinction for myself. The composers of the opera were the Rice brothers. I do not know of any other case where an opera has been written fraternally; and it was such a ·highly suc-cessful little opera that I wish I knew more about the two men who were responsible for it. All that I remember clearly is that they both of them knew music thoroughly and that one of them taught it as a pro-fession.

Our first Cobbler in *Crispino e la Comare* ("The Cobbler and the Fairy") was Rovere, a good Italian buffo baritone. He was one of those extraordinary artists whose art grows and increases with time and, by some law of compensation, comes more and more to take the place of mere voice. Rovere was in his prime in 1852 when he sang in America with Mme. Alboni. Later, when he sang with me, a few of the New York critics remembered him and knew his work and agreed that he was "as good as ever." His voice —no. But his art, his method, his delightful manner— these did not deteriorate. On the contrary, they ma-tured and ripened. Our second Cobbler, Ronconi,

was even more remarkable. He was, I believe, one
of the finest Italian baritones that ever lived, and he
succeeded in getting a degree of genuine high comedy
out of the part that I have never seen surpassed. He
used to tell of himself a story of the time when he was
singing in the Royal Opera of Petersburg. The Czar—
father of the one who was murdered—said to him once:

"Ronconi, I understand that you are so versatile
that you can express tragedy with one side of your
face when you are singing and comedy with the other.
How do you do it?"

"Your Majesty," rejoined Ronconi, "when I sing
Maria de Rohan to-morrow night I will do myself the
honour of showing you."

And, accordingly, the next evening he managed to
turn one side of his face, grim as the Tragic Mask, to
the audience, while the other, which could be seen
from only the Imperial Box, was excessively humorous
and cheerful. The Czar was greatly amused and
delighted with the exhibition.

Once in London, Santley was talking with me about
this great baritone and said:

"Ronconi did something with a phrase in the sextette of *Lucia* that I have gone to hear many and
many a night. I never could manage to catch it or
comprehend how he gave so much power and expression
to

Ronconi was deliciously amusing, also, as the Lord
in *Fra Diavolo*. He sang it with me the first time it
was ever done here in Italian, when Theodor Habel-

mann was our Diavolo.   Though he was a round-
faced German, he was so dark of skin and so finely
built that he made up excellently as an Italian; and he
had been thoroughly trained in the splendid school of
German light opera.   He was really picturesque, especially in a wonderful fall he made from one precipice
to another.   We were not accustomed to falls on the
stage over here, and had never seen anything like it.
Ronconi sang with me some years later, as well, when
I gave English opera throughout the country, and I
came to know him quite well.   He was a man of great
elegance and decorum.

"You know," he said to me once, "I'm a sly dog—
a very sly dog indeed!   When I sing off the key on the
stage or do anything like that, I always turn and look
in an astounded manner at the person singing with me
as if to say 'what on earth did you do that for?' and
the other artist, perfectly innocent, invariably looks
guilty!   O, I'm a *very* sly dog!"

Don Pasquale was another of our "opéra comique"
ventures, as well as *La Dame Blanche* and *Masaniello*.
It was a particularly advantageous choice at the time
because it required neither chorus nor orchestra.   We
sang it with nothing but a piano by way of accompaniment; which possibly was a particularly useful arrangement for us when we became short of cash, for we—
editorially, or, rather, managerially speaking—were
rather given in those early seasons to becoming suddenly "hard up," especially when to the poor operatic
conditions, engendered spasmodically by the war news,
was added the wet blanket of Lent which, in those
days, was observed most rigidly.

Of the three *rôles*, Zerlina, Rosina, and Annetta,
I always preferred that of Rosina.   It was one of

my best *rôles*, the music being excellently placed
for me. *Il Barbiere* had led the school of "opéra
comique" for years, but soon, one after the other, the
new operas—notably *Crispino*—were hailed as the
legitimate successor of *Il Barbiere*, and their novelty
gave them a drawing power in advance of their rational
value. In addition to my personal liking for the *rôle*
of Rosina, I always felt that, although the other
operas were charming in every way, they musically
were not quite in the class with Rossini's masterpiece.
The light and delicate qualities of this form of operatic
art have never been given so perfectly as by him. I
wish *Il Barbiere* were more frequently heard.

Yet I was fond of *Fra Diavolo* too. I was forever
working at the *rôle* of Zerlina or, rather, playing at
it, for the old "opéra comique" was never really work
to me. It was all infectious and inspiring; the music
full of melody; the story light and pretty. Many of
the critics said that I ought to specialise in comedy,
cut out my tragic and romantic *rôles*, and attempt
even lighter music and characterisation than Zerlina.
People seemed particularly to enjoy my "going to bed"
scene. They praised my "neatness and daintiness"
and found the whole picture very pretty and attractive.
I used to take off my skirt first, shake it well, hang it on
a nail, then discover a spot and carefully rub it out.
That little bit of "business" always got a laugh—I do
not quite know why. Then I would take off my
bodice dreamily as I sang: "To-morrow—yes, to-morrow I am to be married!"

Si, do-ma-ni, Si, do-ma-ni sa-rem ma-ri-to e moghi,

One night while I was carrying the candle in that scene a gust of wind from the wings made the flame gutter badly and a drop of hot grease fell on my hand. Instinctively I jumped and shook my hand without thinking what I was doing. There was a perfect gale of laughter from the house. After that, I always pretended to drop the grease on my hand, always gave the little jump, and always got my laugh.

As I say, nearly everybody liked that scene. I was myself so girlish that it never struck anybody as particularly suggestive or immodest until one night an old couple from the country came to see the opera and created a mild sensation by getting up and going out in the middle of it. The old man was heard to say, as he hustled his meek spouse up the aisle of the opera house:

"Mary, we'd better get out of this! It may be all right for city folks, but it's no place for us. We may be green; but, by cracky,—we're *decent!*"

CHAPTER X

ANOTHER SEASON AND A LITTLE MORE SUCCESS

ONE of the pleasant affairs that came my way that year was Sir Morton Peto's banquet in October. Sir Morton was a distinguished Englishman who represented big railway interests in Great Britain and who was then negotiating some new and important railroading schemes on this side of the water. There were two hundred and fifty guests; practically everybody present, except my mother and myself, standing for some large financial power of the United States. I felt much complimented at being invited, for it was at a period when very great developments were in the making. America was literally teeming with new projects and plans and embryonic interests.

The banquet was given at Delmonico's, then at Fifth Avenue and Fourteenth Street, and the rooms were gorgeous in their drapings of American and English flags. The war was about drawing to its close and patriotism was at white heat. The influential Americans were in the mood to wave their banners and to exchange amenities with foreign potentates. Sir Morton was a noted capitalist and his banquet was a sort of "hands across the sea" festival. He used, I recall, to stop at the Clarendon, now torn down and its site occupied by a commercial "sky scraper," but then the smart hostelry of the town.

99

I sang that night after dinner. My services had not been engaged professionally, so, when Sir Morton wanted to reward me lavishly, I of course did not care to have him do so. We were still so new to *prime donne* in New York that we had no social code or precedent to refer to with regard to them; and I preferred, personally, to keep the episode on a purely friendly and social basis. I was an invited guest only who had tried to do her part for the entertainment of the others. I was honoured, too. It was an experience to which anyone could look back with pride and pleasure.

But, being English, Sir Morton Peto had a solution and, within a day or two, sent me an exquisite pearl and diamond bracelet. It is odd how much more delicately and graciously than Americans all foreigners —of whatever nationality indeed—can relieve a situation of awkwardness and do the really considerate and appreciative thing which makes such a situation all right. I later found the same tactful qualities in the Duke of Newcastle who, with his family, were among the closest friends I had in England. Indeed, I was always much impressed with the good taste of English men and women in this connection.

An instance of the American fashion befell me during the winter of '63–'64 on the occasion of a big reception that was given by the father of Brander Matthews. I was invited to go and asked to sing, my host saying that if I would not accept a stipulated price he would be only too glad to make me a handsome present of some kind. The occasion turned out to be very unfortunate and unpleasant altogether, both at the time and with regard to the feeling that grew out of it. I happened to wear a dress that was nearly new, a handsome and expensive gown, and this was completely ruined by a servant upsetting melted ice cream over it. My host and hostess were all concern, saying that, as they were about to go to Paris, they would buy me a new one. I immediately felt that if they did this, they would consider the dress as an equivalent for my singing and that I should never hear anything more of the handsome present. Of course I said nothing of this, however, to anyone. Well—they went to Paris. Days and weeks passed. I heard nothing from them about either dress or present. I went to Europe. They called on me in Paris. In the course of time we all came home to America; and the night after my return I received a long letter and a set of Castilian gold jewelry, altogether inadequate as an equivalent. There was nothing to do but to accept it, which I did, and then proceeded to give away the ornaments as I saw fit. The whole affair was uncomfortable and a discredit to my entertainers. Not only had I lost a rich dress through the carelessness of one of their servants, but I received a very tardy and inadequate recompense for my singing. I had refused payment in money because it was the custom to do so. But I was a professional singer, and I had been asked to the reception as a professional entertainer. This, however, I must add, is the most flagrant case that has ever come under my personal notice of an American host or hostess failing to "make good" at the expense of a professional.

Well—from time to time after Sir Morton's banquet, I sang in concert. On one occasion I replaced Euphrosyne Parepa—she had not then married Carl Rosa—at one of the Bateman concerts. The Meyerbeer craze was then at its height. Good, sound music it was too, if a little brazen and noisy. *L'Étoile du Nord*

(I don't understand why we always speak of it as *L'Étoile du Nord* when we never once sang it in French) had been sung in America by my old idol, Mme. de la Grange, nearly ten years before I essayed Catarina. My *première* in the part was given in Philadelphia; but almost immediately we came back to New York for the spring opera season and I sang *The Star* as principal attraction.   Later on I sang it in Boston.

It was always good fun playing in Boston, for the Harvard boys adored "suping" and we had our extra men almost without the asking.   They were such nice, clean, enthusiastic chaps!   The reason why I remember them so clearly is that I never can forget how surprised I was when, in the boat at the end of the first act of *The Star of the North*, I chanced to look down and caught sight of Peter Barlow (now Judge Barlow) grinning up at me from a point almost underneath me on the stage, and how I nearly fell out of the boat!

We had difficulty in finding a satisfactory Prascovia.   Prascovia is an important soprano part, and had to be well taken.   At last Albites suggested a pupil of his.   This was Minnie Hauck.   Prascovia was sung at our first performance by Mlle. Bososio who was not equal to the part.   Minnie Hauck came into the theatre and sang a song of Meyerbeer's, and we knew that we had found our Prascovia.   Her voice was very light but pleasing and well-trained, for Albites was a good teacher.   She undoubtedly would add value to our caste.   So she made her *début* as Prascovia, although she afterwards became better known to the public as one of the most famous of the early Carmens.   Indeed, many people believed that she created that *rôle* in America although, as a matter of fact, I sang Carmen several months before she did.

As Prascovia she and I had a duet together, very long and elaborate, which we introduced after the tent scene and which made an immense hit. We always received many flowers after it—I, particularly, to be quite candid. By this time I was called The Flower Prima Donna because of the quantities of wonderful blossoms that were sent to me night after night. When singing *The Star of the North* there was one bouquet that I was sure of getting regularly from a young man who always sent the same kind of flowers. I never needed a card on them or on the box to know from whom they came. Miss Hauck used to help me pick up my bouquets. The only trouble was that every one she picked up she kept! As a rule I did not object, and, anyway, I might have had difficulty in proving that she had appropriated my flowers after she had taken the cards off: but one night she included in her general haul my own special, unmistakable bouquet! I recognised it, saw her take it, but, as there was no card, had the greatest difficulty in getting it away from her. I did, though, in the end.

Minnie Hauck was very pushing and took advantage of everything to forward and help herself. She never had the least apprehension about the outcome of anything in which she was engaged and, in this, she was extremely fortunate, for most persons cursed with the artistic temperament are too sensitive to feel confident. She was clever, too. This is another exception, for very few big singers are clever. I think it is Mme. Maeterlinck who has made use of the expression "too clever to sing well." I am convinced that there is quite a truth in it as well as a sarcasm. Wonderful voices usually are given to people who are, intrinsically, more or less nonentities. One cannot have everything in this world, and people with brains are not obliged to sing! But Minnie Hauck was a singer and she was also clever. If I remember rightly, she married some scientific foreign baron and lived afterwards in Lucerne.

Once I heard of a soldier who was asked to describe Waterloo and who replied that his whole impression of the battle consisted of a mental picture of the kind of button that was on the coat of the man in front of him. It is so curiously true that one's view of important events is often a very small one,—especially when it comes to a matter of mere memory. Accordingly, I find my amethysts are almost my most vivid recollection in connection with *L'Étoile du Nord*. I wanted a set of really handsome stage jewelry for Catarina. In fact, I had been looking for such a set for some time. There are many *rôles*, Violetta for instance, for which rich jewels are needed. My friends were on the lookout for me, also, and it was while I was preparing for *The Star of the North* that a man I knew came hurrying in with a wonderful tale of a set of imitation amethysts that he had discovered, and that were, he thought, precisely what I was looking for.

"The man who has them," he told me, "bought them at a bankrupt sale for ninety-six dollars and they are a regular white elephant to him. Of course, they are suitable only for the stage; and he has been hunting for months for some actress who would buy them. You 'd better take a look at them, anyhow."

I had the set sent to me and, promptly, went wild over it. The stones, that ranged from the size of a bean to that of a large walnut, appeared to be as perfect as genuine amethysts, and the setting—genuine soft, old, worked gold—was really exquisite. There were seventy stones in the whole set, which included a necklace, a bracelet, a large brooch, ear-rings and a most gorgeous tiara. The colour of the gems was very deep and lovely, bordering on a claret tone rather than violet. The crown was apparently symbolic or suggestive of some great house. It was made of roses, shamrocks, and thistles, and every piece in the set was engraved with a small hare's head. I wish I knew heraldry and could tell to whom the lovely ornaments had first belonged. Of course I bought them, paying one hundred and fifty dollars for the set, which the man was glad enough to get. I wore it in *The Star* and in other operas, and one day I took it down to Tiffany's to have it cleaned and repaired.

The man there, who knew me, examined it with interest.

"It will cost you one hundred and seventy dollars," he informed me.

"What!" I gasped. "That is more than the whole set is worth!"

He looked at me as if he thought I must be a little crazy.

"Miss Kellogg," he said, "if you think that, I don't believe you know what you 've really got. What do you think this jewelry is really worth?"

"I don't know," I admitted. "What do you think it is worth?"

"Roughly speaking," he replied, "I should say about six thousand dollars. The workmanship is of great value, and every one of the stones is genuine."

Through all these years, therefore, I have been fearful that some Rip Van Winkle claimant might rise up and take my beloved amethysts away from me!

My general impressions of this period of my life

include those of the two great pianists, Thalberg and Gottschalk. They were both wonderful, although I always admired Gottschalk more than the former. Thalberg had the greater technique; Gottschalk the greater charm. Sympathetically, the latter musician was better equipped than the former. The very simplest thing that Gottschalk played became full of fascination. Thalberg was marvellously perfect as to his method; but it was Gottschalk who could "play the birds off the trees and the heart out of your breast," as the Irish say. Thalberg's work was, if I may put it so, mental; Gottschalk's was temperamental.

Gottschalk was one of the first big pianists to come to New York touring. He was from New Orleans, having been born there in the French Quarter, and spoke only French, like so many persons from that city up to thirty years ago. But he had been educated abroad and always ranked as a foreign artist. He must have been a Jew, from his name. Certainly, he looked like one. He had peculiarly drooping eyelids and was considered to be very attractive. He wrote enchanting Spanish-sounding songs; and gave the banjo quite a little dignity by writing a piece imitating it, much to my delight, because of my fondness for that instrument. He was in no way a classical pianist. Thalberg was. Indeed, they were altogether different types. Thalberg was nothing like so interesting either as a personality or as a musician, although he was much more scholarly than his predecessor. I say predecessor, because Thalberg followed Gottschalk in the touring proposition. Gottschalk began his work before I began mine, and I first sang with him in my second season. He and I figured in the same concerts not only in those early days but also much later.

Gottschalk
Photograph by Case & Getchell

Gottschalk was a gay deceiver and women were crazy about him. Needless to say, my mother never let me have anything to do with him except professionally. He was pursued by adoring females wherever he went and inundated with letters from girls who had lost their hearts to his exquisite music and magnetic personality. I shall always remember Gottschalk and Brignoli comparing their latest love letters from matinée girls. Some poor, silly maiden had written to Gottschalk asking for a meeting at any place he would appoint. Said Gottschalk:

"It would be rather fun to make a date with her at some absurd, impossible place,—say a ferry-boat, for instance."

"Nonsense," said Brignoli, "a ferry-boat is not romantic enough. She would n't think of coming to a ferry-boat to meet her ideal!"

"She would come anywhere," declared Gottschalk, not at all vaingloriously, but as one stating a simple truth. "I 'll make her come; and you shall come too and see her do it!"

"Will you bet?" asked Brignoli.

"I certainly will," replied Gottschalk.

They promptly put up quite a large sum of money and Gottschalk won. That dear, miserable goose of a girl did go to the ferry-boat to meet the illustrious pianist of her adoration, and Brignoli was there to see. If only girls knew as much as I do about the way in which their stage heroes take their innocent adulation, and the wicked light-heartedness with which they make fun of it! But they do not; and the only way to teach them, I suppose, is to let them learn by themselves, poor little idiots.

As I look back I feel a continual sense of outrage

that I mixed so little with the people and affairs that were all about me; interesting people and important affairs. My dear mother adored me. It is strange that we can never even be adored in the particular fashion in which we would prefer to be adored! My mother's way was to guard me eternally; she would have called it protecting me. But, really, it was a good deal like shutting me up in a glass case, and it was a great pity. My mother was an extraordinarily fine woman, upright as the day and of an unusual mentality. Uncompromising she was, not unnaturally, according to her heritage of race and creed and generation. Yet I sometimes question if she were as uncompromising as she used to seem to me, for was not the life she led with me, as well as her acceptance of it in the beginning, one long compromise between her nature and the actualities? At any rate, where she seemed to draw the line was in keeping me as much as possible aloof from my inevitable associates. I led a deadly dull and virtuous life, of necessity. To be sure, I might have been just as virtuous or even more so had I been left to my own devices and judgments; but I contend that such a life is not up to much when it is compulsory. Personal responsibility is necessary to development. Perhaps I reaped certain benefits from my mother's close chaperonage. Certainly, if there were benefits about it, I reaped them. But I very much question its ultimate advantage to me, and I confess freely that one of the things I most regret is the innocent, normal coquetry which is the birthright of every happy girl and which I entirely missed. It is all very well to be carefully guarded and to be made the archetype of American virtue on the stage, but there is a great deal of entirely innocuous amusement that I might have

Jane Elizabeth Crosby
Mother of Clara Louise Kellogg
From a tintype

had and did not have, which I should have been better off for having. My mother could hardly let me
hold a friendly conversation with a man—much less a
flirtation.

CHAPTER XI

THE Civil War was now coming to its close. Abraham Lincoln was the hero of the day, as he has been of all days since, in America. The White House was besieged with people from all walks of life, persistently anxious to shake hands with the War President, and he used to have to stand, for incredible lengths of time, smiling and hand-clasping. But he was ever a fine economist of energy and he flatly refused to talk. No one could get out of him more than a smile, a nod, or possibly a brief word of greeting.

One man made a bet that he would have some sort of conversation with the President while he was shaking hands with him.

"No, you won't," said the man to whom he was speaking, "I'll bet you that you won't get more than two words out of him!"

"I bet I will," said the venturesome one; and he set off to try his luck.

He went to the White House reception and, when his turn came and his hand was in the huge presidential grasp, he began to talk hastily and volubly, hoping to elicit some response. Lincoln listened a second, gazing at him gravely with his deep-set eyes, and then he laid an enormous hand in a loose, wrinkled white glove across his back.

"Don't dwell!" said he gently to his caller; and shoved him along, amiably but relentlessly, with the rest of the line. So the man got only his two words after all.

One week before the President was murdered I was in Washington and sat in the exact place in which he sat when he was shot. It was the same box, the same chair, and on Friday too,—one week to the day and hour before the tragedy. When I heard the terrible news I was able to picture exactly what it had been like. I could see just the jump that Booth must have had to make to get away. I never knew Wilkes Booth personally nor saw him act, but I have several times seen him leaving his theatre after a performance, with a raft of adoring matinée girls forming a more or less surreptitous guard afar off. He was a tremendously popular idol and strikingly handsome. Even after his wicked crime there were many women who professed a sort of hysterical sympathy and pity for him. Somebody has said that there would always be at least one woman at the death-bed of the worst criminal in the world if she could get to it; and there were hundreds of the sex who would have been charmed to watch beside Booth's, bad as he was and crazy into the bargain. It is a mysterious thing, the fascination that criminals have for some people, particularly women. Perhaps it is fundamentally a respect for accomplishment; admiration for the doing of something, good or evil, that they would not dare to do themselves.

We had all gone to Chicago for our spring opera season and were ready to open, when the tragic tidings came and shut down summarily upon every preparation for amusement of any kind. Every city in the Union went into mourning for the man whom the

country idolised; of whom so many people spoke as *our*
"Abraham Lincoln." Perhaps it was because of this
universal and almost personal affection that the authori-
ties did such an odd thing—or, at least, it struck me as
odd,—with his body. He was taken all over the
country and "lay-in-state," as it is called, in different
court houses in different states.

I was stopping in the Grand Pacific Hotel when the
body was brought to Chicago, and my windows overlooked the grounds of the Court House of that city.
Business was entirely suspended, not simply for a few
memorial moments as was the case when President
McKinley was killed, but for many hours during the
"lying-in-state." This, however, was probably only
partly official. Everyone was so afraid that he would
not be able to see the dead hero's face that business
men all over the town suspended occupation, closed
shops and offices, and made a pilgrimage to the Court
House. All citizens were permitted to go into the
building and look upon the Martyr President, and
vast numbers availed themselves of the privilege—
waited all night, indeed, to claim it. From sunset to
sunrise the grounds were packed with a silent multi-
tude. The only sound to be heard was the shuffling
echo of feet as one person after another went quietly
into the Court House, shuffle, shuffle, shuffle,—I can
hear it yet. There was not a word uttered. There
was no other sound than the sound of the passing feet.
One thing that must have been official was that, for
quite a long time, not a wheel in the city was allowed
to turn. This was an impressive tribute to a man
whom the whole American nation loved and counted a
friend.

The only diversion in the whole melancholy solemnity of it all was the picking of pockets. The crowds were enormous, the people in a mood of sentiment and off their guard, and the army of crooks did a thriving business. It is a sickening thing to realise that in all hours of great national tragedy or terror there will always be people degenerate enough to take advantage of the suffering and ruin about them. Burning or plague-stricken cities have to be put under military law; and it is said that to the multiplied horrors of the San Francisco earthquake the people look back with a shudder to the ghastly system of looting which prevailed afterwards in the stricken city.

Every imaginable kind of flowers were sent to the dead President, splendid wreaths and bouquets from distinguished personages, and many little cheap humble nosegays from poor people who had loved him even from afar and wanted to honour him in some simple way. No man has ever been loved more in his death than was Abraham Lincoln.

I sent a cross of white camellias. I do not like camellias when they are sent to me, because they always seem such heartless, soulless flowers for living people to wear. But just for that reason, just because they are the most perfect and the most impersonal of all flowers that grow and blossom they seem right and suitable for death. Ever since that time I have associated white camellias with the thought of Abraham Lincoln and with my strange, impressive memory of those days in Chicago.

However, nations go on even after the beloved rulers of them are laid in the ground. Our Chicago season opened soon—I in Lucia—and everything went along as though nothing had happened. The only difference was that the end of the war had made

8

the nation a little drunk with excitement and our performances went with a whirl.

Finally the victorious generals, Lieutenant-General Grant and Major-General Sherman, came to Chicago as the guests of the city and we gave a gala performance for them. As the *Daughter of the Regiment* had been our choice to inaugurate the commencement of the great conflict, so the *Daughter of the Regiment* was also our choice to commemorate its close. The whole opera house was gay with flags and flowers and decorations, and the generals were given the two stage boxes, one on each side of the house. The audience began to come in very early; and it was a huge one. The curtain had not yet risen—indeed, I was in my dressing-room still making-up—when I heard the orchestra break into *See the Conquering Hero Comes*, and then the roof nearly came off with the uproar of the people cheering. I sent to find out what was happening, and was told that General Grant had just entered his box. We were ridiculously excited behind the scenes, all of us; even the foreigners. They were such emotional creatures that they flung themselves into a mood of general excitement even when it was based on a patriotism to which they were aliens. The wild and jubilant state of the audience infected us. I had felt something of the same emotion in Washington at the beginning of the war, when we had done *Figlia* before, to the frantically enthusiastic houses there. Yet that was different. Mingled with that feeling there had been a grimness and pain and apprehension. Now everyone was triumphant and happy and emotionally exultant.

General Sherman came into his box early in the first act and the orchestra had to stop while the house cheered him, and cheered again. Sherman was always just a bit theatrical and loved applause, and he, with his staff, stood bowing and smiling and bowing and smiling. The whole proceeding took almost the form of a great military reception. As I look back at it, I think one of the moments of the evening was created by our basso, Susini. Susini—himself a soldier of courage and experience, a veteran of the Italian rebellion—made his entrance, walked forward, stood, faced one General after the other and saluted each with the most military exactness. They were both plainly delighted; while the house, in the mood to be moved by little touches, broke into the heartiest applause.

I had a moment of triumph also when we sang the *Rataplan, rataplan.* Since the early hit I had made with my drum I always played it as the Daughter of the Regiment, and when we came to this scene I directed the drum first toward one box and then toward the other, as I gave the rolling salute. The audience went mad again; and again the orchestra had to stop until the clapping and the hurrahs had subsided. It may not have been a great operatic performance but it was a great evening! Such moments written about afterwards in cold words lose their thrill. They bring up no pictures except to those who have lived them. But on a night such as that, one's heart seems like a musical instrument, wonderfully played upon.

Between the acts the two distinguished officers came behind the scenes and were introduced to the artists, making pleasant speeches to us all. Immediately, I liked best the personality of General Grant. There was nothing the least spectacular or egotistical about him; he was absolutely simple and quiet and

unaffected. He bewildered me by apologising courteously for not being able to shake hands with me.
"You have had an accident to your hand!" I exclaimed.

"Not exactly an accident," he said, smiling. "I
think I may call it design!"

He explained that he had shaken hands with so
many people that he could not use his right hand for
a while. He held it out for me to see and, sure enough,
it was terribly swollen and inflamed and must have
been very painful.

The great evening came to an end at last. We were
not sorry on the whole for, thrilling as it had been, it
had been also very tiring. I wonder if such mad,
national excitement could come to people to-day? I
cannot quite imagine an opera performance being
conducted on similar lines in the Metropolitan Opera
House. Perhaps, however, it is not because we are
less enthusiastic but because our events are less
dramatic.

In recalling General Sherman I find myself thinking
of him chiefly in the later years of my acquaintance
with him. After that Chicago night, he never failed
to look me up when I sang in any city where he was
and we grew to be good friends. He was always quite
enthusiastic about operatic music; much more so than
General Grant. He confided to me once that above
all songs he especially disliked *Marching through
Georgia*, and that, naturally, was the song he was constantly obliged to listen to. People, of course, thought
it must be, or ought to be, his favourite melody. But
he hated the tune as well as the words. He was
desperately tired of the song and, above all, he detested
what it stood for, and what it forced him to recall.

General William Tecumseh Sherman, 1877
From a photograph by Mora

Like nearly all great soldiers, Sherman was naturally a gentle person and saddened by war. Everything connected with fighting brought to him chiefly the recollection of its horrors and tragedies and always filled him with pain. So it was that his real heart's preference was for such simple, old-fashioned, plantation-evoking, country-smelling airs as *The Little Old Log Cabin in the Lane*. One day during his many visits to our home he asked me to sing this and, when I informed him that I could not because I did not know and did not have the words, he said he would send them to me. This he did; and I took pains after that never to forget his preference.

In de lit-tle old log cab-in in de lane.

One night when I was singing in a concert in Washington, I caught sight of him sitting quietly in the audience. He did not even know that I had seen him. Presently the audience wanted an encore and, as was my custom in concerts, I went to the piano to play my own accompaniment. I turned and, meeting the General's eyes, smiled at him. Then I sang his beloved *Little Old Log Cabin*. My reward was his beaming expression of appreciation. He was easily touched by such little personal tributes.

"Why on earth did you sing that queer old song, Louise," someone asked me when I was back behind the scenes again.

"It was an official request," I replied mysteriously.

The end of the war was a strenuous time for the

nation; and for actors and singers among others. The combination of work and excitement sent me up to New Hartford in sore need of my summer's rest. But I think, of all the many diverse impressions which that spring made upon my memory, the one that I still carry with me most unforgetably, is a *sound*:—the sound of those shuffling feet, shuffle, shuffle, shuffle,— in the Court House grounds in Chicago: a sound like a great sea or forest in a wind as the people of the nation went in to look at their President whom they loved and who was dead.

CHAPTER XII

THE following season was one of concerts and not remarkably enjoyable. In retrospect I see but a hurried jumble of work until our decision, in the spring, to go to England.

For two or three years I had wanted to try my wings on the other side of the world. Several matters had interfered and made it temporarily impossible, chiefly an unfortunate business agreement into which I had entered at the very outset of my professional career. During the second season that I sang, an *impresario*, a Jew named Ulman, had made me an offer to go abroad and sing in Paris and elsewhere. Being very eager to forge ahead, it seemed like a satisfactory arrangement, and I signed a contract binding myself to sing under Ulman's management *if I went abroad* any time in three years. When I came to think it over, I regretted this arrangement exceedingly. I felt that the *impresario* was not the best one for me. To say the least, I came to doubt his ability. At any rate, because of this complication, I voluntarily tied myself up to Max Maretzek for several years and felt it a release as now I could not tour under Ulman even if I cared to. By 1867, however, my Ulman contract had expired and I was free to do as I pleased. I had no contract abroad to be sure, nor any very definite prospects, but I determined to go to England on a chance and see what developed. At any rate I should have the advantage of being able to consult foreign teachers and to improve my method. The uncertainties of my professional outlook did not disturb me in the least. Indeed, what I really wanted was, like any other girl, to go abroad, as the gentleman in the old-fashioned ballad says:

> . . . to go abroad;
> To go strange countries for to see!

I greatly enjoyed the voyage as I have enjoyed every voyage that I have made since, even including the channel crossing when everyone else on board was seasick, and also the one in which I was nearly ship-wrecked off the Irish coast. I have crossed the Atlantic between sixty and seventy times and every trip has given me pleasure of one kind or another. I am never nervous when travelling. Like poor Jack, I have a vague but sure conviction that nothing will happen to *me;* that I am protected by "a sweet little cherub that sits up aloft!"

At Queenstown, where we touched before going on to our regular port of Liverpool, a man came on board asking for Miss Clara Louise Kellogg. He was from Jarrett, the agent for Colonel Mapleson who was then *impresario* of "Her Majesty's Opera" in London, and he brought me word that Mapleson wanted me to call on him as soon as I reached London and, until we could definitely arrange matters, to please give him the refusal of myself, if I may so express it. Perhaps I was n't a proud and happy girl! Mapleson, I heard later, was then believed to be on the verge of failure and it was hoped that my appearance in his company would revive his fortunes. I grew afterwards cordially to detest and to distrust him, and we had more troubles than I can or care to keep track of: and, as for Jarrett, he was a most unpleasant creature with a positive genius for making trouble. But on that day in Queenstown harbour, with the sun shining and the little Irish fisher boats—their patched sails streaming into the blue off-shore distance,—the man Jarrett had sent to meet me on behalf of Colonel Mapleson seemed like a herald of great good cheer.

When we reached London we went to Miss Edward's Hotel in Hanover Square. It was a curious institution, distinctive of its day and generation, a real old-fashioned English hotel, behind streets that were "chained-up" after nightfall. It was called a "private hotel" and unquestionably was one; deadly dull, but maintained in the most aristocratic way imaginable, like a formal, pluperfect, private house where one might chance to be invited to visit. Everyone dined in his own sitting-room, which was usually separated from the bedroom, and never a soul but the servants was seen. The Langham was the first London hotel to introduce the American style of hotel and it, with its successors, have had such an influence upon the other hostelries of London as gradually to undermine the quaint, old, truly English places we used to know, until there are no more "private hotels" like Miss Edward's in existence.

We had friends in London and quickly made others. Commodore McVickar, of the New York Yacht Club, had given me a letter to a friend of his, the Dowager Duchess of Somerset. Her cards, by the way, were engraved in just the opposite fashion—"Duchess Dowager." McVickar told me that, if she liked, she could make things very pleasant for me in London.

It appeared that she was something of a lion hunter and was always on the lookout for celebrities either arriving or arrived. She went in for everything foreign to her own immediate circle—art, intellect, and Americans—chiefly Americans, in fact, because they were more or less of a novelty, and she had the thirst for change in her so strongly developed that she ought to have lived at the present time. Every night of her life she gave dinners to hosts of friends and acquaintances. Indeed, it is a fact that her sole interest in life consisted of giving dinner parties and making collections of lions, great and small. I have been told that after dinner she sometimes danced the Spanish fandango toward the end of the evening. I never happened to see her do it, but I quite believe her to have been capable of that or of anything else vivacious and eccentric, although she was seventy or eighty in the shade and not entirely built for dancing.

I was somewhat impressed by the prospect of meeting a real live Duchess, and had to be coached beforehand. In the early part of the eighteenth century the mode of address "Your Grace" was used exclusively, and very pretty and courtly it must have sounded. Nowadays it is only servants or inferiors who think of using it. Plain "Duke" or "Duchess" is the later form. At the period of which I am writing the custom was just betwixt and between, in transition, and I was duly instructed to say "Your Grace," but cautioned to say it *very* seldom!

On the nineteenth of November, Colonel Stebbins and I went to call. Maria, Dowager Duchess of Somerset lived in Park Lane in a house of indifferent aspect. Its distinctive feature was the formidable number of flunkeys ranged on the steps and standing

Henry G. Stebbins
From a photograph by Grillet & Co.

in front, all in powdered wigs and white silk stockings and wearing waistcoats of a shade carrying out the dominant colour of the ducal coat of arms. It was raining hard when we got there, but not one of these gorgeous functionaries would demean himself sufficiently to carry an umbrella down to our carriage. In the drawing-room we had to wait a long time before a sort of gilt-edged Groom of the Chambers came to the door and announced,

"Her Grace, the Duchess!"

My youthful American soul was prepared for someone quite dazzling, a magnificent presence. What is the use of diadems and coronets if the owner does not wear them? Of course I knew, theoretically, that duchesses did not wear their coronets in the middle of the day, but I did nevertheless hope for something brilliant or impressive.

Then in walked Maria, Dowager Duchess of Somerset. I cannot adequately describe her. She was a little, dumpy, old woman with no corsets, and dressed in a black alpaca gown and prunella shoes—those awful things that the present generation are lucky enough never to have even seen. She furthermore wore a *fichu* of a style which had been entirely extinct for fifty years at least. I really do not know how there happened to be anyone living even then who could or would make such things for her. No modern modiste could have achieved them and survived. Her whole appearance was certainly beyond words. But she had very beautiful hands, and when she spoke, the great lady was heard instantly. It was all there, of course, only curiously costumed, not to say disguised.

After Colonel Stebbins had presented me and she had greeted me kindly, he said:

"I am sure Miss Kellogg will be glad to sing for you."
"O," said Her Grace, carelessly, "I have n't a
piano. I don't play or sing and so I don't need one.
But I 'll get one in."

I was amazed at the idea of a Duchess not owning a
piano and having to hire one when, in America, most
middle-class homes possess one at whatever sacrifice,
and every little girl is expected to take music lessons
whether she has any ability or not. Even yet I do not
quite understand how she managed without a piano
for her musical lions to play on.

She did get one in without delay and I was speedily
invited to come and sing. I thought I would pay a
particular compliment to my English hostess on that
occasion by choosing a song the words of which were
written by England's Poet Laureate, so I provided
myself with the lovely setting of *Tears, Idle Tears;*
music written by an American, W. H. Cook by name,
who besides being a composer of music possessed a
charming tenor voice. In my innocence I thought
this choice would make a hit. Imagine my surprise
therefore when my hostess's comment on the text was:
"Very pretty words. Who wrote them?"

"Why," I stammered, "Tennyson."

"Indeed? And, my dear Miss Kellogg, who *was*
Tennyson?"

Almost immediately after Colonel Stebbins bought
her a handsome set of the Poet Laureate's works with
which she expressed herself as hugely pleased, although
I am personally doubtful if she ever opened a single
volume.

She did not forget the *Tears, Idle Tears* episode,
however, and had the wit and good humour often to
refer to it afterwards and, usually, quite aptly. One

of her most charming notes to me touches on it gracefully. She was a great letter-writer and her epistles,
couched in flowery terms and embellished with huge
capitals of the olden style, are treasures in their way:
" . . . I know all I feel; and the Tears (*not idle
Tears*) that overflow when I read about that Charming
and Illustrious 'glorious Queen' . . . who is winning
all hearts and delighting everyone . . ."

Another letter, one which I think is a particularly
interesting specimen of the Victorian style of letter-
writing, runs:

> . . . I read with great delight the "critique" of you
> in *The London Review*, which your Mamma was good
> enough to send me. The Writer is evidently a man of
> highly Cultivated Mind, capable of appreciating Excellency
> and Genius, and like the experienced Lapidary knows a
> pearl and a Diamond when he has the good fortune to fall
> in the way of one of high, pure first Water, and great
> brilliancy. Even *you* must now feel you have captivated
> the "élite" of the British Public, and taken root in the
> country, deep, deep, deep. . . .

My mother and I used often to go to see the Duchess
and, through her met many pleasant English people;
the Duke and Duchess of Newcastle, Lady Susan
Vane-Tempest who was Newcastle's sister, Lord Dudley, Lord Stanley, Lord Derby, Viscountess Combermere, Prince de la Tour D'Auvergne, the French Ambassador,—I cannot begin to remember them all—
and I came really to like the quaint little old Duchess,
who was always most charming to me. One small
incident struck me as pathetic,—at least, it was half
pathetic and half amusing. One day she told me with
impressive pride that she was going to show me one

of her dearest possessions, "a wonderful table made from a great American treasure presented to her by her dear friend, Commodore McVickar." She led me over to it and tenderly withdrew the cover, revealing to my amazement a piece of rough, cheap, Indian beadwork, such as all who crossed from Niagara to Canada in those days were familiar with. It was about as much like the genuine and beautiful beadwork of the older tribes as the tawdry American imitations are like true Japanese textures and curios. This poor specimen the Duchess had had made into a table-top and covered it with glass mounted in a gilt frame, and had given it a place of honour in her reception room. I suppose Mr. McVickar had sent it to her to give her a rough general idea of what Indian work looked like. I cannot believe that he intended to play a joke on her. She was certainly very proud of it and, so far as I know, nobody ever had the heart to disillusion her.

More than once I encountered in England this incongruous and inappropriate valuation of American things. I do not put it down to a general admiration for us but, on the contrary, to the fact that the English were so utterly and incredibly ignorant with regard to us. The beadwork of the Duchess reminds me of another somewhat similar incident.

At that time there were only two really rich bachelors in New York society, Wright Sandford and William Douglass. Willie Douglass was of Scotch descent and sang very pleasingly. Women went wild over him. He had a yacht that won everything in sight. While we were in London, he and his yacht put in an appearance at Cowes and he asked us down to pay him a visit. It was a delightful experience. The Earl of Harrington's country seat was not far away and the Earl with his daughters came on board to ask the yacht's party to luncheon the day following. Of course we all went and, equally of course, we had a wonderful time. Lunch was a deliciously informal affair. At one stage of the proceedings, somebody wanted more soda water, when young Lord Petersham, Harrington's eldest son, jumped up to fetch it himself. He rushed across the room and flung open, with an air of triumph, the door of a common, wooden ice-box,—the sort kept in the pantry or outside the kitchen door by Americans.

"Look!" he cried, "did you ever see anything so splendid? It's our American refrigerator and the joy of our lives! I suppose you've seen one before, Miss Kellogg?"

I explained rather feebly that I had, although not in a dining-room. But the family assured me that a dining-room was the proper place for it. I have seldom seen anything so heart-rendingly incongruous as that plain ugly article of furniture in that dining-room all carved woodwork, family silver, and armorial bearings!

They were dear people and my heart went out to them more completely than to any of my London friends. I soon discovered why.

"You are the most cordial English people I've met yet," I said to Lady Philippa Stanhope, the Earl's charming daughter. Her eyes twinkled.

"Oh, we're not English," she explained, "we're Irish!"

Yet even if I did not find the Londoners quite so congenial, I did like them. I could not have helped it, they were so courteous to my mother and me. Probably they supposed us to have Indians in our back-yards at home; nevertheless they were always courteous, at times cordial. One of the most charming of the Englishwomen I met was the Viscountess Combermere. She was one of the Queen's ladies-in-waiting, a very vivacious woman, and used to keep dinner tables in gales of laughter. Just then when anyone in London wanted to introduce or excuse an innovation, he or she would exclaim, "the Queen does it!" and there would be nothing more for anyone to say. This became a sort of catch-word. I recall one afternoon at the Dowager Duchess of Somerset's, a cup of hot tea was handed to the Viscountess who, pouring the liquid from the cup into the saucer and then sipping it from the saucer, said:

"Now ladies, do not think this is rude, for I have just come from the Queen and saw her do the same. Let us emulate the Queen!" Then, seeing us hesitate, "the Queen does it, ladies! the Queen does it!"

Whereupon everyone present drank tea from their saucers.

It was the Viscountess, also, who so greatly amused my mother at a luncheon party by saying to her with the most polite interest:

"You speak English remarkably well, Mrs. Kellogg! Do they speak English in America?"

"Yes, a little," replied mother, quietly.

CHAPTER XIII

AT HER MAJESTY'S

ADELINA PATTI came to see us at once. I had known her in America when she was singing with her sister and when, if the truth must be told, many people found Carlotta the more satisfactory singer of the two. I was glad to see her again even though we were *prime donne* of rival opera organisations. Adelina headed the list of artists at Covent Garden under Mr. Gye, among whom were some of the biggest names in Europe. Indeed, I found myself confronted with the competition of several favourites of the English people. At my own theatre, Her Majesty's, was Mme. Titjiens, always much beloved in England and still a fine artist. Christine Nilsson was also a member of the company; had sung there earlier in that year and was to sing there again later in the season.

A *tour de force* of Adelina's was my old friend *Linda di Chamounix*. She was supposed to be very brilliant in the part, especially in the *Cavatina* of the first act. As for Marguerite it was considered her private and particular property at Covent Garden, and Nilsson's private and particular property at Her Majesty's.

I have been often asked my opinion of Patti's voice. She had a beautiful voice that, in her early days, was very high, and she is, on the whole, quite the most remarkable singer that I ever heard. But her voice has not been a high one for many years. It has changed, changed in pitch and register. It is no longer a soprano; it is a mezzo and must be judged by quite different standards. I heard her when she sang over here in America thirteen years ago. She gave her old *Cavatina* from *Linda* and sang the whole of it a tone and a half lower than formerly. While the public did not know what the trouble was, they could not help perceiving the lack of brilliancy. Ah, those who have heard her in only the last fifteen years or so know nothing at all about Patti's voice! Yet it was always a light voice, although I doubt if the world realised the fact. She was always desperately afraid of overstraining it, and so was Maurice Strakosch for her. She never could sing more than three times in a week and, of those three, one *rôle* at least had to be very light. A great deal is heard about the wonderful preservation of Patti's voice. It *was* wonderfully preserved thirteen years ago. How could it have been otherwise, considering the care she has always taken of herself? Such a life! Everything divided off carefully according to *régime:*—so much to eat, so far to walk, so long to sleep, just such and such things to do and no others! And, above all, she has allowed herself few emotions. Every singer knows that emotions are what exhaust and injure the voice. She never acted; and she never, never felt. As Violetta she did express some slight emotion, to be sure. Her *Gran Dio* in the last act was sung with something like passion, at least with more passion than she ever sang anything else. Yes: in *La Traviata*, after she had run away with Nicolini, she did succeed in putting an unusual amount of warmth into the *rôle* of Violetta.

Adelina Patti
From a photograph by Fredericks

But her great success was always due to her wonderful voice. Her acting was essentially mechanical. As an intelligent actress, a creator of parts, or even as an interesting personality, she could never approach Christine Nilsson. Nilsson had both originality and magnetism, a combination irresistibly captivating. Her singing was the embodiment of dramatic expression.

In September of that year we went down to Edinburgh to see the ruins of Melrose Abbey. To confess the truth, I remember just two things clearly about Scotland. One was that, at the ruins, Colonel Stebbins picked up a piece of crumbling stone, spoke of the strange effect of age upon it, and let it drop. Around turned the showman, or guide, or whatever the person was called who crammed the sights down our throats.

"You Americans are the curse of the country!" he exclaimed sharply.

My other distinct memory—with associations of much discomfort and annoyance—is that I left one rubber overshoe in Loch Lomond.

So much for Scotland. We did not stay long; and were soon back in London ready for work.

Our rehearsals were rather fun. It seemed strange to be able to walk across a stage without getting the hem of one's skirt dirty. English theatres are incredibly clean when one considers what a dirty, sooty, grimy town London is. Our opera was at the old Drury Lane, although we always called it Her Majesty's because that was the name of the opera company. I was amused to find that a member of the company, a big young basso named "Signor Foli," turned out to be none other than Walter Foley, a boy from my old home in the Hartford region. I always called him "the Irish Italian from Connecticut."

We opened on November 2d in *Faust*. There was
rather a flurry of indignation that a young American
prima donna should dare to plunge into Marguerite
the very first thing.   The fact that the young American
had sung it before other artists had, with the exception
of Patti and Titjiens, and that she was generally
believed to know something about it, mattered not at
all.   English people are acknowledged idolaters and
notoriously cold to newcomers.   They cling to some
imperishable memory of a poor soul whose voice
has been dead for years: and it was undoubtedly an
inversion of this same loyalty to their favourites that
made them so dislike the idea of Marguerite being
selected for the new young woman's *début*.   But,
really, though on a slightly different scale, it was not so
unlike the early days of *Linda* over again when the
Italians accused me with so much animosity of taking
the bread out of their mouths.   It can easily be believed
that, with Nilsson holding all records of Marguerite
at Her Majesty's, and with Adelina waiting at Covent
Garden with murderous sweetness to see what I
was going to do with her favourite *rôle*, I was wretch-
edly nervous.   When the first night came around no
one had a good word for me; everybody was indifferent; and I honestly do not know what I should have
done if it had not been for Santley—dear, big-hearted
Santley.   He was our Valentine, that one, great,
incomparable Valentine for whom Gounod wrote
the *Dio possente*.   I was walking rather shakily
across the stage for my first entrance, feeling utterly
frightened and lonely, and looking, I dare say, nearly
as miserable as I felt, when a warm, strong hand was
laid gently on my shoulder.

"Courage, little one, courage," said Santley, smiling

at me and patting me as if I had been a very small, unhappy, frightened child.

I smiled back at him and, suddenly, I felt strong and hopeful and brave again. Onto the stage I went with a curiously sure feeling that I was going to do well after all.

I suppose I must have done well. There was a packed house and very soon I felt it with me. I was called out many times, once in the middle of the act after the church scene, an occurrence that was so far as I know unprecedented. Colonel Keppel, the Prince of Wales's aide (I did not dream then how well-known the name Keppel was destined to be in connection with that of his royal master), came behind during the *entr'acte* to congratulate me on behalf of the Prince. In later performances his Highness did me the honour of coming himself. The London newspapers—of which, frankly, I had stood in great dread—had delightful things to say. This is the way in which one of them welcomed me: ". . . She has only one fault: if she were but English, she would be simply perfect!" The editorial comments in *The Athenæum* of Chorley, that gorgon of English criticism, included the following paragraph:

Miss Kellogg has a voice, indeed, that leaves little to wish for, and proves by her use of it that her studies have been both assiduous and in the right path. She is, in fact, though so young, a thoroughly accomplished singer—in the school, at any rate, toward which the music of M. Gounod consistently leans, and which essentially differs from the florid school of Rossini and the Italians before Verdi. One of the great charms of her singing is her perfect enunciation of the words she has to utter. She never sacrifices sense to sound; but fits the verbal text to the music, as if she attached equal importance to each. Of the Italian language she seems to be a thorough mistress, and we may well believe that she speaks it both fluently and correctly. These manifest advantages, added to a graceful figure, a countenance full of intelligence, and undoubted dramatic ability, make up a sum of attractions to be envied, and easily explain the interest excited by Miss Kellogg at the outset and maintained by her to the end.

But, oh, how grateful I was to that good Santley for giving the little boost to my courage at just the right moment! He was always a fine friend, as well as a fine singer. I admired him from the bottom of my heart, both as an artist and a man, and not only for what he was but also for what he had grown from. He was only a ship-chandler's clerk in the beginning. Indeed, he was in the office of a friend of mine in Liverpool. From that he rose to the foremost rank of musical art. Yet that friend of mine never took the least interest in Santley, nor was he ever willing to recognise Santley's standing. Merely because he had once held so inferior a position this man I knew—and he was not a bad sort of man otherwise— was always intolerant and incredulous of Santley's success and would never even go to hear him sing. It is true that Santley never did entirely shake off the influences of his early environment, a characteristic to be remarked in many men of his nationality. In addition to this, some men are so sincere and simple-hearted and earnest that they do not take kindly to artificial environment and I think Santley was one of these. And he was a dear man, and kind. His wife, a relative of Fanny Kemble, I never knew very well as she was a good deal of an invalid.

Clara Louise Kellogg as Linda, 1868

From a photograph by Stereoscopic Co.

On the 9th we repeated *Faust* and on the 11th we gave *Traviata*. This also, I feel sure, must have irritated Adelina. It is a curious little fact that, while the opera of *Traviata* was not only allowed but also greatly liked in London, the play *La Dame aux Camilias*—which as we all know is practically the *Traviata* libretto—had been rigorously banned by the English censor! *Traviata* brought me more curtain calls than ever. The British public was really growing to like me!

Martha followed on the 15th. This was another *rôle* in which I had to challenge comparison with Nilsson, who was fond of it, although I never liked her classic style in the part. It was given in Italian; but I sang *The Last Rose of Summer* in English, like a ballad, and the people loved it. I wore a blue satin gown as Martha which, alas! I lost in the theatre fire not long after.

Then came *Linda di Chamounix*, the second *rôle* that I had ever sung. I was glad to sing it again, and in England, and the newspapers spoke of it as "a great and crowning success" for me. As soon as we had given this opera, Gye, the *impresario* at Covent Garden, decided it was time to show off Patti in that *rôle*. So he promptly—hastily, even—revived Linda for her. I have always felt, however, that Linda was tacitly given to me by the public. Arditi, our conductor at Her Majesty's, wrote a waltz for me to sing at the close of the opera, *The Kellogg Waltz*, and I wore a charming new costume in the part, a simple little yellow gown, with a blue moiré silk apron and tiny pale pink roses. The combination of pink and yellow was always a favourite one with me. I wore it in my early appearance as Violetta and, later,

also in *Traviata*, I wore a variant of the same colour
scheme that was called by my friends in London my
"rainbow frock." It was composed of a *grosgrain*
silk petticoat of the hue known as apricot, trimmed
with mauve and pale turquoise shades; the overskirt
was caught back at either side with a turquoise bow
and the train was of plain turquoise. I took a serious
interest in my costumes in those days—and, indeed,
in all days! This latter gown was one of Worth's
creations and met with much admiration. More than
once have I received letters asking where it was made.

The English public was most cordial and kindly
toward me and unfailingly appreciative of my work.
But I believe from the bottom of my heart that,
inherently and permanently, the English are an un-
musical people. They do not like fire, nor passion,
nor great moments in either life nor art. Mozart's
music, that runs peacefully and simply along, is precisely what suits them best. They adore it. They
likewise adore Rossini and Handel. They think that
the crashing emotional climaxes of the more advanced
composers are extravagant; and, both by instinct and
principle, they dislike the immoderate and the extreme
in all things. They are in fact a simple and primitive
people, temperamentally, actually, and artistically. I
remember that the first year I was in London all the
women were singing:

> My mother bids me bind my hair
> And lace my bodice blue!

It wandered along so sweetly and mildly, not to say
insipidly, that of course it was popular with Victorian
England.

Finally, came *Don Giovanni* on December 3d. I played Zerlina as I had done in America. Later I came to prefer Donna Anna. But in London Titjiens did Donna Anna. Santley was the Almaviva and Mme. Sinico was the Donna Elvira. The following spring when we gave our "all star cast" Nilsson was the Elvira. I had no Zerlina costume with me and the decision to put on the opera was made in a hurry, so I got out my old Rosina dress and wore it and it answered the purpose every bit as well as if I had had a new one.

The opera went splendidly, so splendidly that, two days later, on the 5th, we gave it again at a matinée, or, as it was the fashion to say then, a "morning performance." The success was repeated. I caught a most terrible cold, however, and returned in a bad temper to Miss Edward's Hotel to nurse myself for a few days and get in condition for the next performance. But there was destined to be no next performance at the old Drury Lane.

The following evening at about half-past ten, my mother, Colonel Stebbins, and I were talking in our sitting-room with the window-shades up. Suddenly I saw a red glow over the roofs of the houses and pointed it out.

"It's a fire!" I exclaimed.

"And it's in the direction of the theatre!" said Colonel Stebbins.

"Oh, I hope that Her Majesty's is in no danger!" cried my mother.

We did not think at first that it could be the theatre itself, but Colonel Stebbins sent his valet off in a hurry to make enquiries. While he was gone a messenger arrived in great haste from the Duchess of Somerset asking for assurances of my safety. Then came other messages from friends all over London and soon the man servant returned to confirm the reports that were reaching us. Her Majesty's had caught fire from the carpenter's shop underneath the stage and, before morning, had burned to the ground.

Arditi had been holding an orchestra rehearsal there at the time and the last piece of music ever played in the old theatre was *The Kellogg Waltz.*

Mr. McHenry
From a photograph by Brady

CHAPTER XIV

TITJIENS had smelled smoke and she had been told that it was nothing but shavings that were being burned. Luckily, nobody was hurt and, although some of our costumes were lost, we artists did not suffer so very much after all. But of course our season was summarily put an end to and we all scattered for work and play until the spring season when Mapleson would want us back.

My mother and I went across to Paris without delay. I had wanted to see "the Continent" since I was a child and I must say that, in my heart of hearts, I almost welcomed the fire that set me free to go sightseeing and adventuring after the slavery of dressing-rooms and rehearsals. Crossing the Channel I was the heroine of the boat because, while I was just a little seasick, I was not enough so to give in to it. I can remember forcing myself to sit up and walk about and even talk with a grim and savage feeling that I would die rather than admit myself beaten by a silly and disgusting *malaise* like that; and after crossing the ocean with impunity too. Everyone else on board was abjectly ill and I expect it was partly pride that kept me well.

In Paris we went first to the Louvre Hotel where we were nearly frozen to death. As soon as we could, we moved into rooms where we might thaw out and become almost warm, although we never found the temperature really comfortable the whole time we lived in French houses. We saw any number of plays, visited cathedrals and picture galleries, and bought clothes. In fact we did all the regulation things, for we were determined to make the most of every minute of our holiday. Rather oddly, one of the entertainments I remember most distinctly was a production of *Gulliver's Travels* at the Théâtre Châtelet. It was the dullest play in the world; but the scenery and effects were splendid.

I was not particularly enthusiastic over the French theatres. Indeed, I found them very limited and disappointing. I had gone to France expecting every theatrical performance in Paris to be a revelation. Probably I respect French art as much as any one; but I believe it is looked up to a great deal more than is justified. Consider Mme. Carvalho's wig for example, and, as for that, her costume as well. Yet we all turned to the Parisians as authority for the theatre. The pictures of the first distinguished Marguerite give a fine idea of the French stage effects in the sixties. A few years ago I heard *Tannhäuser* in Paris. The manner in which the pilgrims wandered in convinced me in my opinion. The whole management was inefficient and Wagner's injunctions were disregarded at every few bars. The French Gallicise everything. They simply cannot get inside the mental point of view of any other country. Though they are popularly considered to be so facile and adaptable, they are in truth the most obstinate, one-idead, single-sided race on earth barring none except, possibly, the Italians. Gounod's *Faust* is a good example—a German story treated by Frenchmen. Remarkably little that is Teutonic has been left in it. Goethe has been eliminated so far as possible. The French were held by the drama, but the poetry and the symbolism meant nothing at all to them. Being German, they had no use for its poetry and its symbolism. The French colour and alter foreign thought just as they colour and alter foreign phraseology. They do it in a way more subtle than any usual difficulties of translation from one tongue to another. The process is more a form of transmuting than of translating—words, thoughts, actions—into another element entirely. How idiotic it sounds when Hamlet sings:

Être—ou n'être pas!

Perhaps this, however, is not entirely the fault of the French. Shakespeare should never be set to music.

There is also the question of traditions. I may seem to be contradicting myself when I find fault with a certain French school for its blind and bigoted adherence to traditions; but there should be moderation in all things and a hidebound rigidity in stupid old forms is just as inartistic as a free-and-easy elasticity in flighty new ones. It is possible to put some old wine in new bottles, but it must be poured in very gently. French artists learn most when once they get away from France. Maurel is a good example. Look at the way he grew and developed when he went to England and America and was allowed to work problems and ideas out by himself.

Once when in Paris I wanted to vary and freshen my costume of Marguerite, give it a new yet consistent touch here and there. I was not planning to renovate the *rôle*, only the girl's clothes. Having always felt that the Grand Opera was a Mecca to us artists from afar, I hastened there and climbed up the huge stairway to pay my respects to the Director. Monsieur had never heard of me. Frenchmen make a point never to have heard of any one outside of France. The fact that I was merely the first and the most famous Marguerite across the sea did not count. He was, however, very polite. He brought out his wonderful costume books that were full of new ideas to me and delighted me with numberless fresh possibilities. I saw unexplored fields in the direction of correct costuming and exclaimed over the designs, Monsieur watching my enthusiasm with bored civility. There was one particularly enchanting design for a silver chatelaine, heavy and mediæval in character. I could see it with my mind's eye hanging from Marguerite's bodice. This I said to M. le Directeur: but he shook his dignified head with a frown.

"Too rich. Marguerite was too poor," he said with weary brevity.

"Oh, no!" I explained volubly and eagerly, "she was of the well-to-do class—the burghers—don't you remember? Marguerite and Valentine owned their house and, though they were of course of peasant blood, this sort of chatelaine seems to me just the thing that any German girl might possess."

"Too rich," Monsieur put in imperturbably.

"But," I protested, "it might be an heirloom, you know, and——"

"Too rich," he repeated politely; and he added in a calm, dreamy voice as he shut up the book, "I think that Mademoiselle will make a mistake *if she ever tries anything new!*"

As for sightseeing in France, my mother and I did

any amount of it on that first visit. Sometimes I was charmed but more often I was disillusioned. There have been few "sights" in my life that have come up to my "great expectations" or been half as wonderful as my dreams. This is the penalty of a too vivid imagination; nothing can ever be as perfect as one's fancy paints it. The view of Mont Blanc from the terrace of Voltaire's house near the borderland of France and Switzerland is one of the few in my experience that I have found more lovely than I could have dreamed it to be. Of all the palaces that I have been in—and they have numbered several—the only one that ever seemed to me like a real palace was Fontainebleau. Small but exquisite, it looked like a haven of rest and loveliness, as though its motto might well be: "How to be happy though a crowned head!"

Speaking of crowned heads reminds me that while we were in Paris Mr. McHenry, our English friend from Holland Park, made an appointment for me to be presented to the ex-Queen of Spain, the Bourbon princess, Christina, so beloved by many Spaniards. I was delighted because I had never been presented to royalty and a Spanish queen seemed a very splendid sort of personage even if she did not happen to be ruling at the moment. Christina had withdrawn from Spain and had married the Duke de Rienzares. They lived in a beautiful palace on the Champs Élysées. There are nothing but shops on the site now but it used to be very imposing, especially the formal entrance which, if I remember correctly, was off the Rue St. Honoré. Mrs. and Mr. McHenry went with me and, after being admitted, we were shown up a marble staircase into what was called the Cameo Room, a small, austere apartment filled with cameos of the Bourbons. Queen

Christina liked to live in small and unpretentious rooms; they seemed less suggestive of a palace.

I found that "royalty at home" was about as simple as anything could conceivably be; not quite as plain as the old Dowager Duchess of Somerset to be sure but quite plain enough. The Queen and the Duke de Rienzares entered without ceremony. The Queen wore a severe and simple black gown that cleared the floor by an inch or two. It was a perfectly practical and useful dress, admirably suited for housekeeping or tidying up a room. Around the royal lady's shoulders hung a little red plaid shawl such as no American would wear. She was Spanishly dark and her black hair was pulled into a knot about the size of a silver dollar in the middle of the back of her head. I have never seen her *en grande toilette* and so do not know whether or not she ever looked any less like a respectable housekeeper. She had a delightful manner and was most gracious. She had, with all the Bourbon pride, also the Bourbon gift of making herself pleasant and of putting people at their ease. Of course she was immensely accomplished and spoke Italian as perfectly as she did Spanish. The Duke seemed harmless and amiable. He had little to say, was thoroughly subordinate, and seemed entirely acclimated to his position in life as the ordinarily born husband of a Queen.

Our visit was not much of an ordeal after all. It was really quite instinctively that I courtesied and backed out of the room and observed the other points of etiquette that are correct when one is introduced to royalty. As it was a private presentation, it had not been thought necessary to coach me, and as I backed myself out of the august presence, keeping myself as nearly as possible in a courtesying attitude, I caught Mr. McHenry looking at me with amused approval.

"Well," said he, when we were safe in the hall and I had straightened up, "I should say that you had been accustomed to courts and crowned heads all your life! You acted as if you had been brought up on it!"

"Ah," I replied, "that comes from my opera training. We learn on the stage how to treat kings and queens."

Not more than a fortnight after this I had an offer for an engagement at the Madrid Opera for $400.00 a night, very good for Spain in those days. I suppose that it came indirectly through the influence of Queen Christina. I wanted to go to Spain, but my mother would not let me accept. We were almost pioneers of travel in the modern sense and had no one to give us authoritative ideas of other countries. People alarmed us about the climate, declaring it unhealthy; and about the public, which they said was capricious and rude. The warning about the public particularly frightened me. I should never object to my efforts being received in silence in case of disapproval, but I felt that I could not survive what I had been told was the Spanish custom of hissing. I was also told that Spanish audiences were very mercurial and difficult to win. So we refused the Madrid Opera offer, and I have never sung in either Spain or Italy principally because of my dread of the hissing habit.

That same year I heard Christine Nilsson for the first time, in *Martha* at the Théâtre Lyrique and, later, in *Hamlet* at the same theatre with Faure. Shortly after both Nilsson and Faure were taken over by the Grand Opera. Ophélie had been written for Nilsson and composed entirely around her voice. She created

10

the part, singing it exquisitely, and Ambrose Thomas paid her the compliment of taking his two principal soprano melodies from old Swedish folk-songs. Nilsson could sing Swedish melodies in a way to drive one crazy or break one's heart. I have been quite carried away with them again and again. There was one delicious song that she called *Le Bal* in which a young fellow asks a girl to dance and she is very shy. It was slight, but ever so pretty, and it had a minor melody that was typically northern. These were the good days before her voice became impaired. In this connection I may mention that it was Christine Nilsson who, having heard the Goodwin girls sing *Way Down upon the Swanee River*, first introduced it on the stage as an *encore*.

While speaking of Nilsson, I want to record that I was present on the night, much later, when she practically murdered the high register of her voice. She had five upper notes the quality of which was unlike any other I ever heard and that possessed a peculiar charm. The tragedy happened during a performance of *The Magic Flute* in London and I was in the Newcastles' box, which was near the stage. Nilsson was the Queen of the Night, one of her most successful early *rôles*. The second *aria* in *The Magic Flute* is more famous and less difficult than the first *aria* and, also, more effective. Nilsson knew well the ineffectiveness of the ending of the first *aria* in the two weakest notes of a soprano's voice, A natural and B flat. I never could understand why a master like Mozart should have chosen to use them as he did. There is no climax to the song. One has to climb up hard and fast and then stop short in the middle. It is an appalling thing to do: and that night Nilsson took those two notes at the last in *chest tones*.

Christine Nilsson as Queen of the Night
From a photograph by Pierre Petit

"Great heavens!" I gasped, "what is she doing? What is the woman thinking of!"

Of course I knew she was doing it to get volume and vibration and to give that trying climax some character. But to say that it was a fatal attempt is to put it mildly. She absolutely killed a certain quality in her voice there and then and she *never recovered it*. Even that night she had to cut out the second great *aria*. Her beautiful high notes were gone for ever. Probably the fatality was the result of the last stroke to a continued strain which she had put upon her voice. After that she, like Mario, began to be dramatic to make up for what she had lost. She, the classical and cold artist, became full of expression and animation. But the later Nilsson was very different from the Nilsson whom I first heard in Paris during the winter of 1868, when, besides singing the music perfectly, she was, with her blond hair and broad brow, a living Ophélie. As I have said, Faure, the baritone, was her Hamlet in that early performance. He was a great artist, a great actor in whatever *rôle* he took. His voice was not wonderful, but he was saved, and more than saved, by his style and his art. He was a particularly cultivated, musicianly man whose dignity of carriage and elegance of manner could easily make people forget a certain ungrateful quality in his voice. It was Faure who had the brains and perseverance to learn how to sing a particular note from a really bad singer. The bad singer had only one good note in his voice and that happened to be the worst one in Faure's. So, night after night, the great artist went to hear and to study the inferior one to try and learn how he got that note. And he succeeded, too. This is a fair sample of his careful and finished way of doing anything. He was a big artist, and to big artists, especially in singing, music is almost mathematical in its exactness.

Adelina Patti, who had also left London for the winter, was singing at the *Italiens* in Paris. I went to hear her give an indifferent performance of *Ernani*. It was never one of her advantageous *rôles*. Adelina had a most extraordinary charm and a great power over men of very diverse sorts. De Caux, Nicolini, Maurice Strakosch, who married Adelina's sister Amelia, all adored her and felt that whatever she did must be right because she did it. Nicolini, who had been a star tenor singing all over Italy before she captured him, was willing to forget that he ever had a wife or children. Maurice was for years her "manager and representative," and as such put up with incredible complexities in the situation. There is a long and lurid tale about Nicolini's wife appearing in Italy when Nicolini, Maurice, and Adelina were all there. The story ended with Nicolini being kicked downstairs and the press commented upon the episode with an apt couplet from Schiller to the effect that "life is hard, but merry is art!"

The names of Paris and of Maurice Strakosch in conjunction conjure up the thought of Napoleon III, who, in his young days of exile, used to be very intimate with Maurice. Louis Napoleon, after he had escaped from the fortress of Ham, spent some time in London, and he and Maurice frequently lunched or dined together. By the way, some years later, at a dinner at the McHenrys' in Holland Park, I was told by Chevalier Wyckoff that it was he who rescued Napoleon from the prison of Ham by smuggling clothes in to him and by having a boat waiting for him. Maurice used to tell of one rather amusing incident that occurred during the London period. Louis Napoleon's dress clothes were usually in pawn, and one night when he wanted to go to some party, he presented himself at Maurice's rooms to borrow his. Maurice was out; but nevertheless Louis Napoleon took the dress clothes anyway, adding all of Maurice's orders and decorations. When he was decked out to his satisfaction he went to the party. Shortly after, in came Maurice, to dress for the same party, and called to his valet to bring him his evening clothes.

"Mr. Bonaparte's got 'em on, sir," said the man: and Maurice stayed at home!

Napoleon III was a man of many weaknesses. Yet he kept his promises and remembered his friends—when he could. As soon as he became Emperor he sent for Maurice Strakosch and offered him the management of the *Italiens;* but Maurice declined the honour. He was too busy "representing" Patti in those days to care for any other engagement. He did give singing lessons to the Empress Eugénie however, and was always on good terms with her and with the Emperor.

When I was in Paris in '68 Napoleon and Eugénie were in power at the Tuileries and day after day I saw them driving behind their splendid horses. Paris was extremely gay and yet somewhat ominous, for there was a wide-spread feeling that clouds were gathering about the throne. When thinking of that period I sometimes quote to myself Owen Meredith's poem, *Aux Italiens,*

At Paris it was at the opera there . . .

The Emperor there in his box of state
Looked grave, as if he had just then seen
The red flag wave from the city gate,
Where his eagles in bronze had been.

The Tuileries court was a very brilliant one and we were accustomed to splendid costumes and gorgeous turnouts in the Bois, but one day I came home with a particularly excited description of the "foreign princess" I had seen. Her clothes, her horses (she drove postilion), her carriage, her liveries, her servants, all, to my innocent and still ignorant mind, proclaimed her some distinguished visiting royalty. How chagrined I was and how I was laughed at when my "princess" turned out to be one of the best known *demi-mondaines* in Paris! Even then it was difficult to tell the two *mondes* apart.

A unique character in Paris was Dr. Evans, dentist to the Emperor and Empress. He was an American and a witty, talented man. I remember hearing him laughingly boast:

"I have looked down the mouth of every crowned head of Europe!"

When disaster overtook the Bonapartes, he proved that he could serve crowned heads in other ways besides filling their teeth. It was he who helped the Empress to escape, and the fact made him an exile from Paris. He came to see me in London years afterwards and told me something of that dark and dramatic time of flight. He felt very homesick for Paris, which had been his home for so long, but the dear man was as merry and charming as ever.

We spent in all only a short time in Paris. Two months were taken out of the middle of that winter for travelling on the Continent, after which we returned to the French city for March. When we first started from Paris on our trip we were headed for Nice. It was Christmas Day, and cold as charity. Why *did* we choose that day of all others on which to begin a journey? Our Christmas dinner consisted of cold soup swallowed at a station. Christmas!—I could have wept!

CHAPTER XV

IT seemed very odd to be really idle. From the time I was thirteen I had been working and studying so systematically that to get the habit of leisure was like learning a new and a difficult lesson. It took time, for one thing, to find out how to relax; nervous persons never acquire this art naturally nor possess it instinctively. It is with them the artificial product of painful experience. All my life I had been expending energy at top pressure and building it up again as fast as I could instead of sometimes letting it lie fallow for a bit. When I became exhausted my mother would speedily make strong broths with rice and meat and vegetables and anything else that she considered nourishing to stimulate my jaded vitality; then I would go at my work again harder than ever. When I had finished one thing I plunged, nerves, body, and brain, into another. To be an artist is bad enough; but to be an American artist—! To the temperamental excitability and intensity is added the racial nervousness; and lucky are such, if they do not go up in a final smoke of over-energised effort. When I was singing I was always in a fever before the curtain rose. All the day before I was restless to the point of desperation. Instead of letting myself go and becoming comfortably limp so that I might conserve my strength for the performance itself, I would cast about for a hundred secondary ways in which to waste my nervous force. I was nearly as bad as the Viennese *prima donna*, Marie Willt. The story is told of her that a reporter from a Vienna newspaper went to interview her the afternoon before she was to sing in *Il Trovatore* at the Royal Opera and enquired of the scrubwoman in the hall where he could find Frau Willt.

"Here," responded the scrubwoman, sitting up to eye him calmly.

When the young man expressed surprise and incredulity she explained, as she continued to mop the soapy water, that she invariably scrubbed the floor the day she was going to sing. "It keeps me busy," she concluded sententiously.

Think of the force that went into that scrubbing-brush which might have gone into the part of Leonora! But it is not for me to find fault with such a course of action because I followed a very similar one. If I did not exactly scrub floors, I did, somehow, contrive to find other equally adequate ways of dissipating my strength before I sang. Yet here I was, actually taking a holiday, with no chance at all to work even if I wanted to!

When we arrived in Nice the lemons and oranges on the trees and a sky as blue as painted china made the place seem to me somewhat unnatural, like a stage setting. Not yet having learned my lesson of relaxation, I soon became restless and wanted to be again on the move. Nevertheless we stayed there for nearly a month. My mother seemed to like it. She made many friends and spent hours every day painting little pictures—quite dear little pictures they were—of the bright coloured wild flowers that grew roundabout. But possibly a few extracts from the diary kept by my mother of this visit will not be out of place here. The capital letters and italics are hers.

Dec. 25—Christmas morning. Sun shone for two hours. Left for Nice. Arrived at 5 P.M. A very cold night. Cars warmed by zink hollow planks [boxes] filled with Boiling water which are replaced every three hours at the different stations. Notwithstanding shawls and wraps suffered with the cold. Nothing to eat until we arrived at twelve at Marseilles, where [we] got a poor, cold soup and miserable cup of tea. Arrived at the Hotel Luxembourg in Nice at 6.30 P.M. The city and hotels crowded with people from all parts of the world. Rheumatic people rush here to get into the *sunshine*—a *thing* seldom seen in Paris or London in winter. Nice is simply a watering-place *without the water*, unless one means the Sea Mediterranean which almost rushes into the Halls of the Hotels. All languages are here spoken; therefore no trouble for any nation to obtain what it desires. The streets are pulverised magnesia. Everybody looks after walking as though they had been to mill "turning hopper."

In our promenade [to-day, Dec. 27] we meet in less than twenty minutes as many different nationalities, or representatives of each. Poor in soil, poor in colour, poor in taste is Nice. The Hotels compose the City. Roses bloom by the roadsides in abundance. The gardens of the Hotels are yellow with Oranges. Palm trees line the streets, none of which have shade trees that ever grow enough to shade but *one person at a time*—no soil—no vigour—sun does all the maturing. Things ripen from necessity, not from the soil.

Saturday 28—Clear beautiful morning. Beach covered with promenaders. At twelve Louise and I took a long walk towards Villa Franca—sun very hot—met Richard Palmer who had just arrived. Enjoyed the morning;

were refreshed by our walk. Mr. Stebbins and Charlie called. Drive at 5. Evening had a light wood fire upon the hearth, making rooms and hearts cheerful in direct opposition to the roaring of the wild sea at our very feet. Proprietor of Hotel sent up his Piano for Louise. Basket Phaetons—2 ponies—are hired here for one franc an hour—fine woods but dusty.

29th.—Sunday—Magnificent morning. The sea smooth as glass. Women line the beach spreading clothes to bleach. There is a short diluted Season of Italian Opera here. *Ernani* was announced for last evening. There is no odor from the Mediterranean, no sea weeds, no shells, a perfectly clean barren beach. I don't believe it is even salt. Shall go and sip to satisfy Yankee curiosity. There are two Irish heiresses here whose combined weight in gold is 9000 lbs., and the way the nobs and snobs tiptoe, bow, and scrape is something to behold. They are always dressed alike. We are cold enough to have a small wood fire morning and evening in a very primitive style fireplace 18 inches square. Handirons made of 2 cast iron virgins' heads and busts. Bellows thrown in.

One P.M.—Took a double Pony Basket Phaeton, Louise and I on the front seat, she driving a grey and bay pony. Drove to Villa Franca where the American fleet is anchored. Saw the old flag once more, which brought home most vividly to my heart and roused the old longing for the dear old spot.

30th. No letters. No news of trunks. The Monotonous sea singing *Hush* at measured intervals, not one wave even an inch higher than another. This cannot be a real sea, the Mediterranean, *or it would sometime change its tone.* Yesterday rode through the old Italian part of the City. Houses 6 or 7 stories high. Streets just wide enough for a donkey cart to get through. Never can pass each other. One has to back out.

Tuesday 31. Took our usual walk. Listened to the band in the Public Gardens. This is a poor, barren country.

I believe the plates are *licked by the inhabitants instead of the dogs*. This place is too poor for *them*. The only good conditioned looking people here are the priests. They are bursting with inward satisfaction and joy. When in Paris last October we heard of a most wonderful pair of earrings that had been presented to Adelina Patti by a Gent who glided under the name of Khalil Bey, worth Millions! When in Paris again in December there was a great stir about the Private Picture Gallery of a very wealthy man who had met with severe and great losses at the gaming table. Our friends tried to obtain admission for us to see them, but through some slip we failed. Upon our arrival in Nice, one day there was great confusion and agitation among the Eager. Servants were standing in corners and evidence of something was very vivid. Finally the mystery was solved. And we learned that a great Prince had arrived from St. Petersburg. A Turk! Who was sharing our fate (the order of things is all reversed in Nice. You commence life there by beginning at the top and working your way down) and taken rooms on the 6th floor, accompanied by 2 servants, one especially to take care of the Pipe. His name is Khalil Bey—about 50 years old—a hard, Chinese, cast-iron face run when the iron was very hot—sinking well into the mould—one eye almost blind—short small feet—he seemed to commence to grow at the feet and grew bigger and wider as he went up.

3rd. He moves in the best "society" over here—has his Box at the Opera—tells frankly his losses at cards—so many million francs—is a man of influence even among a certain class and that far above mediocre. Met him at an evening entertainment. Found him a great admirer of Patti in certain *rôles*—very good judgment upon musical matters in general—and a professed *Gambler*.

4th. Rained all day. A lost day to comfort outside and in.

5th. Another day of the same sort. Weary with looking at the sea.

6th. Clearing. Sunshine at intervals.

7th. Mr. Kinney called in afternoon. Conversation related to Americans in Europe. Came to the conclusion that as a general rule none but the class denominated "fast" come to Europe and like it. Mr. —— said he would give any American young gentleman or lady just 18 months in European society to lose all refinement and all moral principle, young ladies in particular. The moral principle cannot be strong when one is *laughed at for blushing!*

8th. Mr. and Mrs. L —— came over in the evening. Sat two hours. Discussed Europe generally and decided *America* was the *only place for decent people to live in.* *Death* is all over Europe, an epidemic that has no cure, Death of all moral responsibility. Death of ambition in the way of virtue. Death of all comforts of life. The last man that dies will be carried from the *card table.*

In my own recollection of Nice the two men principally mentioned in my mother's diary, Khalil Bey and Admiral Farragut, stand out strikingly. Khalil Bey was a fabulously rich Turk who spent his life wandering luxuriously over the face of the earth with a huge retinue of retainers nearly as picturesque as he was. He was a big, dark, murderous looking creature, not unattractive in a sinister, strange, and piratical way. He had a wild and lurid record and was especially notorious for his reckless gambling, at which his luck was said to be miraculous. He was an opera enthusiast, having heard it in every city in Europe, and was one of Adelina's admirers. My mother disliked him exceedingly, declaring he was like a big snake. But my mother never had any tolerance for foreign noblemen. There were many of them at Nice and her comments were caustic and often apt. I remember her casual summing up of the Marquis de Talleyrand (the particular friend of Mrs. Stevens, an American woman from Hoboken whom he afterwards married) as "a young man belonging to some goose pond or other!"

Admiral Farragut, who was in the harbour with his flagship the *Hartford* and several other American battle-ships, was greatly fêted, being just then a great hero of the war. The United States Consul gave a reception for him which he explained in advance was to be "characteristically American." The only noticeable thing about the entertainment seemed to be the quantity and variety of drinkables that were unceasingly served by swift and persuasive waiters. The Continentals must have had a startling impression of American thirst! The Admiral himself, however, was hardly given time to swallow anything at all, people were so anxious to ask him questions and to shake hands.

The Stebbinses and McHenrys joined us when we had been in Nice only a short time, and, after a little stay there together, we went on by way of Genoa and the Corniche Road to Pisa, and thence to Florence. At Florence we met the Admiral again and found him more charming the better we knew him. In Florence, too, we had several glimpses of the Grisi family, Madame and her three daughters. Grisi was, I think, a striking example of a singer being born and not made. When she sang Adalgisa in *Norma* in Milan, she made a sudden and overwhelming hit. Next day every one was rushing about demanding, "Who was her teacher? Who gave her this wonderful style and tone?" Grisi herself was asked about it and she gave the names of several teachers under whom she had worked. But, needless to say, another Grisi was never made. In her case it did n't happen to be the teacher. Often the credit is given to the master when it really belongs to the pupil, or, rather, to *le bon Dieu* who made the vocal chords in the first place. For, however we may agree or disagree about fundamental requirements for an artist—breath control, voice placing, tone colour, interpretation,—the simple fact remains that the one great essential for a singer is a voice! One little story that I recall of Grisi interested me. It was said that, when she was growing old and severe exertion told on her, she always, after her fall as Lucretia Borgia, had a glass of beer come up through the floor to her and would drink it as she lay there with her back half turned to the audience. This is what was *said;* and it seemed to me like a very good scheme.

The director of the railway between Rome and Naples, M. De la Haute, put his private car at our disposal. In the present era of cars equipped with baths and barber shops, libraries and writing rooms, it would seem primitive, but it was quite the last word in the railroad luxury of that period. I was charmed with the Italian scenery as we steamed through it and, above all, with the highly pictorial peasants that we passed. Their clothes, of quaint cut and vivid hues, were exactly like stage costumes.

"Why," I exclaimed excitedly, peering from the car window, "they are all just out of scenes from *Fra Diavolo!*"

We were, indeed, going through the mountains of the *Fra Diavolo* country, where the inhabitants lived in continual fear of the bands of brigands that infested the mountains. Zerlina and Fra Diavolo were literally in their midst.

M. De la Haute gave a delightful breakfast for us on one of the terraces outside Naples with the turquoise blue bay beneath, the marvellous Italian sky overhead, and Vesuvius before us. Albert Bierstadt, the American artist, was of the company, and afterwards turned up in Rome, whither we went next. When we made the ascent of Vesuvius, my mother recounts in her diary: "There must have been at least a hundred Italian devils jumping about and screaming to take us up. It seemed as if they must have just jumped out of the burning brimstone."

In Rome we dined with Charlotte Cushman. This was, of course, some years before her death and she was not yet ravaged by her tragic illness. She was very full of anecdotes of her friends, the Carlyles, Tennyson, and others, whom she had just left in England. To our little party was added Emma Stebbins, who had been doing famously in sculpture, and, also, Harriet Hosmer, the artist, as well as one or two clever men. It was Carnival Week, and so I had my first glimpse of a true Continental *festa*. I had never before seen any real Latin merriment. The Anglo-Saxon variety is apt to be heavy, rough, or vulgar. But those fascinating people had the wonderful power of being genuinely and innocently gay. They became like happy children at play. They threw confetti, sang and laughed, and tossed flowers about. It was a veritable lesson in joy to us more sober and commonplace Americans who looked on.

While I was in Rome I was presented to the Pope, Pius IX, a most lovely and genial personality with a delightful atmosphere about him. I was told that he had very much wanted to be made Pope and had played the invalid so that the Cardinals would not think it was very important whether they elected him or not; so that they could say (as they did say), "Let us elect him:—he'll die anyhow!" He was duly elected and, just as soon as he was in the Pontifical Chair, his health became miraculously restored! When we were presented I could not help being amused at the extraordinary articles brought by people for the good man to bless. One woman had a pair of marble hands. Another offered the Pontiff a photograph of himself; and his Holiness had evident difficulty in keeping a straight face as he explained to her that really he could not bless a likeness of himself. Etiquette at these Vatican receptions is very strict as to what one must wear, what one must do, and where one must stand. Sebasti, of Sebasti e Reali, the famous Roman bankers, has the tale to tell of a Hebrew millionaire from America who contrived to secure an invitation to one of these select audiences and, not being able to see the Pope clearly on account of the crowd, climbed upon a chair to get a better view. In the twinkling of an eye a dozen attendants were after him, whispering harshly, "Giù! Giù! Giù!" ("Get down! Get down! Get down!") and the Israelite climbed down exclaiming in crestfallen accents: "How did you know it?"

I have never been presented to the present Pope, but I gather from my friends in Rome that his administration is, as usual, a rather complicated affair. The ruling power is Cardinal Rampolla, the Mephisto of the Church, for whom a distinguished Marchesa has a *salon* and entertains, so that, in this way, he can meet people on neutral ground.

On our return trip we crossed Mont Cenis by diligence. From Lombardy, with the smell of orange flowers all about us, we mounted up and up until the green growing things became fewer and frailer, and the air chillier and more rarified. Between six and seven thousand feet up we struck snow and changed to a

sleigh. We made the whole trip in eleven hours—
a record in those days. Think of it, you modern
tourists who cross Mont Cenis in three! But you
will do well to envy us our diligence and sleigh just the
same, for you—oh, horrors!—have to do it through a
tunnel instead of over a mountain pass! We felt
quite adventurous, for it was generally considered a
rather hazardous undertaking. By March first we
were back again in Paris and, before the end of the
month, Mr. Jarrett and Arditi joined us with my
renewed contract with Colonel Mapleson.

It seemed to me a very short period before it was
time for me to go back to Drury Lane for the real
London season. Spring had come and Mapleson was
ready to make a record opera season; so we said good-
bye to our friends in Paris and turned once more
toward England.

CHAPTER XVI

FELLOW-ARTISTS

MY mother's diary reads as follows:

March 25. Left Paris for London accompanied by Arditi and Mr. Jarrett. Came by Dover and Calais. Very sick. Had a band on the boat to entice the passengers into the idea that everything was lovely and there is no such thing as seasickness. Arrived in London at ten minutes before six.

28. Went out house-hunting. Rooms too small.

29. House-hunting. Dirty houses. A vast difference between American and English housekeeping. Could n't stand it. Visited ten. Col. Chandler came in the evening. Miss Jarrett went with us.

30. Went again. Saw a highfalutin Lady who said she wanted to get a *fancy price* for her house. Could n't see it.

April 1st. Miss Jarrett, Lou and I started again and had about given up the ship when Louise discovered a house with "to let" on it. So we ventured in without cards. Lovely! *Neat* and *nice.* Beautiful large garden, lawn, etc. We were taken to see the Agent who had it in charge. When we got outside we 3 embraced each other and I screamed with *joy.* She (the Landlady) was the first to have a house "to let" that was not painted and powdered an inch thick.

2. Rehearsal of *Traviata* for the 4th. Three hours long. Bettini, Santley, Foley and "Miss Kellogg."

3. Stage rehearsal.

4. First appearance in the regular season of Miss
Kellogg in *Traviata.* Prince of Wales came down end of
2nd act and congratulated her warmly. Also brought
the warmest congratulations from the Princess—splendid—
called out three times—received 8 bouquets. Forgot powder—sent Annie home—too late—hurried, daubed, nervous,
out of breath. Could n't get champagne opened quick
enough—rushed and tore—delayed orchestra 5 minutes—
got on all right—at last—went off splendidly. Miss
Jarrett, Mr. Jarrett, Arditi, Mr. Bennett of the Press
[critic of *The Daily Telegraph*] came and congratulated
Louise. The Prince of Wales was very kind—said he
remembered the hospitality of the Americans to him years
agone. [Louise] Had a new ball room dress—all white
with red camilias.

This somewhat incoherent record as jotted down by
my mother is sketchy but true in spirit. Never in my
life, before or since, was I ever so nervous as at our
opening performance in London of *Traviata;* no, not
even had my American *début* tried me so sorely. Everything in the world went wrong that could go wrong on
this occasion. I forgot my powder and the skirt of my
dress, and Annie, my maid, had to rush home in a
cab to get them. I tore my costume while making my
first entrance and had to play the entire act with a
streamer of silk dangling at my feet. I went on half
made up, daubed, nervous, out of breath. *Never* was
I in such a state of nerves. But to my astonishment I
made a very big success. There was a burst of applause
after the first act and I could hardly believe my ears.
It struck me as most extraordinary that what I considered so unsatisfactory should please the house.
Several of the artists singing with me came to me
during the evening much upset.

"Don't you know why everything on the stage has been going so badly to-night?" they said. "We've a *jettatura* in front!"

Madame Erminie Rudersdorf, the mother of Richard Mansfield, was in one of the boxes; and she was generally believed to have the Evil Eye. The Italian singers took it very seriously indeed and made horns all through the opera (that is, kept their fingers crossed) to ward off the satanic influence! Madame Rudersdorf was a tall, heavy, and swarthy Russian with ominously brilliant eyes; and one of the most commanding personalities I ever came in contact with. Although she had a dangerously bad temper, I never saw any evidences of it, nor of the *jettatura* either. She came that night and congratulated me:—and it meant something from her.

My professional vocation has brought me up against almost every conceivable superstition, from Brignoli's stuffed deer's head to the more commonplace fetish against thirteen as a number. But I never saw any one more obsessed by an idea of this sort than Christine Nilsson. She actually would not sing unless some one "held her thumbs" first. "Holding thumbs" is quite an ancient way of inviting good luck. One promises to "hold one's thumbs" for a friend who is going through some ordeal, like a first night or an operation for appendicitis or a wedding or anything else desperate. Nilsson was the first person I ever knew who practised the charm the other way about. Before she would even go on the stage somebody, if only the stage carpenter, had to take hold of her two thumbs and press them. She was convinced that the mystic rite brought her good fortune. Many of the Italian artists that I knew believed in the efficacy of coral as a talis-

man and always kept a bit of it about them to rub
"for luck" just before they went on for their part of
the performance. Somebody has told me that Emma
Trentini had a queer individual superstition: when
she was singing for Hammerstein she would never go
on the stage until he had given her a quarter of a
dollar! Ridiculous as all these *idées fixes* appear when
writing them down, I am convinced that they do help
some people. A sense of confidence is a great, an
invaluable thing, and whatever can bring that about
must necessarily, however foolish in itself, make for a
measure of success. I caught Nilsson's "holding
thumbs" trick myself without ever believing in it,
and often have done it to people since in a sort of
general luck-wishing, friendly spirit. The last time I
was in Algiers I entered an antique shop that I always
visit there and found the little woman who kept it
in a somewhat indisposed and depressed state of mind:
—so much so in fact that when I left I pinched her
thumbs for luck. Not long afterwards I had the sweetest letter from her. "I cannot thank you enough,"
she wrote; "you did something—whatever it was—
that has brought me luck. I feel sure it is all through
you!"

To return to my mother's diary after our first
performance of *Traviata* in London:

Sunday. Sat around. Afternoon drove through Hyde
Park.

Monday 6th. Rehearsal of *Gazza Ladra*. I went all over
to find dress for Linda—failed.

Tuesday. Moved out to 48 Grove End Road—8 guineas
a week. Received check on County Bank from Mapleson
for £100. Drew the money.

Wednesday 8th. Heard rehearsal of *Gazza Ladra.* Remained in theatre till 5.25 P.M. fitting costume. Rode home in 22 minutes.

Thursday 9th. Saw Linda. Magnificent. Best thing. Called out three times. Bouquet—dress—yellow. *Moire* blue satin apron—pink roses—gay!

Friday—Good Friday. Regulated house. In the evening *Don Giovanni* was performed. Louise wore her Barber dress—pink satin one—made by Madame Vinfolet in New York—splendid! Foli told me that in the height of the Messiah Season he often made 75 guineas a week. He looked at his operatic engagement as secondary.

Sunday 12. Louise received basket of Easter eggs with a beautiful bluebird over them from Mrs. McHenry—Paris—beautiful—shall take it to America. Mrs. G—— dined with us at 5.

13th. Rehearsal of *G. Ladra*—3 hours. I took cold waiting in cold room. No letters.

Tuesday 14. Letters from Mary Gray, Nell and Leonard and Carter. Pay day at Theatre but it did n't come. 3 hours rehearsal. At 4 P.M. Louise, Mr. S—— and I called by appointment upon the Duchess of Somerset. Met her 3 nieces and the Belgian Minister—a splendid affair—tea was served at 5—went home—dined at 6—went to Covent Garden to hear Mario & Fionetti, the latter said to be the best type of Italian school. Louise thought little of it. Did n't know whether to think less of Davidson's judgment or more of her own.

    .   .   .   .

21st. Green room rehearsal of *Gazza Ladra. Don Giovanni* in the evening—fine house.

22nd. Rehearsed one act of *Gazza Ladra.* Louise tired and nervous. Rained. Santley rode part way home with us.

23rd. Rigoletto—full house—Duke of Newcastle brought Lord Duppelin for introduction. Opera went off splendidly.

Check for £100. Saw the Godwins—Bryant's son-in-law.
24th. Friday. Drew the money. Reception at the
Langs.

25th. Louise went to new Philharmonic to rehearsal.
In the evening went to Queen's Theatre to see Toole in
Oliver Twist—splendid. Mr. Santley went to Paris.

26th. Sunday. Dr. Quinn, Mr. Fechter and Arditi called.
Louise and Miss Jarrett washed the dog! [This pet was
one of the puppies of Titjiens's tiny and beautiful Pomeran-
ian and I had it for a long time and adored it.] The 3
Miss Edwards called. Letter from Sarah.

27. Louise and I go to Rehearsal of *Gazza Ladra* and
to hear Mr. Fechter in *No Thoroughfare*. He thinks more
of himself than of the thoroughfare—good performance
though. Letter from George Farnsworth.

28. Clear and cold. Rehearsed *Gazza Ladra*.

29. [Louise] sang at Philharmonic—duet *Nozze di
Figaro* with Foli.

30th. Long rehearsal of *Gazza*. Dined at Duchess of
Somerset's at 8 P.M. Met many best men of London.
Duke of Newcastle took Louise in to dinner. Col. Williams
took me. Duchess is an old tyrant—sang Louise to death—
unmerciful—I despise her for her selfishness.

Indeed, every minute of those spring weeks was
occupied and more than occupied. I never was so
busy before and never had such a good time. The
"season" was a delightful one; and certainly no one
had a more varied part in it than I. Thanks to the
Dowager Duchess and our friends we went out frequently; and I was singing four and five times a week
counting concerts. Private concerts were a great fad
that season and I have often sung at two or three
different ones in the same evening.

Colonel Mapleson was in great feather, having three
prime donne at his disposal at once, for Christine

Nilsson had soon joined us, that curious mixture of "Scandinavian calm and Parisian elegance" as I have heard her described. No two singers were ever less alike, either physically or temperamentally, than she and I; yet, oddly enough, we over and over again followed each other in the same *rôles*. Titjiens, Nilsson, and I sang together a great deal that season, not only in opera but also in concert. Our voices went well together and we always got on pleasantly. Madame Titjiens was no longer at the zenith of her great power, but she was very fine for all that. I admired Titjiens greatly as an artist in spite of her perfunctory acting. Cold and stately, she was especially effective in purely classic music, having at her command all its traditions:—Donna Anna for instance, and Fidelio and the Contessa. I sang with her in the Mozart operas. Particularly do I recall one night when the orchestra was under the direction of Sir Michael Costa. Both Titjiens and Nilsson were singing with me, and the former had to follow me in the *recitative*. Where Susanna gives the attacking note to the Contessa Sir Michael's 'cello gave me the wrong chord. I perceived it instantly, my absolute pitch serving me well, but I hardly knew what to do. I was singing in Italian, which made the problem even more difficult; but, as I sang, my sixth sense was working subconsciously. I was saying over and over in my brain: "*I've got to give Titjiens the right note or the whole thing will be a mess. How am I going to do it?*" I sang around in circles until I was able to give the Contessa the correct note. Titjiens gratefully caught it up and all came out well. When the number was over, both Titjiens and Nilsson came and congratulated me for what they recognised as a good piece of musicianship. But Sir Michael was in a rage.

"What do you mean," he demanded, "by taking liberties with the music like that?"

One cannot afford to antagonise a conductor and he was, besides, so irascible a man that I did not care to mention to him that his 'cello had been at fault. He was a most indifferent musician as well as a narrow, obstinate man, although London considered him a very great leader. He only infuriated me the more by remarking indulgently, one night not long after, as if overlooking my various artistic shortcomings: "Well, well,—you 're a very pretty woman anyway!" It was his "anyway" that irrevocably settled matters between us. He disliked Nilsson too. He declared both in public and in private that her use of her voice was mere "charlatanry and trickery" and not worthy to be called musical. Nilsson was not, in fact, a good musician; few *prime donne* are. On one occasion she did actually sing one bar in advance of the accompaniment for ten consecutive measures. This is almost inconceivable, but she did it, and Sir Michael never forgave her.

Mapleson was planning as a *tour de force* with which to stun London a series of operas in which he could present all of us. "All-star casts" were rare in those days. Most managers saved their singers and doled them out judiciously, one at a time, in a very conservative fashion. But Mapleson had other notions. Our "all-star" Mozart casts were the wonder of all London. Think of *Don Giovanni* with Santley as the Don and Titjiens as Donna Anna; Nilsson as Donna Elvira, Rockitanski of Vienna the Leporello, and myself as Zerlina! Think of *Le Nozze di Figaro* with Titjiens as the Countess, Nilsson Cherubino, Santley the Count, and me as Susanna! These were casts unequalled in all Europe—almost, I believe, in all time!

Gye, of Covent Garden, declared that we were killing the goose that laid the golden egg by putting all our *prime donne* into one opera. He said that this made it not only impossible for rival houses to draw any audiences, but that it also cut off our own noses. Nobody wanted to go on ordinary nights to hear operas that had only one *prima donna* in them when they could go on star nights and hear three at once. However, Colonel Mapleson found that the scheme paid and our "triple-cast" performances brought us most sensational houses. Personally, as I have already said, I never liked Mapleson, and I had many causes for resentment in a business way. I remember one battle I had with him and the stage manager about a dress I was to wear in *Le Nozze di Figaro*. I do not recall what it was they wanted me to wear; but I know that, whatever it was, I would not wear it. I left in the middle of rehearsal, drove home in an excited state of indignation, and seized upon poor Colonel Stebbins, always my steady help in time of trouble. He went, saw, fought, and conquered, after which the rehearsals went on more or less peaceably.

Undoubtedly we had some fine artists at Her Majesty's, but occasionally Mapleson missed a big chance of securing others. One day we were putting on our wraps after rehearsal when my mother and I heard a lovely contralto voice. On inquiry, we learned that Colonel Mapleson and Arditi were trying the voice of a young Italian woman who had come to London in search of an engagement. The Colonel and the Director sat in the orchestra while the young woman sang an *aria* from *Semiramide*. When the trial was over the girl went away at once and I rushed out to speak to Mapleson.

"Surely you engaged that enchanting singer!" I exclaimed.

"Indeed I did n't," he replied.

She went directly to Gye at Covent Garden, who engaged her promptly and, when she appeared two weeks later, she made a sensation. Her name was Sofia Scalchi.

Besides the private concerts of that season there were also plenty of public concerts, a particularly notable one being a Handel Festival at the Crystal Palace on May 1st, when I sang *Oh, had I Jubal's Lyre!* Everything connected with that occasion was on a large scale. There were seven thousand people in the house, the largest audience by far that I had ever sung to before. The place was so crowded that people hung about the doors trying to get in even after every seat was filled; and not one person left the hall until after I had finished—a remarkable record in its way! Some time later, when I was on my way home to America and wanted to buy some antiques, I wandered into a little, odd Dickens-like shop in Wardour Street. I wanted to have some articles sent on approval to meet me at Liverpool, but hesitated to ask the old man in the shop to take such a risk without knowing me. To my surprise he smiled at me a kindly, wrinkled smile and said, with the prettiest old-fashioned bow:

"Madame, you are welcome to take any liberties you will with my entire stock. I heard you sing 'Jubal's Lyre.' I shall never forget it, nor be able to repay you for the pleasure you gave me!"

I always felt this to be one of my sincerest tributes. Perhaps that is partly why the night of my first Crystal Hall Concert remains so clearly defined in my memory.

My mother's diary of this period continues:

May 4. Mr. Santley dined with us. Played Besique in the evening. *I beat.*

5. Louise and I went to St. James Hall rehearsal. After went to Theatre. Learned Nilsson did not have as good a house 2nd night as Louise's first one in *La Gazza Ladra.* Mr. Arditi came to rehearse the waltz.

6th. La Gazza Ladra. Full house—enthusiasm—Duke of Newcastle came in.

7. Arditi's rehearsal for his concert at his house at 5 P.M.—went—house full—hot and funny. Mr. S—— came in the evening—played one game Besique.

8. Intended to go to Haymarket Theatre but Miss J—— had headache. Santley came in the afternoon to practise Susanna.

9. Santley called. McHenry and Stebbins, with another Budget of disagreeables from Mapleson who, not satisfied with cheating her [Louise] out of $500., deliberately asked her to give him 3 nights more! Shall have his money if we have to go to law about it.

Monday. [Louise] Sang at Old Philharmonic flute song from *The Star.* Mr. Stebbins went to Jarrett and told him Miss Kellogg would sing no longer than the 15th—her engagement closes then—but that Mapleson must pay her what he owed her—that he would have the checks that day or sue him.

Tuesday. Just got the second check of £150, showing that a little *hell fire and brimstone administered in large doses* is a good thing. The Englishman has not outwitted the Yankee yet!

12. Louise sang *Don Giovanni* — Titjiens "Donna Anna," Santley "Don Giovanni," Nilsson "Elvira." Crowded house—seats sold at a premium—Louise received all the honours—everything encored—4 bouquets. Nilsson and Titjiens were encored only for the grand trio. The applause on *Batti Batti* was something unequalled.

13. Went to photographers. Miss Jarrett, Santley and ourselves dined at Mr. Stebbins'—went to hear Lucca in *Fra Diavolo*—was delighted—she was not pretty but intelligent—sang well—not remarkable, but showed great cleverness—full of talent—acted it well—filled out the scenes—kept the thing going. The Tenor was good. I remained through the second act. Dropped my fan onto a bald head. Went over to Drury Lane—heard one act of *The Hugenots*.

14. Mr. S—— dined with us—played Besique in the evening—Louise beat of course.

15. [Louise] Sang *Don Giovanni* to a full house. Bennett came and Smith and Mapleson and Duke of Newcastle.

16. Santley sang in rehearsal *Le Nozze di Figaro*. Mr. Stebbins dined with us. Played solitaire in the evening with the new Besique box.

I sang several times at the Crystal Palace Concerts with Sims Reeves, the idolised English tenor. Never have I heard of or imagined an artist so spoiled as Reeves. The spring was a very hot one for London, although to us who were accustomed to the summer heat of America, it seemed nothing. But poor Sims Reeves evidently expected to have heat prostration or a sunstroke, for he always wore a big cork helmet to rehearsals, the kind that officers wear on the plains of India. The picture he made sitting under his huge helmet with a white puggaree around it, fanning himself feebly, was one never to be forgotten. He had a somewhat frumpy wife who waited on him like a slave. I had little patience with him, especially with his trick of disappointing his audiences at the eleventh hour. But he could sing! He was a real artist, and, when he was not troubling about the temperature, or his diet, he was an artist with whom it was a privilege to sing. I remember singing with him and Mme. Patey at a concert at Albert Hall. Mme. Patey was an admirable contralto and gifted with a superb technique. We three sang a trio without a rehearsal and, when it was over, Reeves declared that it was really wonderful the way in which we all three had "taken breath" at exactly the same points, showing that we were all well trained and could phrase a song in the only one correct way. This was also noticed and remarked upon by several professionals who were present.

I also sang with Alboni. At an Albert Hall concert on my second visit to England a year or two later, I said to her:

"Madame, I cannot tell you how honoured I feel in singing on the same programme with you."

She bowed and smiled. She was a very, very large woman, heavily built, but she carried her size with remarkable dignity. I was considerably amused when she replied:

"Ah, Mademoiselle, I am only a shadow of what I have been!"

My most successful song that season was my old song *Beware*. It was unusual to see a *prima donna* play her own accompaniment, which I always did to this song and to most *encores*. The simple, rather insipid melody was written by Moulton, the first husband of the present Baronne de Hegeman, and it was not long before it was the rage in the sentimental younger set of London. How tired I became of that ridiculous sign-post cover and the "As Sung by Miss Clara Louise Kellogg" staring up at me! And how much more tired of the foolish tune:

I know a maid-en   fair to see, Take care! Take care!

One of the greatest honours paid me was the command to sing in one of the two concerts at Buckingham Palace given each season by the reigning sovereign. I have always kept the letter that told me I had been chosen for this great privilege.   Cusins, from whom it came, was the Director of the Queen's music at the Palace.

CHAPTER XVII

THE ROYAL CONCERTS AT BUCKINGHAM

THE Royal Private Concerts at Buckingham Palace formed in those days, and I believe still form, the last word in exclusiveness. Many persons who have been presented at court, in company with a great crowd of other social aspirants, never come close enough to the inner circle of royalty to get within even "speaking distance" of these concerts. In them the court etiquette is almost mediæval in its brilliant formality; and yet a certain intimacy prevails which could not be possible in a less carefully chosen gathering. So sacred an institution is the Royal Concert that they have a fixed price—twenty-five guineas for all the solo singers, whatever their customary salaries, —the discrepancies between the greater and the lesser being supposedly filled in with the colossal honour done the artists by being asked to appear.

Queen Victoria seldom presided at these or similar functions. The Prince of Wales usually represented the Crown and did the honours, always exceedingly well. I have been told by people who professed to know that his good nature was rather taken advantage of by his august mother, who not only worked him half to death in his official capacity, but never allowed him enough income for the purpose. Personally, I always liked the Prince. He was a tactful, courteous man with real artistic feeling and cultivation. He filled a difficult position with much graciousness and good sense. More than once has he come behind the scenes during an operatic performance to congratulate and encourage me. The Princess was good looking, but was said to be both dull and inflexible. The former impression might easily have been the result of her deafness that so handicapped her where social graces were concerned. She could not hear herself speak and, therefore, used a voice so low as to be almost inaudible. When she spoke to me I could not hear a word of what she said. I hope it was agreeable.

My mother's entries in her diary at this point are:

Monday. 17. 3 P.M. Rehearsal at Anderson's for Buckingham Palace Concert. Met Lucca there. A perfect original. Private concert in the evening at No. 7 Grafton Street. Pinsuti conducted. Louise *encored* with *Beware*. Concert commenced at eleven. Closed at 2 A.M. Saw about five bushels of diamonds.

18th. Tuesday. Went to Buckingham Palace. Rehearsed at eleven. Very good palace, but dirty.

19. Rehearsal of Somnambula. Got home at 4. Mr. S—— came in the evening.

20. Buckingham Palace Concert.

The rehearsal at Buckingham Palace was held in the great ballroom with the Queen's orchestra, under Cusins, and the artists were Titjiens, Lucca, Faure, and myself. These concerts were composed of picked singers from both Covent Garden and Her Majesty's and were supposed to represent the best of each. As my mother notes, I first met Pauline Lucca there— such an odd little creature. She amused me immensely. She was always doing absurd things and making quaint, entertaining speeches. She was not pretty, but her eyes were beautiful. On this occasion, I remember, Titjiens was rehearsing one of her great, classic *arias.* When she had finished we all, the orchestra included, applauded. Lucca was sitting between Faure and myself, her feet nowhere near touching the floor, and she applauded rhythmically and quite indifferently, slap-bang! slap-bang! slinging her arms out so as to hit both of us and then slapping them together, the while she kicked up her small feet like a child of six. She was regardless of appearances and was applauding to please herself.

Lucca used to warn me not to abuse my upper notes. We knew her as almost a mezzo. She told me, however, that she had once had an exceedingly high voice, and that one of her best parts was Leonora in *Trovatore.* She had abused her gift; but she always had a delightful quality of voice and put a great deal of personality into her work.

The approach to the Palace on concert nights was very impressive, for the Grenadier Guards were drawn up outside, and inside were other guards even more gorgeously arrayed than the cavalry. In the concert room itself was stationed a royal bodyguard of the Yeomen of the Guards. The commanding officer was called the Exon-in-Waiting. The proportions of the room were magnificent and there were some fine frescoes and an effective way of lighting up the stained glass windows from the outside; but the general impression was not particularly regal. The decorations were plain and dull—for a palace. The stage was arranged with chairs, rising tier above tier, very much like a stage for oratorio singers. Before royalty appears, the singers seat themselves on the stage and remain there until their turn comes to sing. This is always a trial to a singer, who really needs to get into the mood and to warm up to her appearance. To stand up in cold blood and just *sing* is discouraging. The prospect of this dreary deliberateness did not tend to raise our spirits as we sat and waited.

At last, after we had become utterly depressed and out of spirits, there was a little stir and the great doors at the side of the ballroom were thrown open. First of all entered the Silver-Sticks in Waiting, a dozen or so of them, backing in, two by two. All were, of course, distinguished men of title and position; and they were dressed in costumes in which silver was the dominant note and carried long wands of silver. They were followed by the Gold-Sticks in Waiting—men of even more exalted rank—and, finally, by the Royal Party. We all arose and curtesied, remaining standing until their Highnesses were seated.

The concerts were called informal and therefore long trains and court veils were not insisted on; but the men had to appear in ceremonial dress—knee breeches and silk stockings—and the women invariably wore gorgeous costumes and family jewels, so that the scene was one full of colour and glitter. The uniforms of the Ambassadors of different countries made brilliant spots of colour. The Prince of Wales and his Princess simply sparkled with orders and decorations. I happened to hear the names of a few of her Royal Highness's. They were the Orders of Victoria and Albert, the Star of India, St. Catherine of Russia, and the Danish Family Order. She also wore many of the crown jewels, and with excellent taste on every occasion I have seen her. With a black satin gown and court train of crimson, for example, she wore only diamonds;

while another time I remember she wore pearls and sapphires with a velvet gown of cream and pansy colour. Such good sense and discretion in the choice of gems is rare. So many women seem to think that any jewels are appropriate to any toilet.

Tremendously august personages used to be in the audiences of those Buckingham Palace concerts at which I sang then and later, such as the Duke and Duchess of Teck, the Prince and Princess Christian of Schleswig-Holstein, the Duke and Duchess of Cambridge, the Crown Prince of Sweden and Norway, the Duke and Duchess of Edinburgh. Indeed, royalty, peers of the realm and ambassadors or representatives, and members of the court were the only auditors. In spite of this the concerts were deadly dull, partly, no doubt, because everybody was so enormously impressed by the ceremony of the occasion and by the rigours of court etiquette that they did not dare move or hardly breathe. There was one woman present at my first Buckingham Palace concert, a lady-in-waiting (she looked as if she had become accustomed to waiting) who was even more stiff than any one else and about whose décolleté there seemed to be no termination. Never once, to my certain knowledge, did she move either head or body an inch to the right or to the left throughout the performance.

A breach of etiquette was committed on one occasion by a friend of mine, a compatriot, who had accompanied me to one of these gilt-edged affairs. She stood up behind the very last row of the chorus and—used her opera-glasses! Not unnaturally, she wanted for once, poor girl, to get a good look at royalty; but it is needless to say that she was hastily and summarily suppressed.

When the Prince and Princess were seated the

concert could begin. There were two customs that made those functions particularly oppressive. One was that all applause was forbidden. An artist, particularly a singer or stage person of any kind, lives and breathes through approbation: and for a singer to sing her best and then sit down in a dead and stony silence without any sort of demonstration, is a very chilling experience. The only indication that a performance had been acceptable was when the Prince of Wales wriggled his programme in an approving manner. A hand-clap would have been a terrific breach of etiquette. The other drawback—and the one that affected the guests even more than the artists—was that, when once the Prince and Princess were seated, no one could rise on any pretext or provocation whatever. I think it was at my second appearance at the Royal Concerts that an amusing incident occurred which impressed the inconvenience of this regulation upon my memory. The Duchess of Edinburgh, daughter of the Czar, entered in the Prince of Wales's party. She looked an irritable, dissatisfied, bilious person; and I was told that she was always talking about being "the daughter of the Czar of all the Russias" and that it galled her that even the Princess of Wales took precedence over her. Those were the good old days of tie-backs, made of elastic and steel, a sort of modified hoop-skirt with all of the hoop in the back. The tie-back was the passing of the hoop and its management was an education in itself. I remember mine came from Paris and I had had a bit of difficulty in learning to sit down in it gracefully. Well—the Duchess of Edinburgh had not mastered the art. She was all right until she sat down and looked very regal in a gown of thick, heavy white silk and the most gorgeous of jewels—encrusted diamonds and Russian rubies, the latter nearly the size of a pigeon's eggs. Her tiara and stomacher were so magnificent that they appalled me. The Prince and Princess sat down and every one else followed suit, the daughter of the Czar of all the Russias among the others in the front row. And she sat down wrong. Her tie-back tilted up as she went down; her skirt rose high in front, revealing a pair of large feet, clad in white shoes, and large ankles, nearly up to her knees. There was a footstool under the large feet and they were very much in evidence the whole evening, posing, entirely against their owner's will, on a temporary monument. The awful part of it was that the Duchess knew all about it and was so furious that she could hardly contain herself. It was a study to watch the daughter of the Czar of all the Russias in these circumstances. Her face showed how much she wanted to get up and pull down her dress and hide her robust pedal extremities, but court etiquette forbade, and the Duchess suffered.

The end of everything, as a matter of course, was *God Save the Queen* and, as there were nearly always two *prime donne* present, each of us sang one verse. All the artists and the chorus sang the third, which constituted "Good-night" and was the official closing of the performance. I usually sang the first verse. When the concert was over, the Prince and Princess with the lesser royalties filed out. They passed by the front of the stage and always had some agreeable thing to say. I recall with much pleasure Prince Arthur—the present Duke of Connaught— stopping to compliment me on a song I had just sung— the Polonaise from *Mignon*—and to remind me that I had sung it at Admiral Dahlgren's reception at the Navy Yard in Washington during his American visit.

"You sang that for me in Washington, did n't you, Miss Kellogg?" he said; and I was greatly pleased by the slight courteous remembrance.

After royalty had departed every one drew a long breath of partial relaxation. The guests could then move about with more or less freedom, talk with each other, and speak with the artists if they felt so inclined. I was impressed by the stiffness, the shyness and awkwardness of the English people—of even these very great English people, the women especially. One would suppose that authority and ease and graciousness would be in the very blood of those who are, as the saying is, "to the manner born," but they did not seem to have that "manner." Finally I came to the conclusion that they really *liked* to appear shy and *gauche*, and deliberately affected the stiffness and the awkwardness.

So much has been said about the Victorian prejudice against divorce and against scandal of all sorts that no one will be surprised when I say that, on one occasion when I sang at the Palace, I was the only woman singer whom the ladies present spoke to, although the gentlemen paid much attention to the others. The Duchess of Newcastle was particularly cordial to me, as were also the wife of our American Ambassador and Consuelo, Duchess of Manchester. My fellow-artists on that occasion were Adelina Patti and Trebelli Bettina and, as each of them had been associated with scandal, they were left icily alone. At that time Patti and Nicolini were not married and the papers had much to say about the tenor's desertion of his family. I have sung with Nilsson and Patti and Lucca at these concerts. I have sung with Faure and Santley and Capoul (nice little Capoul, known in America as "the ladies' man") and I have sung with Scalchi and Titjiens. I have sung there with even the great Mario.

There was a supper at the palace after the Royal Concerts—two supper tables in fact—one for the royal family and one for the artists. I caught a glimpse on my first appearance there of the table set for the former with the historic gold plate, with which English crowned heads entertain their guests. It was splendid, of course, although very heavy and ponderous, and the food must needs have been something superlative to have fitted it. I doubt if it was, however, as British cooks are apt to be mediocre, even those in palaces. Cooking is a matter of the Epicurean temperament or, rather, with the British, the lack of it. Our supper was not at all bad in spite of this, although little Lucca did turn up her nose at it and at the arrangements.

"What!" she exclaimed tempestuously, "stay here to 'second supper'! Never! These English prigs want to make us eat with the servants! You may stay for their horrid supper if you choose. But I would rather starve—" and off she went, all rustling and fluttering with childish indignation.

It was at one of these after-concert "receptions" at the palace that I had quite a long chat with Adelina Patti about her coming to America. I urged it, for I knew that a fine welcome was awaiting her here. But Nicolini,—her husband for the moment,—who was sitting near, exclaimed: "*Vous voulez la tuer!*" ("Do you want to kill her!") It seems that they were both terribly afraid of crossing the ocean, although they apparently recovered from their dread in later years.

There was one Royal Concert which will always remain in my memory as the most marvellous and brilliant spectacle, socially speaking, of my whole life. It was the one given in honour of the Queen's being made Empress of India and among the guests were not only the aristocracy of Great Britain, but all the Eastern princes and rajahs representing her Majesty's new empire. At that time hardly any one had been in India. Nowadays people make trips around the world and run across to take a look at the Orient whenever they feel inclined. But then India sounded to us like a fairy-tale place, impossibly rich and mysterious, a country out of *The Arabian Nights* at the very least.

My mother and I were then living in Belgrave Mansions, not far from the palace nor from the Victoria Hotel where the Indian princes put up, and we used to see them passing back and forth, their attendants bearing exquisitely carved and ornamented boxes containing choice jewels and decorations and offerings to "The Great White Queen across the Seas,"—offerings as earnest of good faith and pledges of loyalty. I was glad to be "commanded" for the Royal Concert at which they were to be entertained, for I knew that it would be a splendid pageant. And it turned out to be, as I have said, the richest display I ever saw. The rich stuffs of the costumes lent themselves most fittingly to a lavish exhibition of jewels. The ornaments of the royal princesses and peeresses that I had been admiring up to that occasion seemed as nothing compared to this array. Every Eastern potentate appeared to be trying to vie with all the others as to the gems he wore in his turban.

It would be impossible for me to say how interesting I found all this sort of thing. It was like a play to me —a delicious play, in which I, too, had my part. I am an imperialist by nature.   I love pomp and ceremony and circumstance and titles.   The few times that I have ever been dissatisfied with my experiences in the lands of crowned heads, it was merely because there was n't quite grandeur enough to suit my taste!

CHAPTER XVIII

THE LONDON SEASON

OUR house in St. John's Wood that we rented for our first London season was small, but it had a front door and a back garden and, on the whole, we were very happy there. Whenever my mother became bored or dissatisfied she thought of the hotels on the Continent and immediately cheered up. There many people sought us out, and others were brought to see us. Newcastle was always coming with someone interesting in tow. Leonard Jerome, who built the Jockey Club, came with Newcastle, I remember, and so did Chevalier Wyckoff, who had something to do with *The Herald*, and did not use his title.

It was always said of the Duke and Duchess of Newcastle that "he married her for her money and she married him for his title, so that they each got what they wanted." It may have been true and probably was, for they did not seem an ardently devoted couple, and yet it is difficult to believe the rather cruel report— they were both so much too lovable to merit it. The Duchess was a beauty and, when she wore the big, blue, Hope Diamond,—(I have often seen her wearing it) she was a most striking figure. As for Newcastle himself, I always found him a most simple, warm-hearted, generous man, full of delicate and kindly feelings. He had big stables and raced his horses all

Duke of Newcastle

From a photograph by John Burton & Sons

the time, but it was said of him that he generally lost at the races and one might almost know that he would. He was a sort of "mark" for the racing sharks and they plucked him in a shameless manner. I first met the Newcastles at the dinner table of the Dowager Duchess of Somerset, and more than once afterwards has Newcastle whispered to her "hang etiquette" and taken me in to dinner instead of some frumpy marchioness or countess.

We became acquainted with the Tennants of Richmond Terrace. Their house was headquarters for an association of Esoteric Buddhism;—A. P. Sinnett, the author of the book entitled *Esoteric Buddhism,* was a prominent figure there. The family is perhaps best known from the fact that Miss Tennant married the celebrated explorer Stanley. But to me it always stood for the centre of occult societies. The household was an interesting one but not particularly peaceful.

I suppose the world is full of queer people and situations, but I do think that among the queerest of both must be ranked Lord Dudley, who owned Her Majesty's Theatre. He lived in Park Lane and was a very grand person in all ways, and, according to hearsay, firmly believed that he was a teapot, and spent his days in the miserable hope that somebody would be kind enough to put him on the stove! He did not go about begging for the stove exactly; his desire was just an ever-present, underlying yearning! He was a nice man, too, as I remember him. A man by the name of Cowen represented the poor peer and we gave Cowen his legitimate perquisites in the shape of benefit concerts and so forth; but we all felt that the whole thing was in some obscure manner terribly grim and pathetic. Many things are so oddly both comic and tragic.

During the warm weather we went often into the country to dine or lunch at country houses. I shall never forget Mr. Goddard's dinner at his place. He had a glass house at the end of the regular house that was half buried in a huge heliotrope plant which had grown so marvellously that it covered the walls like a vine. The trunk of it was as thick as a man's arm, and the perfume—! My mother wrote in her diary a single line summing up the day as it had been for her: "Lovely day. Strawberries and two black-eyed children." For my part, I gathered all the heliotrope I wanted for once in my life.

Mr. Sampson's entertainment is another notable memory. Mr. Sampson was financial editor of that august journal *The London Times*, much sought after by the large moneyed interests, and lived in Bushy Park, beyond Kensington. Mrs. Heurtly was our hostess; and Lang, who had just been running for Prime Minister, was there and, also, McKenzie, an East Indian importer in a big way who afterwards became Sir Edward McKenzie, through loaning to the Prince of Wales the money for the trousseau and marriage of the Prince of Wales's daughter Louise to the Duke of Fife, and who then was not invited to the wedding! It was through Sampson, too, that I first met the famous critic Davidson, and I think it was on the occasion of his party that I first met Nilsson's great friend Mrs. Cavendish Bentinck.

Among all the memories of that time stands out that of the home of the dear McHenrys in Holland Park, overlooking the great sweep of lawn of Holland House on which, it is said, the plotters of an elder day went out to talk and conspire because it was the only place in London where they could be sure that they would

not be overheard. Alma Tadema lived just around the
corner and we often saw him. Another interesting
character of whom I saw a good deal at that time was
Dr. Quinn, an Irishman, connected through a morgan-
atic marriage with the royal family. He was very
short and jolly, and very Irish. He had asthma horribly
and ought really to have considered himself an invalid.
He gasped and wheezed whenever he went upstairs,
but he simply could n't resist dinner parties. He loved
funny stories, too, not only for his own sake but also
because his friend, the Prince of Wales, liked them so
much. My mother was very ready in wit and usually
had a fund of stories and jokes at her command, and
Dr. Quinn used to exhaust her supply, taking the
greatest delight in hearing her talk. He would come
panting into the house, his round face beaming, and
gasp:

"Any new American jokes ? I 'm dining with the
Prince and want something new for him !"

He loved riddles and conundrums, particularly
those that had a poetical twist in them. One of his
favourites was:

> *Why is a sword like the moon ?*
> *Because it is the glory of the (k)night !*

I have heard him tell that repeatedly, always ending
with a little appreciative sigh and the ejaculation,
"that is *so* poetical, is n't it ?"

One lovely evening we drove out to Greenwich to
dinner, in Newcastle's four-in-hand coach. It was not
the new style drag, but a huge, lumbering affair, all
open, in which one sat sideways. There were postil-
lions in quaint dress and a general flavour of the Middle
Ages about the whole episode. There was nothing of

the Middle Ages about the dinner however. There were twenty-five of us present in all; among the number Lady Susan Vane-Tempest, a beautiful woman with most brilliant black hair, and Major Stackpoole, and dear Lady Rossmore, his wife (who was so impulsive that I have seen her jump up in her box to throw me the flowers she was wearing), and some of the Hopes (Newcastle's own family), that race that always behaves so badly! A little later in the season, my mother and I accepted with delight an invitation from the Duke and Duchess of Newcastle to visit them at their place in Brighton. The Duke naively explained that he had been having "a run of rotten luck" of late, and thought that I might turn it. Apparently I did, for the very day after we got there his horse won in the races.

I sang, of course, in the evening, as their guest. There was no thought of remuneration, nor could there be. The graceful way in which our dear host showed his appreciation was to send me a pin, beautifully executed, of a horse and jockey done in enamel, enclosed in a circle of perfect crystal, the whole surrounded with a rim of superb diamonds and amethysts —purple and white being his racing colours. The brooch was inscribed simply with the date on which his horse ran and won.

I wore that pin for years. When I had it cleaned at Tiffany's a long time afterwards, it made quite a sensation, it was so unique. Once, I remember, I was in the studio dwelling on Fifteenth Street of the Richard Watson Gilders when I discovered that, having dressed in a hurry, I had put my pin in upside-down. I started to change it, and then said:

"O, what's the use. Nobody will ever notice it. They are all too literary and superior around here!"

The first man Mrs. Gilder presented to me was evidently quite too much interested in the pin to talk to me.

"Excuse me," he at last said politely, "but you will like to know, I feel sure, that your brooch is upside-down."

"O, is it," said I sweetly. But I did not take the trouble to change it even then, and, afterwards, I would not have done so for worlds, for I should have been cheated out of a great deal of quiet amusement. One of the contributors to *The Century* was later presented to me, and the effect of that pin upside-down was more irritating than it had been to the first man. He almost stood on his head trying to discover what was the trouble. At last:

"You 've got your pin upside-down," he snapped at me as though a personal affront had been offered him.

"I know I have," I snapped back.

"What do you wear it that way for?" he demanded.

"To make conversation!" I returned, nearly as cross as he was.

"I don't see it," he said curtly. As a matter of fact I had just realised that upside-down was the way to wear the pin henceforward. I said to Jeannette Gilder the next day:

"My upside-down pin was the hit of the evening. I am never going to wear it any other way!"

I have kept my word during all these years. Never have I worn Newcastle's pin except upside-down, and I have never known anyone to whom I was talking to fail to fall into the trap and beg my pardon and say, "you have your brooch on upside-down." Years later I was once talking to Annie Louise Cary in Rome and a perfectly strange man came up and began timidly:

13

"I beg your pardon, but your——"

"I know," I told him kindly. "My pin is upside-
down, is n't it ?"

He retreated, thinking me mad, I suppose. But the
fun of it has been worth some such reputation. Different people approach the subject so differently. Some
are so apologetic and some are so helpful and some,
like my *Century* acquaintance, are so immensely and
disproportionately annoyed.

But I am wandering far afield and quite forgetting
my first London season which, even at this remote
day, is an absorbing recollection to me. I had at that
time enough youthful enthusiasm and desire to "keep
going" to have stocked a regiment of débutantes!
Although I was quite as carefully chaperoned and
looked out for in England as I had been in America,
there was still an unusual sense of novelty and excitement about the days there. I had all of my clothes
from Paris and learned that, as Sir Michael Costa had
insultingly informed me, I was "quite a pretty woman
anyhow." Add to this the generous praise that the
London public gave me professionally, and is it to be
considered a wonder that I felt as if all were a delightful
fairy tale with me as the princess?

As my mother has noted in her diary, we went one
evening to Covent Garden to hear Patti sing. One
really charming memory of Patti is her Juliette. She
was never at all resourceful as an actress and was never
able to stamp any part with the least creative individuality; but her singing of that music was perfect.
Maurice Strakosch came into our box to present to us
Baron Alfred de Rothschild who became one of the
English friends whom we never forgot and who never
forgot us. Maddox, too, called on us in the box that

evening. He was the editor of a little journal that was the rival of the *Court Circular*. Maddox I saw a good deal of later and found him very original and entertaining. He ordered champagne that night, so we had quite a little party in our box between the acts.

As my mother has also noted, I went to Covent Garden to hear Mario for the first time. Fioretti was the *prima donna*, said to be the best type of the Italian school. Altogether the occasion was expected to be a memorable one and I was full of expectations. Davidson, the critic of *The London Times* and the foremost musical critic on the Continent, except possibly Dr. Hanslick of Vienna, was full of enthusiasm. But I did not think much of Fioretti nor, even, of Mario! Yes, Mario the great, Mario the golden-voiced, Mario who could "soothe with a tenor note the souls in Purgatory" was a bitter disappointment to me. I was too inexperienced still to appreciate the art he exhibited, and his voice was but a ghost of his past glory. Yet England adored him with her wonderful loyalty to old idols.

Several distinguished artists and musicians came into our box that night, Randegger the singing teacher for one, and my good friend Sir George Armitage. Sir George was breathless with enthusiasm.

"There is no one like Mario!" he exclaimed, rubbing his hands with delight.

"This is the first time I ever heard him," I said.

"Ah, what an experience!" he cried.

"I should never have suspected he was the great tenor," I had to admit.

"Oh, my dear young lady," said Sir George eagerly, "that 'la' in the second act! Did you hear that 'la' in the second act? There was the old Mario!"

His devotion was so touching that I forebore to remind him that if one swallow does not make a summer, so one "la" does not make a singer. When poor Mario came over to America later he was a dire failure. He could not hold his own at all. He could not produce even his "la" by that time. Like Nilsson, however, he greatly improved dramatically after his vocal resonances were impaired, for I have been told that when in possession of his full voice he was very stiff and unsympathetic in his acting.

Sir George Armitage, by the way, was a somewhat remarkable individual, a typical, well-bred Englishman of about sixty, with artistic tastes. He was a perfect example of the dilettante of the leisure class, with plenty of time and money to gratify any vagrant whim. His particular hobby was the opera; and he divided his attentions equally between Covent Garden with Adelina and Lucca, and Her Majesty's with Nilsson, Titjiens, and Kellogg. When operas that he liked were being given at both opera houses, he would make a schedule of the different numbers and scenes with the hours at which they were to be sung:—9.20 (Covent Garden), *Aria* by Madame Patti. 10 o'clock (Her Majesty's), Duet in second act between Miss Nilsson and Miss Kellogg. 10.30, Sextette at Covent Garden, etc., etc. He kept his brougham and horses ready and would drive back and forth the whole evening, reaching each opera house just in time to hear the music he particularly cared for. He had seats in each house and nothing else in the world to do, so it was quite a simple matter with him, only,—who but an Englishman of the hereditary class of idleness would think of such a way of spending the evening? He was a dear old fellow and we all liked him. He really did not know much about music, but he had a sincere fondness for it and dearly loved to come behind the scenes and offer suggestions to the artists. We always listened to him patiently, for it gave him great pleasure, and we never had to do any of the things he suggested because he forgot all about them before the next time.

My mother's diary reads:

June 13. Last night *Nozze di Figaro.* Mr. and Mrs. McHenry sent five bouquets. Splendid performance.

15. Dined at Duchess of Somerset's.

16. Dined with Mr. and Mrs. McHenry. Stebbins— Vanderbilts.

18. Don Giovanni. Checks from Mr. Cowen. Banker came to see us. Duke of Newcastle—Sir George Armitage.

20. Benedict's Morning Concert, St. James' Hall. *Encore* "Beware"—*Don Giovanni* in the evening.

21. Sunday. Dined with Duke and Duchess of Newcastle. Major Stackpoole, Lady Susan Vane-Tempest and others. Rehearsed *La Figula.*

Monday. Rehearsal of *La Figula.* In the evening went to hear Patti. Did n't like Patti. Received letter from Colonel Stebbins from Queenstown.

Tuesday. Rehearsed *La Figula.* Called at Langham on Godwin—all came out in the evening.

Wednesday 24. Morning performance of *Le Nozze*—got home at 6. P.M. Charity concert for Mr. Cowen at 8.30 at Dudley House.

Thursday. Rehearsal of *La Figula.* Concert in the evening at Lady Fitzgerald's.

Monday. Louise and I went to drive. Do not learn anything definite about the future—where I am to be next winter—no one knows. I do not see any settled home for me any more. Sometimes I am satisfied to have it so—at others—get nervous and uneasy and discontented. Yet I have lost interest in going home—it will be so short a visit --so soon a separation—then to some other stranger place—

new friends—new faces—I want the old. The surface of
life does not interest me.

Tuesday. Dined at Langs'—large party.

Wednesday 15. Went to Crystal Palace—Mapleson's
Benefit. The whole performance closed with the most
magnificent display of Fireworks I ever saw—most
marvellous.

16. Don Giovanni—full house—great success in the part
—Duchess and Lady Rossmore threw splendid bouquets—
house very enthusiastic—papers fine—Mrs. McHenry and
Mr. Sampson came down—Duke of Newcastle and Major
Stackpoole—Miss Jarrett.

Monday. Le Nozze di Figaro.

Tuesday. La Figula.

Thursday. Went to theatre. Saw Nilsson and all the
artists. Went to hear Patti in *Romeo and Juliette*—Strakosch gave us the box. Strakosch introduced Rothschilds.

Friday. Le Nozze di Figaro. Baron Rothschilds, Sir
George Armitage came around.

Saturday. Sir George breakfasted with Louise. Rothschilds called—letter from Mr. Stebbins.

Sunday morning. Dr. Kellogg of Utica called—spent
several hours. Santley called—and McHenry in the
evening.

I was greatly shocked by the heavy drinking in the
'sixties that was not only the fashion but almost the
requirement of fashion in England. My horror when I
first saw a titled and distinguished Englishwoman in
the opera box of the Earl of Harrington (our friend of
the charming luncheon party), call an attendant and
order a brandy and soda will never be forgotten. It
was the general custom to serve refreshments in the
boxes at the opera, and bottles and glasses of all sorts
passed in and out of these private "loges" the entire
evening. Indeed, people never dreamed of drinking

water, although they drank their wines "like water"
proverbially. Such prejudice as mine has two sides,
as I realise when I think of the landlady of our apartment which we rented during a later London season in
Belgrave Mansions. When singing, I had to have a
late supper prepared for me—something very light and
simple and nourishing. Our good landlady used to be
shocked almost to the verge of tears by my iniquitous
habit of drinking water *pur-et-simple* with my suppers.

"Oh, miss," she would beg, "let me put a bit of
sherry or *something* in it for you ! It 'll hurt you that
way, Miss! It 'll make you ill, that it will!"

CHAPTER XIX

HOME AGAIN

MAPLESON asked me to stay on the other side and sing in England, Ireland, and France at practically my own terms, but I refused to do so. I had made my English success and now I wanted to go home in triumph. My mother agreed with me that it was time to be turning homeward. So I accepted an engagement to sing under the management of the Strakosches, Max and Maurice, on a long concert tour.

I have only gratitude for the manner in which my own people welcomed my return. The critics found me much improved, and one and all gave me credit for hard and unremitting work. "Here is a young singer," said one, "who has steadily worked her way to the highest position in operatic art." That point of view always pleased me; for I contend now, as I have contended since I first began to sing, that, next to having a voice in the first place, the great essential is to work; and then *work;* and, after that, begin to WORK!

New York as a city did not please me when I saw it again. I had forgotten, or never fully realised, how provincial it was. Even to-day I firmly believe that it is undoubtedly the dirtiest city in the world, that its traffic regulation is the worst, and its cab service the most expensive and inconvenient. All this struck me with particular force when I came home fresh from London and Paris.

My contract with the Strakosches was for twenty-five weeks, four appearances a week, making a hundred performances in all. This tour was only broken by a short engagement under my old director Maretzek at the Academy of Music in Philadelphia, an arrangement made for me by Max Strakosch when we reached that city in the spring; and, with the exception of *Robert le Diable*, *Trovatore*, and one or two other operas, I spent the next three years singing in concert and oratorio entirely. It was not enjoyable, but it was successful. We went all over the country, North, South, East, West, and everywhere found an enthusiastic public. Particularly was this so in the South as far as I personally was concerned. The poor South had not yet recovered from the effects of the Civil War and did not have much money to spend on amusements, but, when at Richmond the people learned that I was Southern born, more than one woman said to me:

"Go? To hear you! Yes, indeed; we'll hang up all we have to go and hear you!"

One of my popular fellow-artists on the first tour was James M. Wehli, the English pianist. He was known as the "left-handed pianist" and was in reality better suited to a vaudeville stage than to a concert platform. His particular accomplishment consisted in playing a great number of pieces brilliantly with his left hand only, a feat remarkable enough in itself but not precisely an essential for a great artist, and, even as a pianist, he was not inspired.

My first appearance after my European experience was in a concert at the Academy of Music in New York. It was a real welcome home. People cheered and waved and threw flowers and clapped until I was literally in tears. I felt that it did not matter in the least whether New York was a real city or not; America was a real country ! When the concert was over, the men from the Lotus Club took the horses out of my carriage and dragged it, with me in it, to my hotel. And oh, my flowers! My American title of "The Flower *Prima Donna*" was soon reëstablished beyond all peradventure. Flowers in those days were much rarer than they are now; and I received, literally, loads and loads of camellias, and roses enough to set up many florist shops. Without exaggeration, I sent those I received by *cartloads* to the hospitals. And one "floral offering" that I received in Boston was actually too large for any waggon. A subscription had been raised and a pagoda of flowers sent. I had to hire a dray to carry it to my hotel; and then it could not be got up the stairs but had to spend the night downstairs. In the morning I had the monstrous thing photographed and sent it off to a hospital. Even this was an undertaking as I could not, for some reason, get the dray of the night before; and had to hire several able-bodied men to carry it. I hope it was a comfort to somebody before it faded! It is a pity that this tribute on the part of Boston did not assume a more permanent form, for I should have much appreciated a more lasting token as a remembrance of the occasion. It must not be thought that I was unappreciative because I say this. I love anything and everything that blooms, and I love the spirit that offers me flowers. But I must say that the pagoda was something of a white elephant.

While thinking of Boston and my first season at home, I must not omit mention of Mrs. Martin. Indeed, it will have to be rather more than a mere mention, for it is quite a little story, beginning indirectly with Wright Sandford. Wright Sandford was the only man in New York with a big independent fortune, except "Willie" Douglass who spent most of his time cruising in foreign waters. Wright Sandford was more of a friend of mine than "Willie" Douglass, and I used to haul him over the coals occasionally for his lazy existence. He had eighty thousand a year and absolutely nothing to do but to amuse himself.

"What do you expect me to do?" he would demand plaintively. "I 've no one to play with!"

Whenever I was starting on a tour he would send me wonderful hampers put up by Delmonico, with the most delicious things to eat imaginable in them, so that my mother and I never suffered, at least for the first day or two, from the inconveniences of the bad food usually experienced by travellers. A very nice fellow was Wright Sandford in many ways, and to this day I am appreciative of the Delmonico luncheons if of nothing else.

When we were *en route* for Boston on that first tour, —a long trip then, eight or nine hours at least by the fast trains—there sat close to us in the car a little woman who watched me all the time and smiled whenever I glanced at her. I noticed that she had no luncheon with her, so when we opened our Delmonico hamper, I leaned across and asked her to join us. I do not exactly know why I did it for I was not in the habit of making friends with our fellow-travellers; but the little person appealed to me somehow in addition to her being luncheless. She was the most pleased creature imaginable! She nibbled a little, smiled, spoke hardly a word, and after lunch I forgot all about her.

In Boston, as I was in my room in the hotel practis-

ing, before going to the theatre, there came a faint rap
on the door. I called out "Come in," yet nobody came.
I began to practise again and again came a little rap.
"Come in," I called a second time, yet still nothing
happened. After a third rap I went and opened the
door. In the dark hall stood a woman. I did not
remember ever having seen her before; but I could
hardly distinguish her features in the passage.

"I 've come," said she in a soft, small voice, "to
ask you if you would please kiss me?"

Of course I complied. Needless to say, I thought
her quite crazy. After I had kissed her cheek she
nodded and vanished into the darkness while I, much
mystified, went back to my singing. That night at the
theatre I saw a small person sitting in the front row,
smiling up at me. Her face this time was somewhat
familiar and I said to myself, "I do believe that 's
the little woman who had lunch with us on the train!"
and then—"I wonder—*could* it also be the crazy woman
who wanted me to kiss her?"

During our week's engagement in Boston we were
confronted with a dilemma. Max Strakosch came to
me much upset.

"What are we going to do in Providence—the only
decent hotel in the town has burned down," he said.
"You 'll have to stop with friends."

"I have n't any friends in Providence," I replied.

"Well, you 'll have to get some," he declared.
"There 's no hotel where you could possibly stay and we
can't cancel your engagement. The houses are sold out."

Presently a cousin of mine, acting as my agent on
these trips, came and told me that a man had called
on him at the theatre whose wife wished to "entertain"
Miss Kellogg while she was in Providence!

The idea appalled me and I flatly refused to accept this extraordinary invitation; but those two men simply forced me into it. Strakosch, indeed, regarded the incident as a clear dispensation from heaven. "Nothing could be more fortunate," he said, "never mind who they are, you go and stay with them anyway. You've wonderful business waiting for you in Providence."

Well—I went. Yet I felt very guilty about accepting a hospitality that would have to be stretched so far. It was no joke to have me for a guest. I knew well that we would be a burden on any household, especially if it were a modest one. When I was singing I had to have dinner at half-past four at the latest; I could not be disturbed by anything in the morning and, besides, it meant three beds—for mother, myself, and maid. In Providence we arrived at a tiny house at the door of which I was met by the little woman of the train who was, as I had surmised, the same one who had wanted me to kiss her. Supper was served immediately. Everything was immaculate and dainty and delicious. Our hostess had remembered some of the contents of the Delmonico hamper that I had especially liked and had cooked them herself, perfectly.

She made me promise never to stay anywhere else than with her when I was in Providence and I never have. In all, throughout the many years that have intervened between then and now, I must have visited her more than twenty times. During this period I have been privileged to watch the most extraordinary development that could be imagined by any psychologist. When I first stopped with her there was not a book in the house. While everything was exquisitely clean and well kept, it was absolutely primitive. On my second visit I found linen sheets upon the beds and the soap and perfume that I liked were ready for me on the dressing-table. She studied my "ways" and every time I came back there was some new and flattering indication of the fact. Have I mentioned her name? It was Martin, Mrs. Martin, and her husband was conductor on what was called the "Millionaire's Train" that ran between Boston and Providence. I saw very little of him, but he was a nice, shy man, much respected in his business connection. He was "Hezzy" and she was "Lizy"—short for Hezekiah and Eliza. They were a genuinely devoted couple in their quiet way although he always stood a trifle in awe of his wife's friends. She was about ten years older than I and had a really marvellous gift for growing and improving. After a while they left the first house and moved into one a little larger and much more comfortable. They had a library and she began to gather a small circle of musical friends about her. Her knowledge of music was oddly photographic. She would bring me a sheet of music and say:

"Please play this part—here; this is the nice part!" But she was, and is, a fine critic. Some big singers are glad to have her approval. As in music so it was with books—the little woman's taste was instinctive but unerring. She has often brought me a book of poetry, pointed out the best thing in it, and said in her soft way:

"Don't you think this is nice? I *do* think it is *so* nice ! It 's a lovely poem."

There was a young telegraph operator in Providence who had a voice. His name was Jules Jordan. Mrs. Martin took him into her house and practically brought him up. He, too, began to grow and develop and is now the head of the Arion Society, the big musical association of Providence that has some of the biggest singers in the country in its concerts. Mrs. Martin entertains Jules Jordan's artistic friends and goes to the concert rehearsals and says whether they are good or not. She knows, too. "I am called the 'Singers'' friend," she said to me not very long ago. She criticises the orchestra and chorus as well as the solos, and she is right every time. I consider her one of the finest critics I know. As for the professional critics, she is acquainted with them all and they have a very genuine respect for her judgment. She is the sort of person who is called "queer." Most real characters are. If she does not like one, the recipient of her opinion is usually fully aware of what that opinion is. She has no social idea at all, nor any toleration for it. This constitutes one point in which her development is so remarkable. Most women who "make themselves" acquire, first of all, the social graces and veneer, the artificiality in surface matters that will enable them to pass muster in the "great world." She has allowed her evolution to go along different lines. She has really grown, not in accomplishments but in accomplishment; not in manners but in grey matter. Indeed, I hardly know how to find words with which to speak of Mrs. Martin for I think her such a wonderful person; I respect and care for her so much that I find myself dumb when I try to pay her a tribute. If I have dared to speak of her humble beginnings in the first little house it is because it seems to me that only so can I really do her justice as she is to-day. She is a living monument of what a woman can do with herself unaided, save by the force and the aspiration that is in her. Meeting her was one of the most valuable incidents that happened to me in the year of my home-coming.

It seems as if I spent most of my time in those days being photographed. Likenesses were stiff and unnatural; and I am inclined to believe that the picture of me that has always been the best known—the one leaning on my hand—marked a new epoch in photography. I had been posing a great deal the day that was taken and was dead tired. There had been much arranging; many attempts to obtain "artistic effects." Finally, I went off into a corner and sat down, leaning my head on my hand, while the photographer put new plates in his camera. Suddenly he happened to look in my direction and exclaimed:

"By Jove—if I could only—I'm going to try it anyway!" Then he shouted, "Don't move, please!" and took me just as I was. He was very doubtful as to the result for it was a new departure in photography; but the attempt was very successful, and other photographers began to try for the same natural and easy effect. Another time I happened to have a handkerchief in my lap that threw a white reflection on my face, and the photographer discovered from it the value of large light-coloured surfaces to deflect the light where it was needed. This, too, I consider, was an unconscious factor in the introduction of natural effects into photography. I never, however, took a satisfactory picture. People who depend on expression and animation for their looks never do. My likenesses never looked the way I really did—except, perhaps, one that a photographer once caught while I was talking about Duse, explaining how much more I admired her than I did Bernhardt.

In those concert and oratorio years I remember very few pleasurable appearances: but unquestionably one of the few was on June 15th, when the Beethoven

Jubilee was held and I was asked to sing as alternative *prima donna* with Parepa Rosa. Although I had done well in the Crystal Palace, I was not a singer who was generally supposed nor expected to fill so large a place as the American Institute Colosseum on Third Avenue, and many people prophesied that I could not be satisfactorily heard there. I asked my friends to go to different parts of the house and to tell me if my voice sounded well. Even some of my friends out in front, though, did not expect to hear me to advantage. But, contrary to what we all feared, my voice proved to have a carrying quality that had never before been adequately recognised. The affair was a great success. Parepa Rosa did not, as a matter of fact, have quite so big a voice as she was usually credited with having. She had power only to *G*. Above the staff it was a mixed voice. She could diminish to an exquisite quality, but she could not reinforce with any particular volume or vibration.

There was another occasion that I remember with a deep sense of its impressiveness:—that of the funeral of Horace Greeley, at which I sang. I knew Horace Greeley personally and recall many interesting things about him; but, naturally perhaps, what stands out in my memory is the fact that, a few days before he died, he came to hear me sing Handel's *Messiah*, being, as he said afterwards, particularly touched and impressed by my rendering of *I know that my Redeemer liveth*. When he came to die, the last words that he said were those, whispered faintly, as if they still echoed in his heart. It may have been because of this fact that it was I who was asked to sing at his funeral.

On my return from abroad I was, of course, wearing only foreign clothes and, as a consequence, found

14

myself the embarrassed centre of much curiosity. American women were still children in the art of dressing. At one time I was probably the only woman in America who wore silk stockings and long gloves. People could not accustom themselves to my Parisian fashions. In Saratoga one dear man, whom I knew very well, came to me much distressed and whispered that my dress was fastened crooked. I had the greatest difficulty in convincing him that it was made that way and that the crookedness was the latest French touch. A recent fashion was that humped-up effect that gave the wearer the attitude then known and reviled as the "Grecian Bend." It was made famous by caricatures and jokes in the funny papers of the time, but I, being a new-comer so to speak, was not aware of its newspaper notoriety. Conceive my injured feelings when the small boys in the street ran after me in gangs shouting "Grecian Bend! Grecian Bend!"

Another point that hurt the delicate sensibilities of the concert-going American public was the fact that at evening concerts I wore low-necked gowns. On the other side the custom of wearing a dress that was cut down for any and every appearance after dark, was invariable, and it took me some time to grasp the cause of the sensation with my modestly décolleté frocks. People, further, found my ease effrontery, and my carriage, acquired after years of effort, "putting on airs." In spite of the cordiality of my welcome home, therefore, I had many critics who were not particularly kind. Although one woman did write, "who ever saw more simplicity on the stage?" there were plenty of the others who said, "Clara Louise Kellogg has become 'stuck up' during her sojourn abroad." As for my innocent desire to be properly and becomingly clothed, it gave rise to comments that were intended to be quite scathing, if I had only taken sufficient notice of them to think of them ten minutes after they had reached my ears. That year there was put on the millinery market a "Clara Louise" bonnet, by the way, that was supposed to be a great compliment to me, but that I am afraid I would not have been seen wearing at any price!

In this connection one champion arose in my defence, however, whose efforts on my behalf must not be overlooked. He was an Ohio journalist, and his love of justice was far greater than his knowledge of the French language. Seeing in some review that Miss Kellogg had "a larger *répertoire* than any living *prima donna*," this chivalrous writer rushed into print as follows:

We do not of course know how Miss Kellogg was dressed in other cities, but upon the occasion of her last performance here we are positively certain that her *répertoire* did not seem to extend out so far as either Nilsson's or Patti's. It may have been that her overskirt was cut too narrow to permit of its being gathered into such a lump behind, or it may have been that it had been crushed down accidentally, but the fact remains that both of Miss Kellogg's rivals wore *répertoires* of a much more extravagant size— very much to their discredit, we think . . .

CHAPTER XX

A MAN whose name I never learned dropped a big, fragrant bunch of violets at my feet each night for weeks. Becoming discouraged after a while because I did not seek him out in his gallery seat, he sent me a note begging for a glance and adding, for identification, this illuminating point: "*You'll know me by my boots hanging over!*"

Who could disregard such an appeal? That night my eyes searched the balconies feverishly. He had not vainly raised my hopes; his boots *were* hanging over, large boots, that looked as if they had seen considerable service. I sang my best to those boots and—dear man! —the violets fell as sweetly as before. I have conjured up a charming portrait of this individual, with a soul high enough to love music and violets and simple enough not to be ashamed of his boots. Would that all "sincere admirers" might be of such an ingenuous and engaging a pattern.

The variety of "admirers" that are the lot of a person on the stage is extraordinary. It is very difficult for the stage persons themselves to understand it. It has never seemed to me that actors as a class are particularly interesting. Personally I have always been too cognisant of the personalities behind the scenes to ever have any theatrical idols; but to a great many there is something absolutely fascinating about

the stage and stage folk. The actor appears to the
audience in a perpetual, hazy, calcium glory. We are,
one and all, children with an inherent love for fairy
tales and it is probably this lôve which is in a great
measure accountable for the blind adoration received
by most stage people.

I have received, I imagine, the usual number of
letters from "your sincere admirer," some of them
funny and some of them rather pathetic. Very few of
them were really impertinent or offensive. In nearly
all was to be found the same touching devotion to an
abstract ideal for which, for the moment, I chanced to
be cast. Once in a while there was some one who, like
a person who signed himself "Faust," insisted that I
had "met his eyes" and "encouraged him from afar."
Needless to say I had never in my life seen him; but he
worked himself into quite a fever of resentment on the
subject and wrote me several letters. There was also
a man who wrote me several perfectly respectful, but
ardent, love letters to which, naturally, I did not
respond. Then, finally, he bombarded me with another
type of screed of which the following is a specimen:

"Oh, for Heaven's sake, say something,—if it is
only to rate me for my importunities or to tell me to go
about my business! Anything but this contemptuous
silence!"

But these were exceptions. Most of my "admirers'"
letters are gems of either humour or of sentiment.
Among my treasures is an epistle that begins:

"Miss Clara Louise Kellogg
   Miss:
Before to expand my feelings, before to make you
known the real intent of this note, in fine before to

disclose the secrets of my heart, I will pray you to pardon my indiscretion (if indiscretion that can be called) to address you unacquainted," etc.

Is n't this a masterpiece?

There was also an absurdly conceited man who wrote me one letter a year for several years, always in the same vein. He was evidently a very pious youth and had "gotten religion" rather badly, for in every epistle he broke into exhortation and urged me fervently to become a "real Christian," painting for me the joys of true religion if I once could manage to "find it." In one of his later letters—after assuring me that he had prayed for me night and morning for three years and would continue to do so—he ended in this impressive manner:

". . . And if, in God's mercy, we are both permitted to walk 'the Golden Streets,' I shall there seek you out and give you more fully my reasons for writing you."

Could anything be more entertaining than this *naïve* fashion of making a date in Heaven?

Not all my letters were love letters. Sometimes I would receive a few words from some woman unknown to me but full of a sweet and understanding friendliness. Mrs. Elizabeth Tilton, then the centre of the stage scandal through her friendship with Henry Ward Beecher, wrote me a charming letter that ended with what struck me as a very pathetic touch:

"I am unwilling to be known by you as the defiant, discontented woman of the age—rather, as an humble helper of those less fortunate than myself——"

I never knew Mrs. Tilton personally, but have often felt that I should have liked her. One of the dearest communications I ever received was from a French working girl, a corset maker, I believe. She wrote:

I am but a poor little girl, Mademoiselle, a toiler in the sphere where you reign a queen, but ever since I was a very little child I have gone to listen to your voice whenever you have deigned to sing in New York. Those magic tone-flowers, scattering their perfumed sweetness on the waiting air, made my child heart throb with a wonderful pulsation. . . .

One of the favourite jests of the critics was my obduracy in matters of sentiment. It was said that I would always have emotional limitations because I had no love affairs like other *prime donne*. Once, when I gave some advice to a young girl to "keep your eyes fixed upon your artistic future," or some such similar phrase, the press had a good deal of fun at my expense. "That" it was declared, "was exactly what was the matter with Clara Louise; she kept her eyes fixed upon an artistic future instead of upon some man who was in love with her!" I was rather a good shot, very fond of target shooting, and many jokes were also made on the supposed damage I did. One newspaper man put it rather more aptly. "Not only in pistol shooting," he said, "but in everything she aims at, our *prima donna* is sure to hit the mark."

My "sincere admirers" were from all parts of the house, but I think I found the "gallery" ones most sincere and, certainly, the most amusing. Max Maretzek used to say that he had no manner of use for an artist unless she could fill the family circle. I am glad to be able to record that I always could. My singing usually appealed to the people. *The Police Gazette* always gave me good notices! I love the family circle.

As a rule the appreciation there is greater because of the sacrifices which they have had to make to buy their seats. When people can go to hear good music every night, they do not care nearly so much about doing it.

I wonder if anybody besides singers get such an extraordinary sense of contact and connection with members of their audiences? I have sometimes felt as if thought waves, reaching through the space between, held me fast to some of those who heard me sing. Who knows what sympathies, what comprehensions, what exquisite friendships, were blossoming out there in the dark house like a garden, waiting to be gathered? Letters—not necessarily love letters—rather, stray messages o appreciation and understanding—have brought me a similar sense of joy and of safe intimacy. After the receipt of any such, I have sung with the pleasant sense that a new friend—yes, friend, not auditor—was listening. I have suddenly felt at home in the big theatre; and often, very often, have I looked eagerly over the banked hosts of faces, asking myself wistfully which were the strangers and which mine own people.

It was not only in the theatre that I found "admirers." My vacations were beset with those who wanted to look at and speak to a genuine *prima donna* at close range. Indeed, I had frequently to protect myself from perfectly strange and intrusive people. Often I have gone to Saratoga during the season. Saratoga was a fashionable resort in those days and I always had a good audience. One incident that I remember of Saratoga was a detestable train that invariably came along in the middle of my performance —the evening train from New York. I always had to stop whatever I was singing and wait for it to go by. One night I thought I would cheat it and timed my song a little earlier so that I would be through before the train arrived. It just beat me by a bar; and I could hear it steaming nearer and nearing as I hurried on. As I came to the end there was a loud whistle from the locomotive;—but, for once, luck was on my side, for it was pitched in harmony with my final note! The coincidence was warmly applauded.

When on the road I not infrequently practised with my banjo at hotels. It was more practicable to carry about than a piano and, besides, it was not always an easy matter to hire a good piano. One time—also in Saratoga—I was playing that instrument preparatory to beginning my morning practice, when an old gentleman who had a room on the same floor, descended to the office in a fine temper. He was a long, slim, wiry old fellow, with a high, black satin stock about his bony neck, very few hairs on his little round head, deep sunken eyes, pinched features, and an extremely nervous manner.

"See here," he burst out in a cracked voice, as he danced about on the marble tiling of the office floor, "have you a band of nigger minstrels in the house, eh! Zounds, sir, there's an infernal banjo tum, tum, tumming in my ears every morning and I can't sleep. Drat banjoes—I hate 'em. And nigger minstrels—I hate 'em too. You must move me, sir, move me at once. That banjo 'll set me crazy. Move me at once, d'ye hear?—or I 'll leave the house!"

"Why, sir," said the clerk suavely, "that banjo player is not a nigger minstrel, at all, sir, but Miss Clara Louise Kellogg, who uses a banjo to practise with."

The hard lines in the old fellow's face relaxed, he looked sharply at the clerk and, leaning over the counter, remarked:

"What, Clara Louise Kellogg! W—why, I 'll go up and listen! Zounds, man, she 's my particular favourite. She 's charmed me with her sweet voice many a time. D—n it, give her another banjo! Tell her to play all day if she wants to! Clara Louise Kellogg, eh? H'm, well, well!"

He tottered off and, as I observed, after that so long as I stayed left the door of his room open down the hall so that he could hear my "tum, tum, tumming."

A very different, though equally ingenuous tribute to my powers was that given by an old Indian trapper who, when in Chicago to sell his hides, went to hear me sing and expressed his emotions to a newspaper man of that city in approximately the following language:

I have heard most of the sweet and terrible noises that natives make. I have heard the thunder among the Hills when the Lord was knocking against the earth until it passed; and I have heard the wind in the pines and the waves on the beaches, when the darkness of night was in the woods, and nature was singing her Evening Song and there was no bird nor beast the Lord has made, and I have not heard a voice that would make as sweet a noise as nature makes when the Spirit of the Universe speaks through the stillness; but that sweet lady has made sounds to-night sweeter than my ears have heard on hill or lake shore at noon, or in the night season, and I certainly believe that the Spirit of the Lord has been with her and given her the power to make such sweet sounds. A man might like to have these sweet sounds in his ears when his body lies in his cabin and his spirit is standing on the edge of the great clearing. I wish she could sing for me when my eyes grow dim and my feet strike the trail that no man strikes but once, nor travels both ways.

Surely among my friends, if not among my "sincere admirers," I may include Okakura, who came over here with the late John La Farge as an envoy from the Japanese Government to study the art of this country as well as that of Europe. His dream was to found some sort of institution in Japan for the preservation and development of his country's old, national ideals in art. His criticisms of Raphael and Titian, by the way, were something extraordinary. As for music, he had a marvellous sense for it. La Farge took him to a Thomas Concert and he was vastly impressed by the music of Beethoven. One might have thought that he had listened to Occidental classics all his life. But, for that matter, I know two little Japanese airs that Davidson of London told me might well have been written by Beethoven himself; so it may be that there is an obscure bond of sympathy, which our less acute ears would not always recognise, between our great master and the composers of Okakura's native land.

Okakura was only twenty-six when I first met him at Richard Watson Gilder's studio in New York, but he was already a professor and spoke perfect English and knew all our best literature. When Munkacsy, the Hungarian painter, came over, his colleague, Francis Korbay, the musician, gave him an evening reception, and I took my Japanese friend. It was a charming evening and Okakura was the success of the reception. When he started being introduced he was nothing but a professor. Before he had gone the rounds he had become an Asiatic prince and millionaire. He had the "grand manner" and wore gorgeous clothes on formal occasions.

Some years later I called on his wife in Tokio. I considered this was the polite thing for me to do although Okakura himself was in Osaka at the time. Okakura had an art school in Tokio, kept up with the aid of the Government, where he was trying to fulfil his old ambition of preserving the individuality of his own people's work and of driving out Occidental encroachments. At the school, where we had gone with a guide who could serve also as interpreter, I asked for Madame. My request to see her was met with consternation. I was asking a great deal—how much, I did not realise until afterwards. Before I could enter, I was requested to take off my shoes. This I considered impossible as I was wearing high-laced boots. Furthermore, we were having winter weather, very cold and raw, and nothing was offered me to put on in their place, as the Japanese custom is at the entrances of the temples. My refusal to remove my shoes halted proceedings for a while; but, eventually, I was led around to a side porch where I could sit on a *chair* (I was amazed at their having such a thing) and speak with the occupants of the house as they knelt inside on their heels. The *shoji*, or bamboo and paper screen, was pushed back, revealing an interior wonderfully clever in its simplicity. The furniture consisted of a beautiful brazier and two rare kakamonos on the wall—nothing more.

In came Madame Okakura in a grey kimono and bare feet. Down she went on her knees and saluted me in the prettiest fashion imaginable. We talked through the interpreter until her daughter entered, who spoke to me in bad, limited French. The daughter was an unattractive girl, with an artificially reddened mouth, but I thought the mother charming, like a most exquisite Parisienne masquerading as a "Japanese Lady."

Not long after my visit I saw Okakura himself and told him how much I had enjoyed seeing his wife. He gave me an annoyed glance and remained silent. I was nonplussed and somewhat mortified. I could not understand what could be the trouble, for he acted as if his honour were offended. In time I learned that the unpardonable breach of good form in Japan was to mention his wife to a Japanese!

So graceful, so delicate in both expression and feeling are the letters that I have received from Okakura, that I cannot resist my inclination to include them in this chapter,—although, possibly, they are somewhat too personal. On January 4, 1887, he wrote:

MY DEAR MISS KELLOGG:

France lies three nights ahead of us. The returning clouds still seek the western shore and the ocean rolls back my dreams to you. Your music lives in my soul. I carry away America in your voice; and what better token can your nation offer? But praises to the great sound like flattery, and praises to the beautiful sound like love. To you they must both be tiresome. I shall refrain. You allude to the Eastern Lights. Alas, the Lamp of Love flickers and Night is on the plains of Osaka. There are lingering lights on the crown of the Himalayas, on the edges of the Kowrous, among the peaks of Hira and Kora. But what do they care for the twilight of the Valley? They stand like the ocean moon, regardless of the tempest below. Seek the light in the mansion of your own soul. Are you not yourself the *Spirit Nightingale of the West?* Are you not crying for the moon in union with your Emersons and Longfellows—with your La Farges and your Gilders? Or am I mistaken? I enclose my picture and submit the translation of the few lines on the back to your *axe of anger and the benevolence of your criticism* as we say at home. I need a great deal of your benevolence and deserve more of your anger, as the lines sound so poor in the English. However they do not appear very grand in the original and so I submit them to your guillotine with a free conscience. The lines are different from the former, for I forget them—or care not to repeat.

Will you kindly convey my best regards to Mrs. Gilder, for I owe so much to her, to say nothing of your friendship! Will you also condescend to write to me at your leisure?

.   .   .   .

(*Translation:*—One star floats into the ocean of Night. Past the back of Taurus, away among the Pleiades, whither dost thou go? Sadly I watch them all. My soul wanders after them into the infinite. Shall my soul return, or—never?)

VIENNA, March 4, 1887.

MY DEAR MISS KELLOGG:

The home of a traveller is in his sweet memories. Under the shadow of Vesuvius and on the waters of Leman my thoughts were always for America, which you and your friends have made so pleasant to me. Pardon me therefore if my pen again turns toward you. How kind of you to remember me! Your letter reached me here last night and I regret that I did not stay longer in Paris to receive it sooner. Will you not favour me by writing again?

Europe is an enigma—often a source of sadness to me. The forces that developed her are tearing her asunder. Is it because all civilisations are destined to have their days and nights of Brahma? Or was the principle that organised the European nations itself a false one? Did they grasp the moon in the waters and at last disturb the image? I know not. I only feel that the Spirit of Unrest is standing beside me. War is coming and must come, sooner or later. Conflicting opinions chase each other across the continent as if the demons fought in the air before the battle of men began. The policy of maintaining peace by increasing the armies is absurd. It is indeed a sad state of things to make such a sophism necessary. I am getting tired of this, though there is some consolation that there are more fools in the world than the Oriental.

I have been rather disappointed in the French music. Perhaps I am too much prejudiced by *The Persian Serenade* to appreciate anything else. The acting was artificial and there was no voice which had anything of the Spirit Nightingale in it. You once told me that you intended to cross the Atlantic this summer. When? My dreams are impatient of your arrival. May you come soon and correct my one-sided impression of Europe!

I am going to Rome after two or three weeks' stay in this place. That city interests me deeply, as yet the spiritual centre of the West, whose voice still influences the politics of Central Europe. In May I shall be at the Paris Salon and cross over to London in the early part of June.

It snows every day in Vienna and I spend my time mostly with the old doctors of the University. Their talks on philosophy and science are indeed interesting, but somehow or other I don't feel the delight I had in your society in New York. Why?

July 12, 1887.

MY DEAR MISS KELLOGG:

I am very glad to hear that you are in Europe. My duties in London end this week and I have decided to start for Munich next morning, thence to Dresden and Berlin. I am thus looking forward to the great pleasure of meeting you again and gathering fragrance from your conversation. Mrs. Gilder wrote to me that you were not quite well since your tour in the West and my anxiety mingles with my hopes. The atmosphere of English civilisation weighs heavily on me and I am longing to be away. It seems that civilisation does not agree with a member of an Eastern barbaric tribe. My conception of music has been gradually changing. The Ninth Symphony has revolutionised it. Where is the future of music to be?

Many questions crowd on me and I am impatient to lay them before you at Carlsbad. Will you allow me to do so?

BERLIN. KAISERHAUF, July 24th.

MY DEAR MISS KELLOGG:

The Spirit of Unrest chases me northward. Dresden glided dimly before me. Holbein was a disappointment. The Sistine Madonna was divine beyond my expectation. I saw Raphael in his purity and was delighted. None of his pictures is so inspired as this. Still my thoughts wandered amid these grand creations. They flitted past in a shower of colours and shadows and I have drifted hither through the hazy forests of Heine and the troubled grey of Millet's twilight. . . .

To me your friendship is the boat that bears me proudly home. I wait with pleasure any line you may send me there. Wishing every good to you, I remain yours respectfully.

KAISERHAUF, July 28th, 1887.

MY DEAR MISS KELLOGG:

Ten thousand thanks for your kind letter. My address in Japan is Monbusho, Tokio, and if you will write to me there I shall be so happy! The task which I have imposed upon myself—the preserving of historical continuity and internal development, etc.,—has to work very slowly. I must be patient and cautious. Still I shall be delighted to confide to you from time to time how I am getting on with my dream if you will allow me to do so. You say that you have a hope of finding what you long for in Buddhism. Surely your lotus must be opening to the dawn. European philosophy has reached to a point where no advance is possible except through mysticism. Yet they ignore the hidden truths on limited scientific grounds. The Berlin University has thus been forced to return to Kant and begin afresh. They have destroyed but have no power to construct, and they never will if they refuse to *see* more into themselves. . . .

Hoping you the best and the brightest, I am

Yours faithfully,

OKAKURA KAKUDZO.

And so I come to one of all these who was really a "sincere admirer," and a faithful lover, although I never knew him. It is a difficult incident to write of, for I feel that it holds some of the deepest elements of sentiment and of tragedy with which I ever came in touch.

I was singing in Boston when a man sent me a message saying that he was connected with a newspaper and had something of great importance about which he wanted to see me. He furthermore said that he wished to see me alone. It was an extraordinary request and, at first, I refused. I suspected a subterfuge—a wager, or something humiliating of that sort. But he persisted, sending yet another message to the effect that he had something to communicate to me which was of an essentially personal nature. Finally I consented to grant him the interview and, as he had requested, I saw him alone.

He was just back from the front where he had been war correspondent during the heart of the Civil War, and he told me that he had a letter to give to me from a soldier in his division who had been shot. The soldier was mortally wounded when the reporter found him. He was lying at the foot of a tree at the point of death, and the correspondent asked if he could take any last messages for him to friends or relatives. The soldier asked him to write down a message to take to a woman whom he had loved for four years, but who did not know of his love.

15

"Tell her," he said, speaking with great difficulty, "that I would not try even to meet her; but that I have loved her, before God, as well as any man ever loved a woman." He asked the reporter to feel inside his uniform for the woman's picture. "It is Miss Kellogg," he added, just before he died. "You—don't think that she will be offended if I send her this message—now—do you?"

He asked the correspondent to draw his sabre and cut off a lock of hair to send to me, and the reporter wrote down the message on the only scraps of paper at his disposal—torn bits scribbled over with reports of the enemy's movements, and the names of other dead soldiers whose people must be notified when the battle was over. And then the soldier—my soldier—died; and the correspondent left him the picture and came away.

The scribbled message and the lock of hair he put into my hands, saying:

"He was very much worried lest you would think him presumptuous. I told him that I was sure you would not."

I was weeping as he spoke, and so he left me.

CHAPTER XXI

ON THE ROAD

O H, those first tours! Not only was it exceedingly uncomfortable to travel in the South and West at that time, but it was decidedly risky as well. Highway robberies were numerous and, although I myself never happened to suffer at the hands of any desperadoes, I have often heard first-hand accounts from persons who had been robbed of everything they were carrying. While I was touring in Missouri, Jesse James and his men were operating in the same region and the celebrated highway man himself was once in the train with me. I slipped quietly through to catch a glimpse of him in the smoking-car. Two of his "aides" were with him and, although they were behaving themselves peacefully enough for the time being, I think that most of the passengers were willing to give them a wide berth. During one concert trip of our company I saw something of a situation which might have developed dramatically. There was a "three card monte" gang working on the train. One of their number pretended to be a farmer and entirely innocent, so as to lure victims into the game. I saw this particularly tough-looking individual disappear into the toilet room and come out made up as the farmer. It was like a play. I also saw him finger a pistol that he was carrying in his right hip pocket: and I experienced a somewhat blood-

227

thirsty desire that there might be a genuine excitement in store for us, but the alarm spread and nobody was snared that trip.

As there were frequently no through trains on Sundays, we had sometimes to have special trains. I never quite understood the idea of not having through trains on Sundays, for surely other travellers besides unfortunate singers need occasionally to take journeys on the Sabbath. But so it was. And once our "special" ran plump into a big strike of locomotive engineers at Dayton, Ohio. Our engine driver was held up by the strikers bivouacked in the railroad yards and we were stalled there for hours. At last an engineer from the East was found who consented to take our train through and there was much excitement while he was being armed with a couple of revolvers and plenty of ammunition, for the strikers had threatened to shoot down any "scab" who attempted to break the strike. We were all ordered to get down on the floor of the car to avoid the stones that might be thrown through the windows when we started; and when the train began to move slowly our situation was decidedly trying. We could hear a hail of shots being fired, as the engine gathered speed, but our volunteer engineer knew his business and had been authorised to drive the engine at top speed to get us out of the trouble, so soon the noise of shooting and the general uproar were left behind. The plucky strike-breaker was barely grazed, but I, personally, never cared to come any closer to lawlessness than I was then.

There were some bright spots on these disagreeable journeys. One day as I was coming out of a hall in Duluth where I had been rehearsing for the concert we were giving that evening, I ran into a man I knew,

an Englishman whom I had not seen since I was in
London.

"There!" he exclaimed, "I knew it was you!"

"Did you see the advertisement?" I asked.

"No," he returned, "I 'm just off the yacht that 's
lying out there in the Lake. I 'm out looking into some
mining interests, you know. I heard your voice from
the boat and I knew it must be you, so I thought I 'd
take a run on shore and look you up."

But such pleasant experiences were the exception.
The South in general was in a particularly blind and
dull condition just then. The people could not conceive of any amusement that was not intended literally
to "amuse." They felt it incumbent to laugh at everything. My *cheval de bataille* was the Polonaise from
Mignon, at the end of which I had introduced some
chromatic trills. It is a wonderful piece and required
a great deal of genuine technique to master. A portion
of the house would appreciate it, of course, but on one
occasion a detestable young couple thought the trills
were intended to be humorous. Whenever I sang a
trill they would poke each other in the ribs and giggle
and, when there was a series of the chromatic trills,
they nearly burst. The chromatics introduced by me
were never written. They went like this:

One disapproving unit in an audience can spoil a
whole evening for a singer. I recall one concert when I
was obsessed by a man in the front row. He would not
even look at me. Possibly he considered that I was a
spoiled creature and he did not wish to aid and abet the

spoiling, or, perhaps, he was really bored and disgusted. At any rate, he kept his eyes fixed on a point high over my head and not with a beatific expression, either. He clearly did not think much of my work. Well—I sang my whole programme to that one man. And I was a failure. Charmed I ever so wisely, I could not really move him. But I *did* make him uncomfortable! He wriggled and sat sidewise and clearly was uneasy. He must have felt that I was trying to win him over in spite of himself. I sometimes wonder if other singers do the same with obdurate auditors? Surely they must, for it is a sort of fetish of the profession that there is always one person present who is by far the most difficult to charm. In that clever play *The Concert* the pianist tells the young woman in love with him that he was first interested in her when he saw her in the audience because she did not cry. He played his best in order to moisten her eyes and, when he saw a tear roll down her cheek, he knew that he had triumphed as an artist. Our audiences were frequently inert and indiscriminating. One night an usher brought me a programme from some one in the audience with a suggestion scribbled on the margin:

"Can't you sing something devilish for a change?"

I believe they really wanted a song and dance, or a tight-rope exhibition. We had a baritone who sang well "The Evening Star" from *Tannhauser* and his performance frequently ended in a chill silence with a bit of half-hearted clapping. He had a sense of humour and he used to come off the stage and say:

"That didn't go very well! Do you think I'd better do my bicycle act next?"

Times change and standards with them. The towns where they yearned for bicycle acts and "something

Clara Louise Kellogg as Carmen
From a photograph

devilish" are to-day centres of musical taste and cultivation. I never think of the change of standards without being reminded of an old tale of my father's which
is curious in itself, although I cannot vouch for it nor
verify it. He said that somewhere in Germany there
was a bell in a church tower which, when it was first
hung, many years before, was pitched in the key of *C*
and which was found to ring, in the nineteenth century,
according to our present pitch, at about our *B* flat.
The musical scientists said that the change was not in
the bell but in our own standard of pitch, which had
been gradually raised by the manufacturers of pianos
who pitched them higher and higher to get a more
brilliant tone.

My throat was very sensitive in those days. I took
cold easily and used, besides, to be subject to severe
nervous headaches. Yet I always managed to sing.
Indeed, I have never had much sympathy with capri-
cious *prime donne* who consider themselves and their
own physical feelings before their obligation to the
public that has paid to hear them. While, of course, in
fairness to herself, a singer must somewhat consider
her own interests, I do believe that she cannot be
too conscientious in this connection. In *Carmen* one
night I broke my collar bone in the fall in the last act.
I was still determined to do my part and went out,
after it had been set, and bought material to match my
costumes so that the sling the surgeon had ordered
should not be noticed. And, for once fortunately, my
audiences were either not exacting or not observing, for,
apparently, no comment was ever made on the fact
that I could not use my right arm. I could not
help questioning whether my gestures were usually so
wooden that an arm, more or less, was not perceptible!

Our experiences in general with physicians on the road were lamentable. As a result my mother carried a regular medicine chest about with her and all of my fellow-artists used to come to her when anything was the matter with them.

Another hardship that we all had to endure was the being on exhibition. It is one of the penalties of fame. Special trains were most unusual, and so were *prime donne*, and crowds used to gather on the station platforms wherever we stopped, waiting to catch a glimpse of us as we passed through.

And the food! Some of our trials in regard to food— or, rather, the lack of it—were very trying. Voices are very dependent on the digestion; hence the need of, at least, eatable food, however simple it may be. On one trip we really nearly starved to death for, of course, there were no dining-cars and the train did not stop at any station long enough to forage for a square meal. Finally, in desperation, I told one of the men in the company that, if he would get some "crude material" at the next stop and bring it in, I would cook it. So he succeeded in securing a huge bundle of raw chops, a loaf of bread and some butter. There was a big stove at one end of the car and on its coals I broiled the chops, made tea and toast, and we all feasted. Indeed, it seemed a feast after ten hours with nothing at all! Another time I got off our "special" to hunt luncheon and was left behind. I raced wildly to catch the train but could not make it. After a while the company discovered that they had lost me on the way and backed up to get me. Speaking of food, I shall never forget the battle royal I once had with a hotel manager on the road in regard to my coloured maid, Eliza. She was a very nice and entirely presentable girl and he would not let her have even a cup of tea in the dining-room. We had had a long, hard journey, and she was quite as tired as the rest of us. So, when I found her still waiting after I had lunched, I made a few pertinent remarks to the effect that her presence at the table was much to be preferred to the men who had eaten there without table manners, uncouth, feeding themselves with their knives.

"And what else did we have the war for!" I finally cried. How the others laughed at me. But Eliza was fed, and well fed, too.

I had always to carry my own bedclothes on the Western tours. When we first started out, I did not realise the necessity, but later, I became wiser. Cleanliness has always been almost more than godliness to me. Before I would use a dressing-room I nearly always had it thoroughly swept out and sometimes cleaned and scrubbed. This all depended on the part of the country we were in. I came to know that in certain sections of the South-west I should have to have a regular house-cleaning done before I would set foot in their accommodations. I missed my bath desperately, and my piano, and all the other luxuries that have become practical necessities to civilised persons. When I could not have a state-room on a train, my maid would bring a cup of cold water to my berth before I dressed that was a poor apology for a bath, but that saved my life on many a morning after a long, stuffy night in a sleeper.

The lesser hardships perhaps annoyed me most. Bad food, bad air, rough travelling, were worse than the more serious ills of fatigue and indispositions. But the worst of all was the water. One can, at a pinch, get along with poor food or with no food at all to speak of, but bad water is a much more serious matter. Even dirt is tolerable if it can be washed off afterwards. But I have seen many places where the water was less inviting than the dirt. When I first beheld Missouri water I hardly dared wash in it, much less drink it, and was appalled when it was served to me at the table. I gazed with horror at the brown liquid in my tumbler, and then said faintly to the waiter:

"Can't you get me some clear water, please?"

"Oh, yes," said he, "it 'll be clearer, ma'am, *but it won't be near so rich!*"

And all the time I was working, for, no matter what the hardships or distractions that may come an artist's way, he or she must always keep at work. Singing is something that must be worked for just as hard after it is won as during the winning process. Liszt is supposed to have said that when he missed practising one day he knew it; when he missed two days his friends knew it; on the third day the public knew it. I often rehearsed before a mirror, so that I could know whether I looked right as well as sounded right; and, *apropos* of this, I have been much impressed by the fact that ways of rehearsing are very different and characteristic. Ellen Terry once told me that, when she had a new part to study, she generally got into a closed carriage, with the window open, and was driven about for two or three hours, working on her lines.

"It is the only way I can keep my repose," she said. "I only wish I had some of Henry's repose when studying a part!"

Sir Henry Irving and Ellen Terry as the Vicar and Olivia
From a photograph by Window & Grove

CHAPTER XXII

AFTER nearly three years of concert and oratorio and racketing about America on tours, it was a joy to go to England again for another season. The Peace Jubilee Association asked me to sing at their celebration in Boston that spring, but I went to London instead. The offer from the Association was a great compliment, however, and especially the wording of the resolution as communicated to me by the secretary.

"Unanimously voted:—That Miss Clara Louise Kellogg, the leading *prima donna* of America, receive the special invitation of the Executive Committee, etc."

The spring season in London was well along when we arrived there and, before I had been in the city a day, I began to feel at home again. Newcastle and Dr. Quinn called almost immediately and Alfred Rothschild sent me flowers, all of which made me realize that this was really England once more and that I was among old and dear friends.

I was again to sing under Mapleson's management. The new opera house, built on the site of Her Majesty's that had burned, was highly satisfactory; and he had nearly all of his old singers again—Titjiens, Nilsson, and myself among others. Patti and Lucca were still our rivals at Covent Garden; also Faure and Cotogni; and there was a pretty, young, new singer from Canada with them, Mme. Albani, who had a light, sweet voice and was attractive in appearance. Our two innovations at Her Majesty's were Marie Roze from the Paris Opera Comique—later destined to be associated with me professionally and with Mapleson personally—and Italo Campanini. Campanini was the son of a blacksmith in Italy and had worked at the forge himself for many years before going on the stage, and was the hero of the hour, for not only was his voice a very lovely one, but he was also a fine actor. It was worth while to see his Don José. People forgot that Carmen herself was in the opera. Our other tenor was Capoul, the Frenchman, Trebelli-Bettini was our leading contralto and my friend Foli—"the Irish Italian from Connecticut"—was still with us.

Campanini, the idol of the town, was, like most tenors, enormously pleased with himself. To be sure, he had some reason, with his heavenly voice, his dramatic gift, and his artistic instinct; but one would like some day to meet a man gifted with a divine vocal organ and a simple spirit both, at the same time. It appears to be an impossible combination. When Mapleson told Campanini that he was to sing with me in *Lucia* he frowned and considered the point.

"An American," he muttered doubtfully. "I have never heard her—do I know that she can sing? I—Campanini—cannot sing with a *prima donna* of whom I know nothing! Who is this Miss Kellogg anyway?"

"You 're quite right," said the Colonel with the most cordial air of assent. "You 'd better hear her before you decide. She 's singing Linda to-night. Go into the stalls and listen to her for a few moments. If you don't want to sing with her, you don't have to."

That evening Campanini was on hand, ready to controvert the very idea of an American *prima donna* daring to sing with him. After the first act he came out into the foyer and ran into the Colonel.

"Well," remarked that gentleman casually, winking at Jarrett, "can she sing?"

"Sing?" said Campanini solemnly, "she has the voice of a flute. It is the absolutely perfect tone. It is a—miracle!"

So, after all, Campanini and I sang together that season in *Lucia* and in other operas. While Campanini was a great artist, he was a very petty man in many ways. A little incident when Capoul was singing *Faust* one night is illustrative. Capoul, much admired and especially in America, was intensely nervous and emotional with a quick temper. Between him and Italo Campanini a certain rivalry had been developing for some time, and, whatever may be asserted to the contrary, male singers are much bitterer rivals than women ever are. On the night I speak of, Campanini came into his box during the *Salve dimora* and set down to listen. As Capoul sang, the Italian's face became lined with a frown of annoyance and, after a moment or two, he began to drum on the rail before him as if he could not conceal his exasperation and *ennui*. The longer Capoul sang, the louder and more irritated the tapping became until most of the audience was unkind enough to laugh just a little. Poor Capoul tried, in vain, to sing down that insistent drumming, and, when the act was over, he came behind the scenes and actually cried with rage.

On what might be called my second *début* in London, I had an ovation almost as warm as my welcome home to my native land had been three years before. I had forgotten how truly the English people were my friends until I heard the applause which greeted me as I walked

onto the stage that night in *Linda di Chamouix.* Sir
Michael Costa, who was conducting that year, was
always an irascible and inflexible autocrat when it
came to operatic rules and ideals. One of the points of
observance upon which he absolutely insisted was that
the opera must never be interrupted for applause.
Theoretically this was perfectly correct; but nearly all
good rules are made to be broken once in a while and
it was quite obvious that the audience intended this
occasion to be one of the times. Sir Michael went on
leading his orchestra and the people in front went on
clapping until the whole place became a pandemonium.
The house at last, and while still applauding, began to
hiss the orchestra so that, after a minute of a tug-of-war
effect, Sir Michael was obliged to lay down his baton—
although with a very bad grace—and let the applause
storm itself out. I could see him scowling at me as I
bowed and smiled and bowed again, nearly crying outright at the friendliness of my welcome. There were
traitors in his own camp, too, for, as soon as the baton
was lowered, half the orchestra—old friends mostly—
joined in the applause! Sir Michael never before had
broken through his rule; and I do not fancy he liked me
any the better for being the person to force upon him
this one exception.

I include here a letter written to someone in America
just after this performance by Bennett of *The London
Telegraph* that pleased me extremely, both for its
general appreciative friendliness and because it was a
résumé of the English press and public regarding my
former and my present appearance in England.

Miss Kellogg has not been forgotten during the years
which intervened, and not a few *habitués* cherished a hope

that she would be led across the Atlantic once more. She was, however, hardly expected to measure herself against the *crème-de-la-crème* of the world's *prime donne* with no preliminary beat of drum and blowing of trumpet, trusting solely to her own gifts and to the fairness of an English public. This she did, however, and all the English love of "pluck" was stirred to sympathy. We felt that here was a case of the real Anglo-Saxon determination, and Miss Kellogg was received in a manner which left nothing of encouragement to be desired. Defeat under such circumstances would have been honourable, but Miss Kellogg was not defeated. So far from this, she at once took a distinguished place in our galaxy of "stars"; rose more and more into favour with each representation, and ended, as Susannah in *Le Nozze di Figaro* by carrying off the honours from the Countess of Mlle. Titjiens and the Cherubino of Mlle. Nilsson. A greater achievement than this last Miss Kellogg's ambition could not desire. It was "a feather in her cap" which she will proudly wear back to her native land as a trophy of no ordinary conflict and success. You may be curious to know the exact grounds upon which we thus honour your talented countrywoman, and in stating them I shall do better than were I to criticise performances necessarily familiar. In the first place, we recognise in Miss Kellogg an artist, and not a mere singer. People of the latter class are plentiful enough, and are easily to be distinguished by the way in which they "reel" off their task—a way brilliant, perhaps, but exciting nothing more than the admiration due to efficient mechanism. The artist, on the other hand, shows in a score of forms that he is more than a machine and that something of human feeling may be made to combine with technical correctness. Herein lies the great charm often, perhaps, unconsciously acknowledged, of Miss Kellogg's efforts. We know at once, listening to her, that she sings from the depth of a keenly sensitive artistic nature, and never did anybody do this without calling out a sympathetic response. It is not less evident that Miss Kellogg is a consummate musician—that "rare bird" on the operatic boards. Hence, her unvarying correctness; her lively appreciation of the composer in his happiest moments, and the manner in which she adapts her individual efforts to the production of his intended effects. Lastly, without dwelling upon the charm of a voice and style perfectly well known to you and ungrudgingly recognised here, we see in Miss Kellogg a dramatic artist who can form her own notion of a part and work it out after a distinctive fashion. Anyone able to do this comes with refreshing effect at a time when the lyric stage is covered with pale copies of traditionary excellence. It was refreshing, for example, to witness Miss Kellogg's Susannah, an embodiment full of realism without coarseness and *esprit* without exaggeration. Susannahs, as a rule, try to be ladylike and interesting. Miss Kellogg's waiting-maid was just what Beaumarchais intended, and the audience recognised the truthful picture only to applaud it. For all these reasons, and for more which I have no space to name, we do honour to the American *prima donna*, so that whenever you can spare her on your side we shall be happy to welcome her on ours.

It was during this season in London that Max Maretzek and Max Strakosch decided to go into opera management together in America; and Maretzek came over to London to get the company together. Pauline Lucca and I were to be the *prime donne* and one of our novelties was to be Gounod's new opera *Mireille*, founded on the poem by the Provençal poet, Mistral. I say "new opera" because it was still unknown in America; possibly because it had been a failure in London where it had already been produced. "The Magnificent" thought it would be sure to do well in "the States" on account of the wild Gounod vogue that had been started by *Faust* and *Romeo and Juliette*.

First edition of the *Faust* score, published in 1859 by Chousens of Paris, now in the Boston Public Library

I was to sing it; and Colonel Mapleson sent Mr. Jarrett with me to call on Gounod, who was then living in London, to get what points I could from the master himself.

Everybody who knows anything about Gounod knows also about Mrs. Welldon. Georgina Welldon, the wife of an English officer, was an exceedingly eccentric character to say the least. Even the most straight-laced biographers refer to the "romantic friendship" between the composer and this lady—which, after all, is as good a way as any of tagging it. She ran a sort of school for choristers in London and had, I believe, some idea of training the poor boys of the city to sing in choirs. Her house was usually full of more or less musical youngsters. She was, also, something of a musical publisher and the organiser of a woman's musical association, whether for orchestral or choral music I am not quite certain. From this it will be seen that she was, at heart, a New Woman, although her activities were in a period that was still old-fashioned. If she were in her prime to-day, she would undoubtedly be a militant suffragette. She was also noted for the lawsuits in which she figured; one particular case dragging along into an unconscionable length of time and being much commented upon in the newspapers.

Gounod and she lived in Tavistock Place, in the house where Dickens lived so long and that is always associated with his name. On the occasion of our call, Mr. Jarrett and I were ushered into a study, much littered and crowded, to wait for the great man. It proved to be a somewhat long drawn-out wait, for the household seemed to be in a state of subdued turmoil. We could hear voices in the hall; some one was asking

16

about a music manuscript for the publishers. Suddenly, a woman flew into the room where we were sitting. She was unattractive and unkempt; she wore a rumpled and soiled kimono; her hair was much tousled; her bare feet were thrust into shabby bedroom slippers; and she did not look in the least as if she had had her bath. Indeed, I am expressing her appearance mildly and politely! She made a dive for the master's writing-table, gathered up some papers—sorting and selecting with lightning speed and an air of authority—and then darted out of the room as rapidly as she had entered. It was, of course, Mrs. Welldon, of whom I had heard so much and whom I had pictured as a fascinating woman. This is the nearest I ever came to meeting this person who was so conspicuous a figure of her day, although I have seen her a few other times. When dressed for the street she was most ordinary looking. Gounod was in the house, it developed, all the time that we waited, although he could not attend to us immediately. He was living like a recluse so far as active professional or social life was concerned, but he was a very busy man and beset with all manner of duties. When he at last came to us, he greeted us with characteristic French courtesy. His manners were exceedingly courtly. He was grey-haired, charming, and very quiet. I think he was really shy. With apologies, he opened his letters, and, while giving orders and hearing messages, a pretty incident occurred. A young girl, very graceful and sweet looking, came into the room. She hurried forward with a little, impulsive movement and, curtseying deeply to Gounod, seized one of his hands in both of hers and raised it to her lips.

"*Cher maître!*" she murmured adoringly, and flitted away, the master following her with a smiling glance.

It was Nita Giatano, an American, afterwards Mrs. Moncrieff, now the widow of an English officer, who was studying with Gounod and living there and who, later, became fairly well known as a singer. Then Gounod proceeded to say pleasant things about my *Marguerite* and was interested in hearing that I was planning to do *Mireille*. We then and there went over the music together and he gave me an annotated score of *Mireille* with his autograph and marginal directions. I treasured it for years afterwards; and a most tragic fate overtook it at last. I sent it to a book-binder to be bound, and, when the score came back, did not immediately look through it. It was some time later, indeed, that I opened it to show it off to someone to whom I had been speaking of the precious notes and autograph. I turned page after page—there were no notes. I looked at the title page—there was no signature. That wretched book-binder had not scrupled to substitute a new and valueless score for my beloved copy, and had doubtless sold the original, with Gounod's autograph and annotations, to some collector for a pretty sum. When I tried to hunt the man up, I found that he had gone out of business and moved away. He was not to be found and I have never been able to regain my score.

Mireille was not given for several years, as affairs turned out, and I rather congratulated myself that this was so, for it was not one of Gounod's best productions. I once met Mme. Gounod in Paris, or, rather, in its environs, at a garden party given at the Menier— the Chocolat Menier—place. She was a well-mannered, commonplace Frenchwoman, rather colourless and uninteresting. I came to understand that even Georgina Welldon, with her untidy kimono and her lawsuits, might have been more entertaining. I asked Gounod, on this occasion, to play some of the music of *Romeo and Juliette*. He did so and, at the end, said: "I see you like my children!"

Gounod was chiefly famous in London for the delightful recitals he gave from time to time of his own music. He had no voice, but he could render programmes of his own songs with great success. Everybody was enthusiastic over the beautiful and intricate accompaniments that were such a novelty. He was so splendid a musician that he could create a more charming effect without a voice than another man could have achieved with the notes of an angel. Poor Gounod, like nearly all creative genuises, had a great many bitter struggles before he obtained recognition. Count Fabri has told me that, while *Faust* (the opera which he sold for twelve hundred dollars) was running to packed houses and the whole world was applauding it, Gounod himself was really in need. His music publisher met him in the streets of Paris, wearing a wretched old hat and looking very seedy.

"Why on earth," cried the publisher, "don't you get a new hat?"

"I did not make enough on *Faust* to pay for one," was the bitter answer.

CHAPTER XXIII

THE SEASON WITH LUCCA

AFTER the London season and before returning to America we went to Switzerland for a brief holiday. During this little trip there occurred a pleasing and somewhat quaint incident. On the Grünewald Glacier we met a young Italian-Swiss mountaineer who earned his living by making echoes from the crags with a big horn and by the national art of yodeling. There was one particular echo which was the pride of the region and, the day we were exploring the glacier, he did not call it forth as well as usual. Although he tried several times, we could distinguish very little echo. Finally, acting on a sudden impulse, I stood up in our carriage and yodeled for him, ending with a long trill. The high, pure air exhilarated me and made me feel that I could do absolutely anything in the world with my voice, and I actually struck one or two of the highest and strongest notes that I ever sang in my life and one of the best trills. The echoes came rippling back to us with wonderful effect.

The young mountaineer took off his Tyrolean hat and bowed to me deeply.

"Ah, mademoiselle!" he said, "if I could call into being such an echo, my fortune here would be made!"

Our stay there was all too short to please me and the day soon came for us to start for home. We crossed on the *Cuba* of the Cunard Line, and a very poor steamer she was. It was not in the least an interesting trip. There was no social intercourse, because all the passengers were too seasick to talk or even to listen. It seemed to them like a personal affront for anyone not to succumb to *mal de mer*.

"You mean thing," one woman said to me, "why are n't you seasick!"

Our passenger list was, however, a somewhat striking one. Rubenstein and Wieniawski were on board and Clara Doria; Mark Smith, the actor; Edmund Yeats and Maddox, the editor whom I had known in London, and, of course, Pauline Lucca. She was registered as the Baroness von Raden and had her baby with her—the one generally believed to have a royal father—and, with her baby and her seasickness, was very much occupied. Her father and mother accompanied her. Lucca, as we know, had been a ballerina. Her toes were all twisted and deformed by her early years of dancing. She once showed them to me, a pitiful record of the triumphs of a ballet dancer. There was something of the ballerina in her temperament, also, which she never entirely outgrew. Certainly she was far from being a *prima donna* type. An irresistible sense of fun made her a most amusing companion; and her charm lay largely in her unexpectedness. One never could guess what she was going to do or say next. I recall an incident that occurred a little later in Chicago that illustrates this. A very handsome music critic—I will not mention his name—came behind the scenes one night to see us. He was a grave young man, with a brown beard and beautiful eyes, and his appearance gave a vague sense of familiarity as if we had seen it in some well-known picture. Yet I could not place

the resemblance. Lucca stood off at a little distance
studying him owlishly for a minute or two as he was
chatting to me in the wings. Presently she whisked
up to him with her brown eyes dancing and, looking
up at him in the drollest way, said laughingly:
"And how do you do, my Jesus Christ!"

On this voyage home I saw more or less of Edmund
Yeats who kept us amused with a steady flow of witty
talk and who kept up an equally steady flow of brandy
and soda, and of Maddox who was not seasick and was
willing to both walk and talk. Maddox was an interesting man, with many strange stories to tell of things and
people famous and well-known. Among other personalities we discussed Adelaide Neilson, whose real name,
by the way, was Mary Ann Rogers. I was speaking
of her refinement and pretty manners on the stage, her
gracious and yet unassuming fashion of accepting
applause, and her general air of good breeding, when
Maddox told me, to my great astonishment, that this
was more remarkable than I could possibly imagine
since the charming actress had come from the most
disadvantageous beginnings. She had, in fact, led a
life that is generally characterised as "unfortunate"
and it was while she was in this life that Maddox first
met her, and, finding the girl full of ambition and
aspirations toward something higher, had put her in
the way of cultivating herself and her talents. These
facts as told me by Maddox have always remained in
my mind, not in the least to Neilson's discredit, but
quite the reverse, for they only make her charming and
artistic achievements all the more admirable. I have
always enjoyed watching her. She was always just
diffident enough without being self-conscious. It used
to be pretty to see her from a box where I could look

at her behind the scenes compose herself before taking
a curtain call. She would slip into the mood of the
part that she had just been playing and that she wished
still to suggest to the audience. Which reminds me
that Henry Irving once told me that he and Miss Terry
did exactly this same thing. "We always try to keep
within the picture even after the act is over," he said.
"An actor should never take his call in his own character, but always in that which he has been personating."

On the whole the particular trip of which I am now
speaking stands out dominantly in my memory because
of Rubenstein. I never, never saw anyone so seasick,
nor anyone so completely depressed by the fact. Poor
creature! He swore, faintly, that he would never cross
the ocean again even to get home! Occasionally he
would talk feebly, but his spirit was completely broken.
I have not the faintest idea what Rubenstein was like
when he was not seasick. He may have sparkled con-
summately in a normal condition; but he did not sparkle
on the *Cuba*.

The Lucca-Kellogg season which followed was not a
comfortable one, but it netted us large receipts. The
work was arduous, the operas heavy, and the management was up to its ears in contentions and jealousies.
New York was in a musical fever during the early
seventies. We were just finding out how to be musical
and it was a great and pleasurable excitement. We
were pioneers, and enjoyed it, and were happy in not
being hide-bound by traditions as were the older
countries, because we had none. One of the season's
sensations was Senorita Sanz, a Spanish contralto,
whose voice was not unlike that of Adelaide Phillips.
She was a beautiful woman and a good actress, and,
above all, she had the true Spanish temperament,

languid, exotic and yet fiery. Her Azucena was a fine performance; and she created a tremendous *furore* with La Paloma, which was then a novelty. She used to sing it at Sunday night concerts and set the audiences wild with:

Cuan-do...... sa - li de lo Ha-ba-na Vál-ga-me Dios !

Lucca's operas for the season were *Faust, Traviata, L'Africaine, Fra Diavolo* and *La Figlia del Regimento.* Mine were *Trovatore, Traviata, Crispano, Linda* and *Martha,* and *Don Giovanni.* It was to Lucca's *Zerlina* that I first sang Donna Anna in *Don Giovanni;* and, as in the big concert at the Coliseum my friends had felt some doubts as to the carrying power of my voice, so now many persons expected the *rôle* to be too heavy for me. But I believe I succeeded in proving the contrary. When we did *Le Nozze di Figaro,* Lucca was the Cherubino, making the quaintest looking of boys and much resembling one of Raphael's cherubs in his painting of the *Sistine Madonna.*

Personally, the relations between Lucca and myself were always amicable enough; but we had certain professional frictions, brought about, indeed, by Jarrett who, although he was nothing but an agent and an indifferent one at that, was generally regarded as an authority, and gave out critiques to the newspapers. It so happened that, without my knowledge, the monopoly of singing in *Faust* was in her contract and I was so prevented from singing Marguerite once during our entire engagement. As Marguerite was my *rôle* pre-eminently, by right of conquest, in America, I felt very hurt and angry about the matter and, at first, wanted to resign from the company, but, of course, was talked out of that attitude. Jarrett would not, however, consent to my even alternating with Lucca in the part; but possibly he was wise in this as Marguerite was never one of her best personations. She played a very impulsive and un-German Gretchen, in spite of herself, being an Austrian by birth. One of the newspapers said that "she fell in love with Faust at first sight and the Devil was a useless article!" Her characterisation of the part was somewhat devilish in itself; her work was striking, effective, and *piquant*, but not touched by much distinction. The difference between our presentations was said to be that I "convinced by a refined perfection of detail" and Lucca by more vivid qualities. Indeed, our voices and methods were so dissimilar that we never felt any personal rivalry, whatever the critics said to the contrary. As one man justly expressed it: "Neither Lucca nor Kellogg has the talent for quarrelling." There were, of course, rival factions in our public. A man one night sent a note behind the scenes to me containing this message: "Poor Kellogg! you have no chance at all with Lucca!" Two days later Mme. Lucca came to me laughing and said that some one had asked her: "How do you dare to sing on the same bill with Miss Kellogg, the American favourite?"

So interesting did our supposed rivalry become, however, as to excite considerable newspaper comment. In reply to one of these in *The Chicago Tribune* a contributor answered:

To the Editor of The Chicago Tribune:

SIR: In your issue of this morning, there is an editorial headed "Operatic Failure," which is, in some respects, so unjust and one-sided as to call for an immediate protest

Newspaper Print of the Kellogg-Lucca Season

Drawn by Jos. Keppler

against its injustice. Having taken your ideas from *The New York Herald*, and having no other source of information, it is not to be wondered at that you should fall into error. For reasons best known to Mr. James Gordon Bennett, *The New York Herald*, since the commencement of the Jarrett-Maretzek season, has undertaken to write up Madame Lucca at the expense of every other artist connected with the troupe; and it is because of *The Herald's* fulsome laudations of Lucca, and its outrageously untruthful criticisms of Kellogg, that much of the trouble has occurred. Of the two ladies, Kellogg is by far the superior singer. Lucca has much dramatic force, but, in musical culture, is not equal to her sister artist, and there is no jealousy on the part of either lady of the other. The facts are these: The management, taking their cue from *The Herald*, and being afraid of the power of Mr. Bennett, tried to shelve Kellogg, and the result has been that the dear public would not permit the injustice, and they, the managers, as well as *The Herald*, are amazed and angered at the result of their dirty work.

OPERA.

Chicago, Oct. 28, 1872.

Lucca and I gave *Mignon* that season together, she playing the part of Mignon and I that of Felina, the cat. Mignon was always a favourite part of my own, a sympathetic *rôle* filled with poetry and sentiment. When I first studied it, I most carefully read *Wilhelm Meister*, upon which it is founded. Regarding the part of Felina, I have often wondered that people have never been more perceptive than they appear to have been of the analogy between her name and her qualities, for she has all of the characteristics of the feline species. Our dual star bill in the opera was highly successful and effective in spite of Jarrett's continual attacks upon me through the press and in every way open to him.

He did me a particularly cruel turn about Felina. I started off in the *rôle*, the opening night, in what I still believe to have been the correct interpretation. *Wilhelm Meister* was set in a finicky period and its characters wore white wigs and minced about in their actions. My part was all comedy and the gestures should have been little and dainty and somewhat constrained. So I played it, until I saw this criticism, written by one of Jarrett's creatures, "Miss Kellogg has no freedom of movement in the *rôle* of Felina, etc."

My mother, always anxious for me to profit by criticism that might have value, said that perhaps the man was right. At any rate, between the two, I became so self-conscious that the next time I sang Felina I could not get into the mood of it at all. Not to seem restricted in gesture, I waved my arms as if I were in *Norma;* and the performance was a very poor one in consequence. Yet, in spite of Jarrett's machinations, it was said of me in the press of the day:

". . . Her rendering of Felina was a magnificent success. From the first scene on the balcony until her light-hearted laughter dies away, she is a vision of beauty and grace, appealing to every high æsthetic emotion and charming all hearts with her sweetness."

Furthermore, an eminent Shakespearean critic, writing then, said:

As an actress, Miss Kellogg's superiority cannot justly be questioned. Some things are exquisitely represented by the fair Swede, Miss Nilsson, such as the dazed look, the stupefaction caused by a great shock, like that of the death of Valentin, for instance; such as the madness to which the distracting conflict of many selfish feelings and passions leads. But she is always circumscribed by her own con-

Clara Louise Kellogg in *Mignon*
From a photograph by Mora

sciousness. Her soul never passes beyond that limit—
never surrounds her—filling the stage and infecting the
audience with a magnetic atmosphere which is a part of
herself, or herself transfused, if such expressions be allow-
able. In this respect Miss Kellogg is very different and
greatly superior. Her sympathies are large. She con-
ceives well the effects of the warmer and more generous
passions upon the person who feels them. She can, by the
force of her imagination, abandon herself to these influences,
and, by her artistic skill, give them apt expression. She
can cease to be self-conscious, and feel but the fictitious
consciousness of the personage whom she represents, while
the force of her own illusion magnetises her auditors till
they respond like well-tuned harps to every chord of
feeling which she strikes.

Such notices, such critiques, were compensations!
Taken as a whole, Felina was a successful part for me;
largely on account of that piece of glittering generalities,
the Polonaise. In this, according to one critic, "she
aroused the admiration of her auditors to a condition
that was really a tempestuous *furore*." So, as I say,
there were compensations for Jarrett's unkindnesses.

CHAPTER XXIV

ENGLISH OPERA

THE idea of giving opera in English has always interested me. I never could understand why there were any more reasons against giving an English version of *Carmen* in New York than against giving a French version of *Die Freischütz* in Paris or a German version of *La Belle Helène* in Berlin. To be sure, it goes without saying, from a purist point of view it is a patent truth, that no libretto is ever so fine after it has been translated. Not only does the quality and spirit of the original evaporate in the process of translating, but, also, the syllables come wrong. Who has not suffered from the translations of foreign songs into which the translator has been obliged to introduce secondary notes to fit the extra syllables of the clumsily adapted English words? These are absolute objections to the performance of any operas or songs in a language other than the one to which the composer first set his music. Wagner in French is a joke; so is Goethe in Italian. A musician of my acquaintance once spoke of Strauss's *Salome* as a case in point, although it is a queerly inverse one. "Oscar Wilde's French poem or play—whichever you like to call it—" he said, "was translated into German; and it was this translation, or so it is generally understood, that Strauss set to music. When the opera—a French opera in spirit, taken from a

254

French text that was most Frenchly treated—was
given with Oscar Wilde's original French words, the
music often seemed to go haltingly, as though it had
been adopted to phrases for which it had not been composed." Several notable singers have recently entered
a protest against giving opera in English. Miss Garden
—admirable and spontaneous artist though she be—
once wrote an article in which she cited *Madame Butter-
fly* as an example of the inartistic effects of English
librettos. I do not recall her exact words, but they
referred to the scene in which Dick Pinkerton offers
Sharpless a whiskey and soda. Miss Garden said, If I
remember correctly, that the very words "whiskey and
soda" were inartistic and spoiled the poetry and picturesqueness of the act. Personally, I do not see that it was
the words that were inartistic, but, rather, the introduction of whiskey and soda at all into a grand opera. My
point is that such objections obtain not more strin-
gently against English translations than against German, French, or Italian translations. Furthermore,
after all is said that can be said against translations
into whatsoever language, the fact remains that countries and races are not nearly so different as they
pretend to be; and a human sentiment, a dramatic
situation, or a lovely melody will permeate the consciousness of a Frenchman, an Englishman, or a German
in approximately the same manner and in the same
length of time. Adaptations and translations are
merely different means, poorer or better as the case
may be, of facilitating such assimilations; and, so soon
as the idea reaches the audience, the audience is going
to receive it joyfully, no matter what nation it comes
from or through what medium:—that is, if it is a good
idea to begin with.

Possibly this may be a little beside the point; but, at least, it serves to introduce the subject of English opera—or, rather, foreign grand opera given in English —the giving of which was an undertaking on which I embarked in 1873. I became my own manager and, with C. D. Hess, organised an English Opera Company that, by its success, brought the best music to the comprehension of the intelligent masses. I believe that the enterprise did much for the advancement of musical art in this country; and it, besides, gave employment to a large number of young Americans, several of whom began their careers in the chorus of the company and soon advanced to higher places in the musical world. Joseph Maas was one of the singers whom this company did much for; and George Conly was another. The former at first played small parts, but his chance came to him as Lorenzo in *Fra Diavolo*, when he made a big hit, and, eventually, he returned to England and became her greatest oratorio tenor. I myself made the versions of the standard operas used by us during the first season of English opera, translating them newly and directly from the Italian and the French and, in some instances, restoring the text to a better condition than is found in English opera generally. My enterprise met with a great deal of criticism and discussion. Usually, public opinion and the opinion of the press were favourable. One of my staunch supporters was Will Davis, the husband of Jessie Bartlett Davis. In *The Chicago Tribune* he wrote:

Unless the public can understand what is sung in opera or oratorio recital, song or ballad, no more than a passing interest can be awakened in the music-loving public. I do not agree with those who claim that language or thought is a secondary consideration to the enjoyment of vocal music. I believe that a superior writer of lyrics can fit words to the music of foreign operas that will not only be sensible but singable. I agree with *The Tribune* that opera in the English language has never had a fair show, but I claim that the reason for this is because of the bad translations that have been given to the artists to sing.

After our success had become assured, one of the press notices read:

Never, in this country, has English opera been so creditably produced and so energetically managed as by the present Kellogg-Hess combination. All the business details being supervised by Mr. Hess, one of the longest-headed and hardest-working men of business to be found in even this age and nation, are thoroughly, systematically and promptly attended to; while all the artistic details, being under the direct personal care of Miss Clara Louise Kellogg, confessedly the best as well as the most popular singer America has produced, are brought to and preserved at the highest attainable musical standard. The performers embraced in the Hess-Kellogg English Opera Company comprise several artists of the first rank. The names of Castle, Maas, Peakes, Mrs. Seguin, Mrs. Van Zandt, and Miss Montague are familiar as household words to the musical world, while the *répertoire* embraces not only all the old established favourites of the public, but many of the most recent or *recherche* novelties, such as *Mignon*, and *The Star of the North*, in addition to such genuine English operas as *The Rose of Castille*.

During the three seasons of our English Opera Company, we put on a great number of operas of all schools, from *The Bohemian Girl* to *The Flying Dutchman*. The former is pretty poor stuff—cheap and insipid—I never liked to sing it. But—the houses it drew! People

17

loved it. I believe there would be a large and sentimental public ready for it to-day. Its extraneous matter,
the two or three popular ballads that had been introduced, formed a part of its attraction, perhaps. Our
Devil's Hoof in *The Bohemian Girl* was Ted Seguin
who became quite famous in the part. His wife Zelda
Seguin was our contralto and they were among the
earliest people to travel with *The Beggar's Opera* and
other primitive performances. George A. Conly was
our basso and a fine one. He was a printer by trade and
he had his first chance with us at the Globe Theatre in
Boston. He was our Deland, too, in *The Flying Dutchman*. Eventually, he was drowned; and I gave a benefit
for his widow. Maurice Grau and Hess had gone to
London to engage singers for my English Opera Company and had selected, among others, Wilfred Morgan
for first tenor and Joseph Maas for second tenor.
Morgan had been singing secondary *rôles* for some time
at Covent Garden. On our opening night of *Faust* he
gave out with a sore throat, and Maas took his place
successfully. William Carlton once told me that when
he was just starting out he bought the theatrical
wardrobe of Alberto Lawrence, a baritone, and was
looking at himself in a mirror, dressed in one of his
second costumes, in the green room of the Academy of
Music early during our English season, when Morgan
came up to him and said:

"Are you going on in those old rags?"

Carlton had to go on in them. The critics next day
gave him a couple of columns of praise; but Morgan,
whose wardrobe was gorgeous, was a complete failure
in his *début*. Our manager had finally to tell him that
he could be second tenor or resign. In six weeks he was
drawing seventy dollars less salary than Carlton, who

was a baritone and a beginner. Carlton said that about this time Wilfred Morgan came up to him exclaiming,

"Well, Bill, I wish I had your voice and you had my clothes!"

William Carlton was a young Englishman, only twenty-three when he joined us; but he was already married and had two children. When we were rehearsing *The Bohemian Girl*, in the scene where the stolen daughter is recognised and Carlton had to take me in his arms, he said:

"I ought to kiss you here."

"Not lower than *this!*" said I, pointing to my forehead. He was much amused. Indeed, he was always laughing at my mother and me for our prudish ways; and my not marrying was always a joke between us.

"It 's a sin," he declared once, when we were talking on a train, "a woman who would make such a perfect wife!"

"Louise," interrupted my mother sternly, "don't talk so much! You 'll tire your voice!"

My good mother! She was always ruffling up like an indignant hen about me. In one scene of another opera, I remember, the villain and I had been playing rather more strenuously than usual and he caught my arm with some force. I staggered a little as I came off the stage and my mother flew at him.

"Don't you dare touch my daughter so roughly," she cried, much annoyed.

Mr. Carlton has paid me a nice tribute when writing of those days and of me at that time. He has said:

I have the most grateful memory of the sympathetic assistance I received from the gifted *prima donna* when I arrived in this country under the management of Maurice Grau and C. D. Hess, who were conducting the business details of the Kellogg Grand Opera Company. Like many Englishmen, I was quite unprepared for the evidences of perfection which characterised the production of opera in the United States and, as I had not yet attained my twenty-fourth year, I was somewhat awed by the importance of the *rôles* and the position I was imported to fulfil. It was in a great measure due to the gracious help I received from Miss Kellogg that, at my *début* at the Academy of Music, Philadelphia, as Valentine in *Faust* to her Marguerite, I achieved a success which led up to my renewing the engagement for four consecutive years.

In putting on grand opera in English I had, in each case, the tradition of two countries to contend with; but I endeavoured to secure some uniformity of style and usually rehearsed them all myself, sitting at the piano. The singers were, of course, hide-bound to the awful translations that were institutional and to them inevitable. None of them would have ever considered changing a word, even for the better. The translation of *Mignon* was probably the most completely revolutionary of the many translations and adaptations I indulged in. I shall never forget one fearfully clumsy passage in *Trovatore*.

> "To the handle,
> To the handle,
> To the handle
> Strike the dagger!"

There were two modifications possible, either of which was vastly preferable, and without actually changing a word.

> "Strike the dagger,
> Strike the dagger,
> Strike the dagger
> To the handle!"

or, which I think was the better way,

> "Strike the dagger
> To the handle,
> Strike the dagger
> To the handle!"

a simple and legitimate repetition of a phrase. This is a case in illustration of the meaningless absurdity and unintelligibility of the average libretto.

Those were the days in which I devoutly appreciated my general sound musical training. The old stand-bys, *Fra Diavolo*, *Trovatore*, and *Martha* were all very well. Most singers had been reared on them from their artistic infancy. But, for example, *The Marriage of Figaro* was an innovation. To it I had to bring my best experience and judgment as cultivated in our London productions; and we finally gave a very creditable English performance of it. Then there were, besides, the new operas that had to be incepted and created and toiled over:—*The Talisman* and *Lily o'Killarney* among others. *The Talisman* by Balfe, an opera of the Meyerbeerian school, was first produced at the Drury Lane in London, with Nilsson, Campanini, Marie Roze, Rota, and others. Our presentation of it was less pretentious, naturally, but we had an excellent cast, with Joseph Maas as Sir Kenneth, William Carlton as Cœur de Lion, Mme. Loveday as Queen Berengaria, and Charles Turner as De Vaux. I was Edith Plantaganet. When the opera was first put on in London, under the direction of Sir Jules Benedict, it was called *The Knight of the Leopard*. Later, it was translated into Italian under the title of *Il Talismano*, and from that finally re-translated by us and given the name of Sir Walter Scott's work on which it was based. It was not only

Balfe's one real grand opera, but was also his last important work. *Lily o'Killarney*, by Sir Jules Benedict, was not a striking novelty. It had a graceful duet for the basso and tenor, and one pretty solo for the *prima donna*—"I'm Alone"—but, otherwise, it did not amount to much. But we scored in it because of our good artistry. Our company was a good one. Parepa Rosa did tremendous things with her English opera *tournées;* but I honestly think our work was more artistic as well as more painstaking. There were not many of us; but we did our best and pulled together; and I was very happy in the whole venture. Benedict's *Lily o'Killarney* was written particularly for me, and was inspired by *Colleen Bawn*, Dion Boucicault's big London success. I have always understood that Oxenford wrote the libretto of that—a fine one as librettos go—but Grove's Dictionary says that Boucicault helped him.

Perhaps this is as good a place as any in which to mention Sir George Grove and his dictionary. When I was in London I was told that young Grove—he was not "Sir" then—was compiling a dictionary; and, not having a very exalted idea of his ability, I am free to confess that, in a measure, I snubbed him. In his copiously filled and padded dictionary, he punished me by giving me less than half a column; considerably less space than is devoted in the corresponding column to one Michael Kelly "composer of wines and importer of music!" It is an accurate paragraph, however, and he heaped coals of fire on my head by one passage that is particularly suitable to quote in a chapter on English opera:

She organised an English troupe, herself superintending the translation of the words, the *mise en scène*, the training

of the singers and the rehearsals of the chorus. Such was
her devotion to the project that, in the winter of '74-'75,
she sang no fewer than one hundred and twenty-five nights.
It is satisfactory to hear that the scheme was successful.
Miss Kellogg's musical gifts are great . . . She has a
remarkable talent for business and is never so happy as
when she is doing a good or benevolent action.

I have never been able to determine to my own
satisfaction whether the "remarkable talent for business" was intended as a compliment or not! The one
hundred and twenty-five record is quite correct, a
number of performances that tried my endurance to
the utmost; but I loved all the work. This particular
venture seemed more completely my own than anything
on which I had yet embarked.

We put on *The Flying Dutchman*, at the Academy of
Music (New York), and it was a tremendous undertaking. It was another case of not having any traditions
nor impressions to help us. No one knew anything
about the opera and the part of Senta was as unexplored a territory for me as that of Marguerite had
been. One thing I had particular difficulty in learning
how to handle and that was Wagner's trick of long
pauses. There is a passage almost immediately after
the spinning song in *The Flying Dutchman* during which
Senta stands at the door and thinks about the Flying
Dutchman, preceding his appearance. Then he comes,
and they stand still and look at each other while a spell
grows between them. She recognises Vanderdecken
as the original of the mysterious portrait; and he is
wondering whether she is the woman fated to save him
by self-sacrifice. The music, so far as Siegfried Behrens,
my director at the time, and I could see, had no meaning whatever. It was just a long, intermittent mumble,

continuing for eighteen bars with one slight interruption of thirds. I had not yet been entirely converted to innovations such as this and did not fully appreciate the value of so extreme a pause. I knew, of course, that repose added dignity; but this seemed too much.

"For heaven's sake, Behrens," said I, "what's the public going to do while we stand there? Can we hold their interest for so long while nothing is happening?"

Behrens thought there might be someone at the German Theatre who had heard the opera in Germany and who could, therefore, give us suggestions; but no one could be found. Finally Behrens looked up Wagner's own brochure on the subject of his operas and came to me, still doubtful, but somewhat reassured.

"Wagner says," he explained, "not to be disturbed by long intervals. If both singers could stand absolutely still, this pause would hold the public double the length of time."

We tried to stand "absolutely still." It was an exceedingly difficult thing to do. In *rôles* that have tense moments the whole body has to hold the tension rigidly until the proper psychological instant for emotional and physical relaxation. The public is very keen to feel this, without knowing how or why. A drooping shoulder or a relaxed hand will "let up" an entire situation. The first time I sang Senta it seemed impossible to hold the pause until those eighteen bars were over. "I have *got* to hold it! I have *got* to hold it!" I kept saying to myself, tightening every muscle as if I were actually pulling on a wire stretched between myself and the audience. I almost auto-hypnotised myself; which probably helped me to understand the Norwegian girl's own condition of auto-hypnotism! An inspiration led me to grasp the back of a tall Dutch chair on the stage. That chair helped me greatly and, as affairs turned out, I held the audience quite as firmly as I held the chair!

Afterwards I learned the wonderful telling-power of these "waits" and the great dignity that they lend to a scene. There is no hurry in Wagner. His work is full of pauses and he has done much to give leisure to the stage. When I was at Bayreuth—that most beautiful monument to genius—I met many actors from the Théâtre Français who had journeyed there, as to a Mecca, to study this leisurely stage effect among others.

Our production was a fair one but not elaborate. We had, I remember, a very good ship, but there were many shortcomings. There is supposed to be a transfiguration scene at the end in which Senta is taken up to heaven; but this was beyond us and *I* was never thus rewarded for my devotion to an ideal! I liked Senta's clothes and make-up. I used to wear a dark green skirt, shining chains, and a wonderful little apron, long and of white woollen. For hair, I wore Marguerite's wig arranged differently. I should like to be able to put on a production of *Die Fliegende Holländer* now! There is just one artist, and only one, whom I would have play the Dutchman—and that is Renaud, for the reason, principally, that he would have the necessary repose for the part. I had understudies as a matter of course. One of them was wall-eyed; and, on an occasion when I was ill, she essayed Senta. William Carlton, was, as usual, our Dutchman, and he had not been previously warned of Senta's infirmity. He came upon it so unexpectedly, indeed, and it was so startling to him, that he sang the whole opera without looking at her for fear that he would break down!

CHAPTER XXV

ENGLISH OPERA (*Continued*)

NO account of our English Opera would be complete without mention of Mike. He was an Irish lad with all the wit of his race, and his head was of a particularly classic type. He was only sixteen when he joined us, but he became an institution, and I kept track of him for years afterwards. His duties were somewhat arbitrary, and chiefly consisted of calling at the dressing-room of the chorus each night after the opera with a basket to collect the costumes. Beyond this, his principal occupation was watching my scenes and generally pervading the performances with genuine interest. He particularly favoured the third act of *Faust*, I remember; and absolutely considered himself a part of my career, constantly making use of the phrase "Me and Miss Kellogg."

One of the operas we gave in English was my old friend *The Star of the North*. It was quite as much a success in English as it had been in the original. We chose it for our *gala* performance in Washington when the Centennial was celebrated, and my good friends, President and Mrs. Grant, were in the audience. The King of Hawaii was also present, with his suite, and came behind the scenes and paid me extravagant compliments. His Hawaiian Majesty sent me lovely heliotropes, I remember,—my favourite flower and my

favourite perfume. At one performance of *The Star of
the North* at a matinée in Booth's Theatre, New York,
there occurred an incident that was reminiscent of my
London experience with Sir Michael Costa's orchestra.
It was in the third act, the camp scene. There is a
quartette by Peter, Danilowitz and two *vivandières*
almost without accompaniment in the tent on the stage,
and I, as Catherine, had to take up the note they left
and begin a solo at its close. The orchestra was supposed to chime in with me, a simple enough matter to do
if they had not fallen from the key. It is surprising
how relative one's pitch is when suddenly appealed to.
Even a very trained ear will often go astray when some
one gives it a wrong keynote. Music more than almost
any other art is dependent; every tone hangs on other
tones. That particular quartette was built on a musical
phrase begun by one of the sopranos and repeated by
each. She started on the key. The mezzo took it up a
shade flat. The tenor, taking the phrase from the mezzo,
dropped a little more, and when the basso got through
with it, they were a full semitone lower. Had I taken
my *attaque* from their pitch, imagine the situation when
the orchestra came in! My heart sank as I saw ahead
of us the inevitable discord. It came to the last note. I
allowed a half-second of silence to obliterate their false
pitch. Then I *concentrated*—and took up my solo in the
original and correct key. That "absolute pitch" again!
Behrens expressed his amazement after the curtain fell.

The company, after that, was never tired of experimenting with my gift. It became quite a joke with
them to cry out suddenly, at any sort of sound—a
whistle, or a bell:

"Now, what note is that? What key was that in,
Miss Kellogg?"

Most of our travelling on these big western tours of opera was very tiresome, although we did it as easily as we could and often had special cars put at our disposal by railroad directors. We were still looked upon as a species of circus and the townspeople of the places we passed through used to come out in throngs at the stations. I have said so much about the poor hotels encountered at various times while on the road that I feel I ought to mention the disastrous effect produced once by a really good hotel. It was at the end of our first English Opera season and, in spite of the fact that we were all worn out with our experiences, we proceeded to give an auxiliary concert trip. We had a special sleeper in which, naturally, no one slept much; and by the time we reached Wilkesbarre we were even more exhausted. The hotel happened to be a good one, the rooms were quiet, and the beds comfortable. Every one of us went promptly to bed, not having to sing until the next night, and William Carlton left word at the office that he was going to sleep: "and don't call me unless there's a fire!" he said. In strict accordance with these instructions nobody did call him and he slept twenty-four hours. When he awoke it was time to go to the theatre for the performance and—he found he couldn't sing! He had slept so much that his circulation had become sluggish and he was as hoarse as a crow. Consequently, we had to change the programme at the last moment.

Carlton, like most nervous people, was very sensitive and easily put out of voice, even when he had not slept twenty-four consecutive hours. Once in *Trovatore* he was seized with a sharp neuralgic pain in his eyes just as he was beginning to sing "Il Balen" and we had to stop in the middle of it. During this same performance, an unlucky one, Wilfred Morgan, who was Manrico, made both himself and me ridiculous. In the *finale* of the first act of the opera, the Count and Manrico, rivals for the love of Leonora, draw their swords and are about to attack each other, when Leonora interposes and has to recline on the shoulder of Manrico, at which the attack of the Count ceases. Morgan was burly of build and awkward of movement and, for some reason, failed to support me, and we both fell heavily to the floor. It is so easy to turn a serious dramatic situation into ridicule that, really, it was very decent indeed of our audience to applaud the *contretemps* instead of laughing.

Ryloff, an eccentric Belgian, was our musical director for a short time. He was exceedingly fond of beer and used to drink it morning, noon, and night,— especially night. Even our rehearsals were not sacred from his thirst. In the middle of one of our full dress rehearsals he suddenly stopped the orchestra, laid down his baton, and said to the men:

"Boys, I *must* have some beer!"

Then he got up and deliberately went off to a nearby saloon while we awaited his good pleasure.

I have previously mentioned what a handsome and dashing Fra Diavolo Theodore Habelmann was, and naturally other singers with whom I sang the opera later have suffered by comparison. In discussing the point with a young girl cousin who was travelling with me, we once agreed, I remember, that it was a great pity no one could ever look the part like our dear old Habelmann. Castle was doing it just then, and doing it very well except for his clothes and general make-up. But he was so extremely sensitive and yet, in some ways, so opinionated, that it was impossible to tell him plainly that he did not look well in the part. At last, my cousin conceived the brilliant scheme of writing him an anonymous letter, supposed to be from some feminine admirer, telling him how splendid and wonderful and irresistible he was, but also suggesting how he could make himself even more fascinating. A description of Habelmann's appearance followed and, to our great satisfaction, our innocent little plot worked to a charm. Castle bought a new costume immediately and strutted about in it as pleased as Punch. He really did present a much more satisfactory appearance, which was a comfort to me, as it is really so deplorably disillusioning to see a man looking frumpy and unattractive while he is singing a gallant song like:

Proud - ly   and   wide.... my   stand - ard

flies   O'er dar - ing heads, a   no - ble band!

Naturally these tours brought me all manner of adventures that I have long since forgotten—little incidents "along the road" and meetings with famous personages. Among them stand out two experiences, one grave and one gay. The former was an occasion when I went behind the scenes during a performance of *Henry VIII* to see dear Miss Cushman (it must have been in the early seventies, but I do not know the exact date), who was playing Queen Katherine. She asked me if I would be kind enough to sing the solo for her. I was very glad to be able to do so, of course, and so, on the spur of the moment, complied.

I have wondered since how many people in front ever knew that it was I who sang *Angels Ever Bright and Fair* off stage, during the scene in which the poor, wonderful Queen was dying! The other experience of these days which I treasure was my meeting with Eugene Field. It was in St. Louis, where Field was a reporter on one of the daily papers. He came up to the old Lindell Hotel to interview me; but that was something I would *not* do—give interviews to the press—so my mother went down to the reception room with her sternest air to dismiss him. She found the waiting young man very mild-mannered and pleasant, but she said to him icily:

"My daughter never sees newspaper men."

"Oh," said he, looking surprised, "I'm a singer and I thought Miss Kellogg might help me. I want to have my voice trained." (This is the phrase used generally by applicants for such favours.) Mother looked at the young man suspiciously and pointed to the piano.

"Sing something," she commanded.

Field obediently sat down at the instrument and sang several songs. He had a pleasing voice and an expressive style of singing, and my mother promptly sent for me. We spent some time with him in consequence, singing, playing, and talking. It was an excellent "beat" for his paper, and neither my mother nor I bore him any malice, we had liked him so much, when we read the interview next day. After that he came to see me whenever I sang where he happened to be and we always had a laugh over his "interview" with me—the only one, by the way, obtained by any reporter in St. Louis.

On one concert tour—a little before the English

Opera venture—we had arrived late one afternoon in Toledo where the other members of the company were awaiting me. Petrelli, the baritone, met me at the train and said immediately:

"There is a strange-looking girl at the hotel waiting for you to hear her sing."

"Oh, dear," I exclaimed, "another one to tell that she has n't any ability!"

"She 's *very* queer looking," Petrelli assured me.

As I went to my supper I caught a glimpse of a very unattractive person and decided that Petrelli was right. She was exceedingly plain and colourless, and had a large turned-up nose. After supper, I went to my room to dress, as I usually did when on tour, for the theatre dressing-rooms were impossible, and presently there was a knock at the door and the girl presented herself.

She was poorly clad. She owned no warm coat, no rubbers, no proper clothing of any sort. I questioned her and she told me a pathetic tale of privation and struggle. She lived by travelling about from one hotel to the next, singing in the public parlour when the manager would permit it, accompanying herself upon her guitar, and passing around a plate or a hat afterwards to collect such small change as she could.

"I sang last night here," she told me, "and the manager of the hotel collected eleven dollars. That 's all I 've got—and I don't suppose he 'll let me have much of that!"

Of course I, who had been so protected, was horrified by all this. I could not understand how a girl could succeed in doing that kind of thing. She told me, furthermore, that she took care of her mother, brothers, and sisters.

"I must go to the post-office now and see if there 's a letter from mother!" she exclaimed presently, jumping up. It was pouring rain outside.

"Show me your feet!" I said.

She grinned ruefully as she exhibited her shoes, but she was off the next moment in search of her letter. When she came back to the hotel, I got hold of her again, gave her some clothes, and took her to the concert in my carriage. After I had sung my first song she rushed up to me.

"Let me look down your throat," she cried excitedly, "I 've got to see where it all comes from!"

After the concert we made her sing for us and our accompanist played for her. She asked me frankly if I thought she could make her living by her voice and I said yes. Her poverty and her desire to get on naturally appealed to me, and I was instrumental in raising a subscription for her so that she could come East. My mother immediately saw the hotel proprietor and arranged that what money he had collected the night before should be turned over to her. It has been said that I am responsible for Emma Abbott's career upon the operatic stage, but I may be pardoned if I deny the allegation. My idea was that she intended to sing in churches, and I believe she did so when she first came to New York. She was the one girl in ten thousand who was really worth helping, and of course my mother and I helped her. When we returned from my concert tour, I introduced her to people and saw that she was properly looked out for. And she became, as every one knows, highly successful in opera—appearing in many of my own *rôles*. In a year's time from when I first met her, Emma Abbott was self-supporting. She was a girl of ability and I am glad that I started her off fairly,

18

although, as a matter of fact, she would have got on anyway, whether I had done anything for her or not. Her way to success might have been a longer way, unaided, but she would have succeeded. She was eaten up with ambition. Yet there is much to respect in such a dogged determination to succeed. Of course, she was never particularly grateful to *me*. Of all the girls I have helped—and there have been many—only one has ever been really grateful, and she was the one for whom I did the least. Emma wrote me a flowery letter once, full of such sentences as "when the great *Prima Donna* shined on me," and "I was almost in heaven, and I can remember just how you sang and looked," and "never can I forget all your goodness to me." But in the little ways that count she never actually evinced the least appreciation. Whenever we were in any way pitted against each other, she showed herself jealous and ungenerous. She made enemies in general by her lack of tact, and never could get on in London, for instance, although in her day the feeling there for American singers was becoming most kindly.

Emma Abbott did appalling things with her art, of which one of the mildest was the introduction into *Faust* of the hymn *Nearer My God to Thee!* It was in Italy that she did it, too. I believe she introduced it to please the Americans in the audience, many of whom applauded, although the Italians pointedly did not. And yet she was always trying to "purify" the stage and librettos! I have always felt about Emma Abbott that she had *too much* force of character. Another thing that I never liked about her was the manner in which she puffed her own successes. She was reported to have made five times more than she actually did; but, at that, her earnings were considerable, for she would sacrifice much—except the character—to money-getting. Indeed, she was a very fine business woman.

I have spoken about George Conly's tragic death by drowning and of the benefit the Kellogg-Hess English Opera Company gave for his widow. Conly had also sung with Emma Abbott and, when the benefit was given, she and I appeared on the same programme. She knew my baritone, Carlton, and sent for him before the performance. She explained that she wanted him to appear on the bill with her in *Maritana* and, also, to see that all donations from my friends and colleagues were sent to her, so that her collection should be larger than mine. Carlton explained to her that he was singing with Miss Kellogg and so would send any money that he could collect to her. It seems incredible that any one could do so small an action, and I can only consider it one of many little attempts to be spiteful and to show me that my erstwhile *protégée* was now at the "top of the ladder."

Her thirst for profits finally was the indirect means of her death. When Utah was still a territory, the town of Ogden, where many travelling companies gave concerts, was very primitive. The concert hall had no dressing-room and was cold and draughty. I always refused outright to sing in such theatres, or else dressed in my hotel and drove to the concert warmly wrapped up. Emma Abbott was warned that the stage in the concert hall of the town of Ogden was bitterly cold. The house had sold well, however, and the receipts were considerable. Emma dressed in an improvised screened-off dressing-room, and, having a severe cold to begin with, she caught more on that occasion, and suddenly developed a serious case of pneumonia from which she died, a victim to her own indiscretion.

CHAPTER XXVI

AMATEURS—AND OTHERS

IN the seventies New York was interesting musically, chiefly because of its amateurs. This sounds something like a paradox, but at that time New York had a collection of musical amateurs who were almost as highly cultivated as professionals. It was a set that was extremely interesting and quite unique; and which bridged in a wonderful way the traditional gulf between art and society.

Those of us who were fortunate enough to know New York then look about us with wonder and amazement now. It seems, with our standards of an earlier generation, as if there were no true social life to-day, just as there are left no great social leaders. As for music—but perhaps it behooves a retired *prima donna* to be discreet in making comparisons.

Mrs. Peter Ronalds; Mrs. Samuel Barlow; her daughter Elsie, who became Mrs. Stephen Henry Olin; May Callender; Minnie Parker—the granddaughter of Mrs. Hill and later the wife of M. de Neufville;—these and many others were the amateurs who combined music and society in a manner worthy of the great French hostesses and originators of *salons*. Mrs. Barlow was in advance of everybody in patronising music. She was cultivated and artistic, had travelled a great deal abroad, and had acquired a great many charming foreign graces in addition to her own good American brains and breeding, and her fine natural social tact. When I returned to New York after a sojourn on the other side, she came to see me one day, and said:

"Louise, you 've been away so much you don't know what our amateurs are doing. I want you to come to my house to-night and hear them sing."

Like all professionals, I was a bit inclined to turn up my nose at the very word "amateur," but of course I went to Mrs. Barlow's that evening, and I have rarely spent a more enjoyable three hours. Elsie Barlow sang delightfully. She had a limited voice, but an unusual musical intelligence; I have seldom heard a public singer give a piece of music a more delicate and discriminating interpretation. Then Miss May Callender sang " Nobile Signor " from the *Huguenots*, and astonished me with her artistic rendering of that *aria*. Miss Callender could have easily been an opera singer, and a distinguished one, if she had so chosen. Eugene Oudin, a Southern baritone, also sang with charming effect. Minnie Parker, an eminent connoisseur in music, had her turn. She sang "Bel Raggio" from *Semiramide* with fine execution and all the Rossini traditions. And I must not forget to mention Fanny Reed, Mrs. Paran Stevens's sister, who sang very agreeably an *aria* from *Il Barbiere*. Altogether it was a most startling and illuminating evening, and I was proud of my country and of a society that could produce such amateurs.

Mrs. Peter Ronalds was another charming singer of that group; as was, also, Mrs. Moulton, who was Lillie Greenough before her marriage. Both had delightful and well cultivated voices. Mrs. Moulton had studied abroad, but for the most part the amateurs of that day were purely American products.

I often visited Mrs. Barlow at her country place at Glen Cove, L. I. She was the most tactful of hostesses, and in her house there was no fuss or formality, nothing but kind geniality and courtesy. She was the first hostess in the United States to ask her women guests to bring their maids; and she never once has asked me to sing when I was there. I did sing, of course, but she was too well-bred to let me feel under the slightest obligation. American hostesses are certainly sometimes very odd in this connection. I have mentioned Fanny Reed and Mrs. Stevens in Boston, and the time I had to play "Tommy Tucker" and sing for my supper; and I am now reminded of another occasion even more unpardonable, one that made me indirectly quite a bit of trouble.

Once upon a time when I was visiting in Chicago, and was being made much of as an American *prima donna* freshly arrived from European triumphs, some old friends of my father gave me a reception. I had been for nearly fourteen months abroad, and had come back with the associations and manners of the best people of the older countries: and this I particularly mention to suggest what a shock my treatment was to me.

On the day of the reception I had one of my worst sick headaches. I did not want to go, naturally, but the husband of the woman giving the reception called for me and begged that I would show myself there, if only for a few moments. My mother also urged me to make an effort and go. I made it—and went. In view of what afterwards occurred, I want to say that my costume was a black velvet gown created by Worth, with a heavy, long, handsome coat and a black velvet hat. When I reached the house I was so ill that I could not stand at the door with my hostess to receive the guests, but remained seated, hoping that I would not groan aloud with the throbbing of my head.

The ladies began arriving, and nearly every one of them was in full evening dress—*in the afternoon!* Mrs. Marshall Field, I remember, came in an elaborate point lace shawl, and no hat.

I had not been there half an hour before I was asked to sing! I had brought no music, there was no accompanist, and I was so dizzy that I could hardly see the keys of the piano, yet, as the request was not altogether the fault of my hostess, I did my best, playing some sort of an accompaniment and singing something—very badly, I imagine. Then I went home and to bed.

That episode was served up to me for eight years. I never went to Chicago without reading some reference to it in the newspapers, and my friends have told me that years later it was still discussed with bitterness. It was stated that I was "ungracious," "rude," and that I had "insulted the guests by my plain street attire" (shade of the great Worth!); that I only sang once and then with no attempt to do my best; that I did not eat the elaborate refreshments; did not rise from my chair when people were presented to me; and left the house inside an hour, although the reception was given for me. The bitterest attack was an article printed in one of the morning papers, an article written by a woman who had been among the guests. I never answered that or any other of the attacks because the host and hostess were old friends and felt very badly about the affair; but I have a memory of Chicago that will go with me to the grave. It was very different with the New York hostesses of whom Mrs. Barlow, Mrs. Ronalds, and Mrs. Gilder were the representatives.

By them a singer was treated as a little more, not less, than an ordinary human being!

O you unfortunate people of a newer day who have not the memory of that enchanting meeting-ground in East Fifteenth Street:—the delightful Gilder studio, the rebuilding of which from a carriage house into a studio-home was about the first piece of architectural work done by Stanford White. There was one big, beautiful room, drawing-room and sitting-room combined, with a fine fireplace in it. Many a time have I done some scene from an opera there, in the firelight, to a sympathetic few. Everybody went to the Richard Watson Gilders'—at least, everybody who was worth while. They were in New York already the power that they remained for so many years. Some pedantic enthusiast once said of them that, "The Gilders were empowered by divine right to put the *cachet* of recognition upon distinction."

Miss Jeannette Gilder came into my life as long ago as 1869. I was singing in a concert in Newark and she was in the wings, listening to my first song. My mother and my maid were near her and, when I came off the stage, as we were trying to find a certain song for an *encore*, the pile of music fell at her feet. Promptly the tall young stranger said:

"Please let me hold them for you."

Her whole personality expressed a species of beaming admiration. I looked at her critically; and from this small service began our friendship.

The Gilders were then living in Newark. The father, who was a Chaplain in the 40th New York Volunteers, died during the Civil War. His sons, Richard Watson Gilder and William H. Gilder, were also soldiers in the Civil War. The Richard Watson

Gilders were married in 1874. Mrs. Gilder was Miss Helena de Kay, granddaughter of Joseph Rodman Drake, who was the author of *The Culprit Fay*.

I met many interesting people at the Fifteenth Street studio. Helen Hunt Jackson, I remember well. She was then Mrs. Hunt, long before she had married Mr. Jackson or had written *Ramona*. She was a most pleasing personality, just stout enough to be genuinely genial. And Mrs. Frances Hodgson Burnett I first met there, about the time her *Lass o'Lowrie's* appeared, a story we all thought most impressive. George Cable was discovered by the Gilders, like so many other literary lights, and he and I used to sing Creole melodies before their big fireplace. His voice was queer and light, without colour, but correct and well in tune. He had only one bit of colour in him and that—the poetry of his nature—he gave freely and exquisitely in his tales of Creole life. At a much later time I saw something of the old French Quarter of New Orleans of which he wrote, the whole spirit of which was so lovely. I also first met John Alexander at the Gilders' after he came back from Paris; and John La Farge, who brought there with him Okakura, the Japanese art connoisseur. That was when I first met Okakura; and on the same occasion he was introduced to Modjeska, she and I being the first stage people he had ever met socially.

Later, in '79–'80, I saw a good deal of the Gilders in Paris, where they had a studio in the Quartier Latin. At that time, Mr. Gilder arranged for Millet's autobiography which first made him widely known in America; and in their Paris studio I met Sargent and Bastien Le Page and many other notables. I recall how becomingly Rodman Gilder—then three or four years old—was always dressed, in "Little Lord Fauntleroy" fashion long before the days of his young lordship. It was at this same period that I went to Fontainebleau to study the Barbizon School and met the son of Millet, who was trying to paint and never succeeded.

Speaking of the Gilders reminds me, albeit indirectly, of Helena Modjeska, whom I first saw in Sacramento, playing *Adrienne Lecouvreur*. I was simply enchanted and thought I had never seen such delicate and yet such forcible acting. One reason why I was so greatly impressed was that I had acquired the foreign standard of acting, and had been much disturbed when I came home to find such lack of elegance and ease upon the stage. She had the foreign manner—the grace and, at the same time, the authority of the great French and German players; and it seemed to me that she ought to be heard by the big critics. So I wrote home to Jeannette Gilder in New York an enthusiastic account of this actress who was being wasted on the Sacramento Valley. The public-spirited efforts of the Gilders in promoting anything artistic was so well and so long known that it is almost unnecessary to add that they interested themselves in the Polish artist and secured for her an opportunity to play in the East. She came, saw, and conquered; and I shall always feel, therefore, that I was definitely instrumental in launching Modjeska in theatrical New York.

"Didn't I tell you so?" I said to Jeannette Gilder.

There was always something very odd to me about Helena Modjeska. I never liked her personally half as much as I did as an actress. But she certainly was a wonderful actress. I once met John McCullough and talked with him about Modjeska, and he told me that she first acted in Polish to his English—Ophelia to his Hamlet—out West somewhere, I think it was in San

Francisco. He said that he had been the first to urge
her to learn English, and he was most enthusiastic about
the wonderful effect she created even at that early time.
As I had seen her in Sacramento during, approximately, the same period, I could discuss her with him
sympathetically and intelligently.

Although I never personally liked Helena Modjeska,
I have liked as well as known many stage folk and have
had, first and last, many real friends among them. It
was my good fortune to know the elder Salvini in
America. He happened to be stopping at the same
hotel. He looked like a successful farmer; a very plain
man,—very. He told me, among other interesting
things, that no matter how small his part happened to
be, he always played each succeeding act in a stronger
colour, maintaining a steady *crescendo*, so that the last
impression of all was the climax. I remember him in
Othello, particularly his delicate and lovely *silent* acting. When Desdémona came in and told the court how
he had won her, Salvini only looked at her and spoke
but the one word: "Desdémona!"—but the way he
said it "made the tears rise in your heart and gather
to your eyes."

Irving and Terry, always among my close friends, I
first met in London, at the McHenrys' house in Holland
Park. At that time the McHenrys' Sunday night
dinners were an institution. Later, when they came to
America, I saw a great deal of them; and I remember
Ellen Terry saying once, after a luncheon given by me
at Delmonico's, "What a splendid woman Jeannette
Gilder is! You know—" and she gave me a rueful
glance—"I am *always* wrong about men,—but seldom
about women!"

Dear Ellen Terry! She has always been the freshest,

the most wholesome, and the most spontaneous personality on the stage: a sweet and candid woman, with a
sound, warm heart and a great genius. At Lady
Macmillan's a number of people, most of them literary,
were discussing that deadly worthy and respectable
actress Madge Robertson—Mrs. Kendall. The morals
of stage people was the subject, and Mrs. Kendall was
cited as an example of propriety. One of the women
present spoke up from her corner:

"Well," said she, "all I can say is that if I were
giving a party for young girls I would steer very clear
of Mrs. Kendall and ask Miss Terry instead. The
Kendall lady does nothing but tell objectionable stories
that lead to the glorification of her own purity, but you
will never in a million years hear an indelicate word
from the lips of Ellen Terry!"

The only complaint Henry Irving had to make
against New York was that he "had no one to play
with." He insisted, and quite justly, too, that New
York had no leisure class: that cultivated Bohemia,
the playground for people of intellectual tastes and
varied interests, did not exist in New York. He used
to say that after the theatre, and after supper, he
could not find anybody at his club who would discuss
with him either modern drama or the old dramatic
traditions; or give him any exchange of ideas or intelligent comradeship.

He and I had many delightful talks, and I wish
now that I had made notes of the things he told me
about stagecraft. He had a great deal to say about
stage lighting, a subject he was for ever studying and
about which he was always experimenting. It was his
idea to do away with shadows upon the stage, and he
finally accomplished his effect by lighting the wings

Ellen Terry
From a photograph by Sarony

very brilliantly. Until his radical reforms in this direction the theatres always used to be full of grotesque masses of light and shade. To-day the art of lighting may be said to have reached perfection.

One of the most interesting things about Henry Irving was the way in which he made use of the smallest trifles that might aid him in getting his effects. He knew perfectly his own limitations, and was always seeking to compensate for them. For example, he was utterly lacking in any musical sense; like Dr. Johnson, he did not even possess an appreciation of sweet sounds, and did not care to go to either concerts or operas. But he knew how important music was in the theatre, and he knew instinctively—with that extraordinary stage-sense of his—what would appeal to an audience, even if it did not appeal to him. So, if he went anywhere and heard a melody or sequence of chords that he thought might fit in somewhere, he had it noted down at once, and collected bits of music in this way wherever he went. Sometime, he felt, the need for that particular musical phrase would arrive in some production he was putting on, and he would be ready with it. That was a wonderful thing about Irving— he was always prepared.

Speaking of Irving and his statement about the lack of a cultivated leisure class in New York, reminds me of the Vanderbilts, who were shining examples of this very lack, for they were immensely wealthy and yet did not half understand, at that time, the possibilities of wealth. William H. Vanderbilt was always my very good friend. His father, Cornelius, the founder of the family, used to say of him that "Bill had n't sense enough to make money himself—he had to have it left to him!" The old man was wont to add, "Bill's no good anyway!" The Vanderbilts were plain people in those days, but had the kindest hearts. "Bill" took a course in practical railroading, filling the position of conductor on the Hudson River Railroad, from which "job" he had just been promoted when I first knew him. He did turn out to be some "good" in spite of his father's pessimistic predictions.

My mother and I spent many summers at "Clarehurst," my country home at Cold Spring on the Hudson. The Vanderbilts' railroad, the New York Central, ran through Cold Spring, so that my Christmas present from William H. Vanderbilt each year was an annual pass. He began sending it to me alone, and then included my mother, until it became a regular institution. We saw something of Mr. and Mrs. Vanderbilt at Saratoga also, which was then a fashionable resort, before Newport supplanted it with a higher standard of formality and extravagance. I remember I once started to ask William H. Vanderbilt's advice about investing some money.

"You may know of some good security—" I began.

"I don't! I don't!" he exclaimed with heat.

Then he shook his finger at me impressively, saying:

"Let me tell you something that my father always said, and don't you ever forget it. He said that 'it takes a smart man to make money, but a *damned sight smarter one to keep it!*'"

My place at Cold Spring was where I went to rest between seasons, a lovely place with the wind off the Hudson River, and gorgeous oak trees all about. When the acorns dropped on the tin roof of the veranda in the dead of night they made an alarming noise like tiny ghostly footsteps.

One day when I was off on an herb-hunting expedition, some highwaymen tried to stop my carriage, and that was the beginning of troublous times at Cold Spring. It developed that a band of robbers was operating in our neighbourhood, with headquarters in a cave on Storm King Mountain, just opposite us. They made a specialty of robbing trains, and were led by a small man with such little feet that his footprints were easily enough traced;—traced, but not easily caught up with! He never was caught, I believe. But he, or his followers, skulked about our place; and we were alarmed enough to provide ourselves with pistols. That was when I learned to shoot, and I used to have shooting parties for target practice. My father would prowl about after dark, firing off his pistol whenever he heard a suspicious sound, so that, for a time, what with acorns and pistols, the nights were somewhat disturbed.

During the summers I drove all over the country and had great fun stopping my pony—he was a dear pony, too,—and rambling about picking flowers. I never passed a spring without stopping to drink from it. I've always had a passion for woods and brooks; and was the enterprising one of the family when it came to exploring new roads. Of the beaten track I can stand only just so much; then my spirit rises in rebellion. I love a cowpath.

I used to be an adept, too, at finding flag-root, which was "so good to put in your handkerchief to take to church"! (We carried our handkerchiefs in our hands in those days.) Or dill, or fresh fennel, "to chew through the long service"! Now the dill flavour is called caraway seed; but it isn't the same, or doesn't seem so. And there was fresh, sweet, black birch! Could anything be more delicious than the taste of black birch? The present generation, with its tea-rooms and soda-water fountains, does not know the refreshment of those delicacies prepared by Nature herself. I feel sure that John Burroughs appreciates black birch, being, as he is, one of the survivals of the fittest!

CHAPTER XXVII

"THE THREE GRACES"

IN 1877, I embarked upon a venture that was destined, in spite of much success, to be one of the most unpleasant experiences of my professional career. Max Strakosch and Colonel Mapleson, the younger—Henry Mapleson—organised a Triple-Star Tour all over America, the three being Marie Roze, Annie Louise Cary, and Clara Louise Kellogg. The press called us "The Three Graces" and wrote much fulsome nonsense about "three pure and irreproachable women appearing together upon the operatic stage, etc." The classification was one I did not care for. Here, after many intervening years, I enter and put on record my protest. At the time it all served as advertising to boom the tour and, as it was most of it arranged for by Mapleson himself, I had to let it go by in dignified silence.

Nor was Henry Mapleson any better than he should have been either, in his personal life or in his business relations, as his wives and I have reason to know. I say "wives" advisedly, for he had several. Marie Roze was never really married to him but, as he called her Mrs. Mapleson, she ought to be counted among the number. At the time of our "Three-Star Tour," she was playing the *rôle* of Mapleson's wife and finding it somewhat perilous. She was a mild and gentle woman, very sweet-natured and docile and singularly stupid, frequently incurring her managerial "husband's" rage by doing things that he thought were impolitic, for he had always to manage every effect. She seldom complained of his treatment but nobody could know them without being sorry for her. Previous to this relation with Mapleson, Marie Roze had married an exceedingly fine man, a young American singer of distinction, who died soon after the marriage. She had two sons, one of whom, Raymond Roze, passed himself off as her nephew for years. I believe he is a musical director of position and success in London at the present day. Henry Mapleson did not inherit any of the strong points of his father, Col. J. M. Mapleson of London, who really did know something about giving opera, although he had his failings and was difficult to deal with. Henry Mapleson always disliked me and, over and over again, he put Marie in a position of seeming antagonism to me; but I never bore malice for she was innocent enough. She had some spirit tucked away in her temperament somewhere, only, when we first knew her, she was too intimidated to let it show. When she was singing *Carmen* she was the gentlest mannered gypsy that was ever stabbed by a jealous lover—a handsome Carmen but too sweet and good for anything. Carlton was the Escamillo and he said to her quite crossly once at rehearsal,

"You don't make love to me enough! You don't put enough devil into it!"

Marie flared up for a second.

"I can be a devil if I like," she informed him. But, in spite of this assertion, she never put any devil into anything she did—on the stage at least.

Very few singers ever seem to get really inside

Colonel Henry Mapleson
From a photograph by Downey

Carmen. Some of the modern ones come closer to her; but in my day there was an unwritten law against realism in emotion. In most of the old standard *rôles* it was all right to idealise impulses and to beautify the part generally, but Carmen is too terribly human to profit by such treatment. She cannot be glossed over. One can, if one likes, play *Traviata* from an elegant point of view, but there is nothing elegant about Mérimée's Gypsy. Neither is there any sentiment. Carmen is purely—or, rather, impurely—elemental, a complete little animal. I used to love the part, though. When I was studying the part, I got hold of Prosper Mérimée's novel and read it and considered it until I really understood the girl's nature which, *en passant,* I may say is more than the critic of *The New York Tribune* had done. I doubt if he had ever read Mérimée at all, for he said that my rendering of Carmen was too realistic! The same column spoke favourably in later years, of Mme. Calvé's performance, so it was undoubtedly a case of *autres temps, autres mœurs!* Carmen was, of course, too low for me. It was written for a low mezzo, and parts of it I could not sing without forcing my lower register. The Habanera went very well by being transposed half a tone higher; but the card-playing scene was another matter. The La Morte *encore* lies very low and I could not raise it. Luckily the orchestra is quite light there and I could sing reflectively as if I were saying to myself, as I sat on the bales, "My time is coming!"

Ri- pe - te - rà: l'av - ell. . . . au - cor!

au - cor!. . La Morte au - cor!

In the fortune-telling quartette I arranged with one of the Gypsy girls—Frasquita, I think it was,—to sing my part and let me sing hers, which was very high, and thus relieve me.

A *rôle* in which I made my *début* while I was with Marie Roze and Cary was Aïda. Mapleson was anxious that Roze should have it, but Strakosch gave it to me. One of Mapleson's critics wrote severely about my sitting on a low seat instead of on the steps of the dais during the return of Rhadames, I remember in this connection. But nothing could prevent Aïda from being a success and it became one of my happiest *rôles*. A year or two later when I sang it in London my success was confirmed. Cary was Amneris in it and ranked next to the Amneris for whom Verdi wrote it, although she rather over-acted the part. I have never seen an Amneris who did not. There is something about the part that goes to the head. Speaking of my new *rôles* at that period, I must not forget to mention my mad scene from *Hamlet;* nor my one act of *Lohengrin* that I added to my *répertoire*. Lucia had always been one of my successes; and I believe that one of the points that made my Senta interesting was that I interpreted her as a girl obsessed with what was almost a monomania. She was a highly abnormal creature and that was the way I played her. It was a satisfaction to me that a few people here and there really appreciated this rather subtle interpretation. In commendation of this interpretation there appeared an anonymous letter in *The Chicago Inter-Ocean*, a part of which read:

In her rendering of this strange character (Senta) Miss Kellogg keeps constantly true to the ideal of the great composer, Wagner. In her acting, as well as in her singing, we see nothing of the woman; only the abnormal manifesta-

Clara Louise Kellogg as Aïda
From a photograph by Mora

tions of the subject of a monomania. The writer is informed by a physician whose observations of the insane, extending over many years, enable him to judge of Miss Kellogg's acting in this character, and he does not hesitate to say that she delineates truthfully the victim of a mind diseased. Such a delineation can only be the result of a careful study of the insane, aided by a wonderful intuitive faculty. The representation of the mad Ophelia in the last act of *Hamlet*, given by Miss Kellogg last Saturday, fully confirms the writer in the belief that no woman since Ristori possesses such power in rendering the manifestations of the insane."

The portion of my tour with Roze and Cary under the management of Max Strakosch that took me to the far West, was particularly uncomfortable. Fortunately the financial results compensated in a large measure for the annoyances. Not only did I have Mapleson's influence and his determination to push Marie Roze at all costs to contend with, and the trying actions and personality of Annie Louise Cary, but I also was subjected to much embarrassment from a manager named Bianchi, with whom, early in my career, I had partially arranged to go to California. Our agreement had fallen through because he was unable to raise the sum promised me; so, when I did go, with Roze and Cary and Strakosch, he was exceedingly bitter against me.

Annie Louise Cary was, strictly speaking, a contralto; yet she contrived to be considered as a mezzo and even had a try at regular soprano *rôles* like *Mignon*. It is almost superfluous to state that she disliked me. So far as I was concerned, she would have troubled me very little indeed if she had been willing to let me alone. I would not know her socially, but professionally I always treated her with entire courtesy and would have been satisfied to hold with her the most amicable relations in the world, as I have with all singers with whom I have appeared in public. Annie Louise Cary, however, willed it otherwise. *The Tribune* once printed a long editorial in which Max Strakosch was described as pacing up and down the room distractedly, crying: "Oh, what troubles! For God's sake, don't break up my troupe!" This was rather exaggerated; but I daresay there was more truth than fiction in it. Poor Max did have his troubles!

Max Strakosch was an Austrian by birth and, having lived the greater part of twenty-five years in this country, considered himself an American. He began his career with Parodi, somewhere back in the rosy dawn of our operatic history. Parodi was a great dramatic singer—the only woman of her day—brought over as the rival of Jenny Lind. Later Max Strakosch was with Thalberg, after which he was connected with the importation of various opera troupes having in their lists such singers as Madame Gazzaniga, Madame Coulsen, Albertini, Stigelli, Brignoli, and Susini. In all these early enterprises he was associated with his brother Maurice. He would himself have become a musician, but Maurice advised differently. So, as he expressed it, he always engaged his artists "by ear"; that is, he had them sing to him and in that way judged of their availability. Maurice used to say to him, "If you are merely a technical musician you can only tell what will please musicians. If you have general musical culture, and know the public, you can tell what will please the public." And, as Max sometimes amplified, "I have discovered this to be correct in many cases. Jarrett, who acted as the agent of Nilsson and Lucca, is not a practical musician. Neither is Morelli, who is a great impresario; neither is Mapleson. But they know what the public want and they furnish it." After he separated from his brother in operatic management, Max travelled with Gottschalk, with Carlotta Patti, and first brought Nilsson to America. Capoul, Campanini, and Maurel all made their appearance on the American operatic stage under his guidance.

Do you find your artists difficult to manage? [he was asked by a San Francisco reporter].

In some respects, yes, [was his reply]. They have certain operas which they wish to sing and they decline to learn others. The public get tired of these and demand novelty. With Miss Kellogg there is never this trouble. She knows forty operas and knows them well. She has a wonderful musical memory. She is a student, and learns everything new that is published. She has worked her way to her present high position step by step. She is sure of her position. She has an independent fortune, but loves her art and her country. But she is not obliged to confine herself to America. She has offers from London, Paris, and St. Petersburg, and will probably visit those places next season. She is just now at the zenith of her powers. She has learned *Paul and Virginia*, a very charming opera written for Capoul, and which will be given here for the first time in the United States. If we give our contemplated season of opera here she will sing Valentine in *The Huguenots* for the first time.

This same reporter has described Max as follows:

He can be seen almost at any hour about the Palace Hotel when not engaged with a myriad of musicians— opera singers long ago stranded on this coast, young vocalists with voices to be tried, chorus singers seeking employment, players on instruments wanting to perform in his orchestra, and people who come on all imaginable errands—or looking at the objects of curiosity about the city. He is always in a state of vibration; has a tongue forever in motion and a body never at rest. He is as demonstrative as a Frenchman. He talks with all the oscillations, bobs, shrugs, and nervous twitchings of the most mercurial Parisian. He has a pronounced foreign accent. When speaking, his voice runs over the entire gamut, only stopping at *C* sharp above the lines. In the dining-room he attracts the attention of guests and waiters, by the eagerness of his manner. When interested in the subject of conversation, he throws his arms sideways, endangering the lives of his neighbours with his knife and fork, rises in his seat, makes extravagant gestures . . . His greeting is always cordial, accompanied by a grasp of the hand like a patent vice or the gentle nip of a hay-press.

Mlle. Ilma de Murska, "The Hungarian Nightingale," was with us part of the time on this tour. She was a well-known Amina in *Sonnambula* and appeared in our all-star casts of *Don Giovanni*. She was said to have had five husbands. I know she had a chalk-white face, a belt of solid gold, and a menagerie of snakes and lizards that she carried about with her. This is all I remember with any vividness of Murska.

It all seems long, long ago; and, I find, it is the ridiculously unimportant things that stand out most clearly in my memory. For instance, we gave extra concerts, of course, and one of them lasted so long, thanks to *encores* and general enthusiasm, that Strakosch had to send word to hold the train by which we were leaving. But the audience wanted more, and yet more, and at last I had to go out on the stage and say:

"There's a train waiting for me! If I sing again, I'll miss that train!"

Then the people laughingly consented to let me go.

Another funny little episode happened in San Fran-

cisco, when I did for once break down in the middle of
a scene. It was—let me see—I think it must have been
in our last season of English opera, instead of in "The
Three Graces" tour, for it occurred in *The Talisman*,
but speaking of California suggests it to me. We
carried six Russian singers. They all joined the Greek
Church choir later. One of them was a little man
about five feet high, with a sweet voice, but an extremely nervous temperament. There was an unimportant *rôle* in *The Talisman* of a crusading soldier who
had to rush on and sing a phrase to the effect that St.
George's boats and horses were approaching from both
sides; I do not recall the words. The only man who
could sing the "bit" was our five-foot Russian friend.
He had to wear a large Saracen helmet and carry a
shield six feet high; and his entrance was a running one.
I, playing Lady Edith Plantagenet, looked around to
see the poor little chap come staggering along under
the immense shield and to hear a very shaky and
frightened voice gasp: "Sire, St. George's floats and
boats, and flounts and mounts—" I tried to sing
"A traitor! A traitor!" but got only as far as "A
trai—" when I was overcome with an impulse of
laughter and the curtain had to be rung down!

I recall, too, a visit I had from a Chinese woman.
I had bought something from a Chinese shop in San
Francisco, and the wife of the merchant, dressed most
ceremoniously and accompanied by four servants, came
to see me and expressed her desire to have me call on
her. So a cousin who was with me and I went, expecting to see a Chinese interior; but we found the most
banal of American furnishings and surroundings. Afterwards we visited Chinatown and one of the opium dens,
where we saw the whole process of opium smoking

by the men there, lying in bunks along the wall like shelves. It was on this trip, too, when going West, that, as we reached the Junction in Utah to branch off to Salt Lake City, we found the tracks were all filled up with the funeral train—flat decorated cars with seats —left from the funeral of Brigham Young.

But the strongest recollection of all—yes, even than the troubles between Annie Louise Cary and myself— stands out, of that Western tour, the knowledge of the good friends I won, personally and professionally, a collective testimonial of which remains with me in the form of a large gold brooch shaped like a lyre, across which is an enamelled bar of music from *Faust* delicately engraved in gold and with diamonds used as the notes. On the back is inscribed:

"Farewell from friends who love thee."

The same year I sang at the triennial festival of the Händel and Haydn Society of Boston. Emma Thursby, a high coloratura soprano, was with us. So were Charles Adams and M. W. Whitney. Cary also sang. It was a very brilliant musical event for the Boston of those days. It was in Boston, too, although a little later, that Von Bulow called on me and, speaking of practising on the piano, showed me his fingers, upon the tips of every one of which were very tough corns. In further conversation he remarked, with regard to Wagner, "Ah, he married my widow!" When singing in Boston one night, during "The Three Graces" tour, at a performance of *Mignon*, there was noted by one newspaper man who was present the somewhat curious fact that in singing that Italian opera only one of the principals sang in his or in her native tongue. Cary was an American, Roze a Frenchwoman, Tom Karl (Carroll) an Irishman, Verdi (Green) an

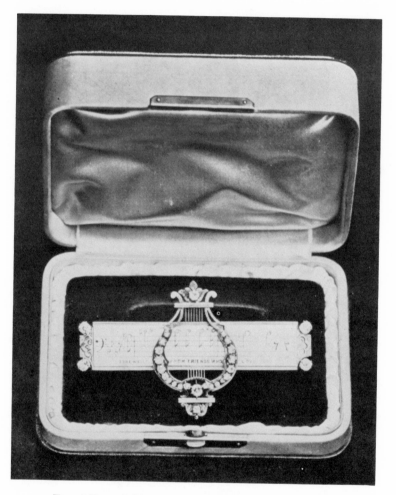

Faust Brooch Presented to Clara Louise Kellogg

American, and myself. The only Italian was Frapoli, the new tenor.

In 1878, on a Western trip, I remember my making a point, in some place in Kansas, of singing in an institute on Sunday for the pleasure of the inmates. We had done this sort of thing frequently before, notably in Utica. So we went to the prison to sing to the prisoners. I said to the company, "I am going to sing to give *pleasure*, and not a hymn is to be in the programme!" When I was told of the desperadoes in the place I was almost intimidated. The guards were particularly imposing. I played my own accompaniments and I sang negro melodies. I never had such an audience, of all my appreciative audiences. Never, I feel sure, have I given quite so much pleasure as to those lawless prisoners out in Kansas.

CHAPTER XXVIII

ACROSS THE SEAS AGAIN

I WAS glad to be going again to England. My farewell to my native land was, however, more like an ovation than a farewell. One long table of the ship's grand saloon was heaped with flowers sent me by friends and "admirers." The list of my fellow passengers on this occasion was a distinguished one, including Bishop Littlejohn, Bishop Scarborough, Bishop Clarkson, and other Episcopal prelates who were going over to attend the conference in London; the Rev. Dr. John Hall; Maurice Grau, Max Strakosch, Henry C. Jarrett, John McCullough, Lester Wallack, General Rathbone of Albany, Colonel Ramsay of the British army, Frederick W. Vanderbilt, and Joseph Andrede, the Cape of Good Hope millionaire. I was interviewed by a *Sun* reporter, on deck, and assured him that I was going abroad for rest only.

"No," I said, "I shall not sing a note. How could I, after such a season—one hundred and fifty nights of constant labour. No; I shall breathe the sea air, and that of the mountains, and see Paris—delightful Paris! With such a lovely summer before me, it would be a little hard to have to work."

It was like old times to be in England once more. Yet I found many changes. One of them was in the state of my old friend James McKenzie who had been

300

in the East Indian trade and had a delightful place in Scotland adjoining that of the Queen, through which she used to drive with the incomparable John Brown. I had been invited up there on my first visit to England, but was not able to accept. When I asked for him this time I learned that he had been knighted for loaning money to the Prince of Wales. A girl I knew quite well told me, this year, a touching little story of a half-fledged romance which had taken place at Sir James's place in Scotland. The Prince who was known in England as "Collars and Cuffs" and who died young, was with the McKenzies for the hunting season and there met my friend,—such a pretty American girl she was! They fell in love with each other and, though of course nothing could come of it, they played out their pathetic little drama like any ordinary young lovers.

"Come down early to dinner," the Prince would whisper. "I 'll have a bit of heather for you!"

And when they met in London, later, he took her to Marlborough House and showed her the royal nurseries and the shelves where his toys were still kept. The girl nearly broke down when she told me about it. I have thought of the little story more than once since.

"He hated to have me courtesy to him," she said. "He used to whisper quite fiercely: 'don't you courtesy to me when you can avoid it—I can't bear to have you do it!' "

My new *rôle* in London that season was Aïda. For, of course, I was singing! It went so well that Mapleson (*père*) wanted to extend my engagement. But I was very, very tired and, for some reason—this, probably,— not in my usual "form," to borrow an Anglicism, so I decided to go to Paris and rest, meanwhile waiting for something to develop that I liked well enough to accept.

Maurice Strakosch had been my agent in England, but it seemed to me that his methods were becoming somewhat antiquated. So I gave him up and decided that I would get along without any agent at all. I also gave up Colonel Mapleson. Mapleson owed me money—although, for that matter, he owed everybody. Poor Titjiens sang for years for nothing. So, when, as soon as I was fairly settled in Paris, the Colonel sent me earnest and prayerful summons to come back to London and go on singing *Aïda*, I turned a deaf ear and sent back word that I was too tired.

My first appearance in London this season was at a Royal Concert at Buckingham Palace to which, as before, I was "commanded." There were present many royalties, any number of foreign ambassadors, dukes, duchesses, marquises, marchionesses, archbishops, earls, countesses, lords, and viscounts. Her Royal Highness, the Princess of Wales wore, I remember, a gown of crème satin brocade trimmed with point d'Alençon, trimmed with pansy-coloured velvet; and her jewels were diamonds, pearls, and sapphires. Her tiara was of diamonds and she was decorated with many orders. Said an American press notice:

Miss Kellogg, it is a pleasure to say, achieved a complete triumph and received the congratulations of the Prince and Princess of Wales and of everyone present. . . . And not a whit behind this was the great triumph she gained on the evening of June 19th, in her character of Aïda, without doubt the most impressive and ambitious of her impersonations, and which has won for her in America the highest praise from musical people and public on account of the intensity of feeling which she throws into the dramatic action and music. The London *Times* critic, who is undoubtedly the best in London, bestows praise in unequivocal language for the excellence of Miss Kellogg's interpretation. That Miss Kellogg has been so successful as a singer will be glad news to her friends, and that she has been so successful as an American singer will be still better news to those people who feel keenly for our national reputation as lovers and promoters of the fine arts.

In an interview in London Max Strakosch was asked with regard to his plans for another season:

"Why do you contemplate giving English opera instead of Italian?"

"For two reasons," he replied. "The first is that English is very popular now and the great generality of people in England and America prefer it. This is especially the case in England. The second reason is that, although Kellogg is the equal of an Italian operatic star, fully as fine as Gerster, immeasurably superior to Hauck, people with set ideas will always have their favourites, and partisanship is possible; whereas in English opera Kellogg stands alone, unapproachable, the indisputable queen."

"What is all this talk I hear about a lot of rich men coming to the front in New York to support Mapleson's operatic ventures with their money?"

"Why, it is all talk; that's just it. That sort of talk has been talked for years back, but they never do anything. Why did n't these rich men that want opera in New York give me any money? I stood ready to bring out any artists they wanted if they would guarantee me against loss. But they never did anything of the kind, and I have brought out the leading artists of our times at my own risks. The only man who's worth anything of all that lot that's talking so much about opera now in New York is Mr. Bennett. He's got the *Herald*, and that has influence."

"What do you think of Americans as an opera-going people?" he was asked.

"While we have many music-lovers in America, it is

nevertheless a difficult matter to cater to our public," Max
replied. "Here in England there is such an immense con-
stituency for opera; people who have solid fortunes, which
nothing disturbs, and who want opera and all other beautiful and luxurious things, and will pay largely for them.
In America hard times may set everybody to economising
and, of course, one of the first things cut off is going to the
opera."

"Was all that gossip about disputes and jealousies between Kellogg and Cary last season a managerial dodge
for notoriety?"

"Dear me, no. I have n't the slightest idea how all that
stuff and nonsense started. Kellogg and Cary were always
good friends. If Cary was n't pleased with her treatment
last year, why should she engage with us again? Besides,
what rivalry could there possibly be between a soprano and
a contralto? The soprano is the *prima donna* incontestably,
the star of the troupe."

In Paris my mother and I took an apartment on the
Rue de Chaillot, just off the Champs Élysées. One
of the first things I did in Paris was to refuse an offer
to sing in Budapesth. While in Paris I, of course, did
sing many times, but it was always unprofessionally.
I had a wonderful stay in Paris, and went to everything
from horse shows to operas. Those were the charming
days when Mme. Adam had her *salon*. I met there
some of the most gifted and brilliant people of the age.
She was the editor of the *Nouvelle Revue*, and it was
through her that I met Coquelin. He frequently
recited at her receptions; and it was a great privilege
to hear his wonderful French and his inimitable intonation in an *intime* way.

The house where I enjoyed visiting more than any
other except the Adams', was that of Theodore Robin,
who had married a rich American widow and had a

beautiful home on Parc Monceau. His baritone voice was a very fine one, and he had studied at first with a view to making a career for himself; but he was naturally indolent and, having married money, his indolence never decreased. Valentine Black was another friend of ours and we spent many an evening at his house listening to Godard and Widor play their songs. Widor was the organist at Saint Sulpice and had composed some charming lyric music. Godard was a very small man, intensely musical. He had the curious gift of being able to copy another composer's style exactly. Few people know, for instance, that he wrote all the recitative music for *Carmen*. It is almost incredible that another brain than Bizet's should have so marvellously caught the spirit and the mood of that music.

The Stanley Club gave me a dinner in the following March at which my mother and I were the only ladies present. Mr. Ryan was the President of the Club and represented the *New York Herald*. The foreign correspondents of the *Evening Post* and the *Boston Advertiser* were there, and next to Ryan sat Richard Watson Gilder who was representing the *Century Magazine*. There were also there several poets and writers, and more than one painter whose picture hung in the *Salon* of that year. No one asked me to sing; but I felt that I wanted to and did so. After the "Jewel Song" and the "Polonaise," someone asked for "Way Down on the Suwanee River." I sang it, and was struck by the incongruous touch of the little negro melody, the brilliant Stanley Club, and all Paris outside.

No one can live in the atmosphere of artistic Paris without being interested in other branches of art besides one's own. That is a charming trait of French

20

people;—they are not a bit prejudiced when it comes to recognising forms of genius that are unfamiliar. The stupidest Parisian painter will weep over Tschaikow-sky's *Pathétique Symphony* or will wildly applaud one of the rather cumbersome Racine tragedies at the Théâtre Français. I knew Cabanel quite well (not, I hasten to add, that he would be apt to cultivate an artistic taste in anybody) and I met Jules Stewart at the Robins', whose father was the greatest collector of Fortuneys in the world. I think it was he who took me to the Loan Exhibition of the Barbizon School of Painting that year. The pictures were hung beautifully, I remember, so that one could see the stages of their development.

It was about the same time that I first heard Joseph-ine de Reszke in Paris. In any case it was somewhere in the seventies. She was a soprano with a beautiful voice but not an attractive personality. Her neck was exceptionally short and set so far down into her shoul-ders that she just escaped deformity. She was very much the blonde, northern type, and still a young woman. I have heard that she did not have to sing for monetary reasons. A few years later she married a wealthy Polish banker and left the stage. At the time I first heard her the de Reszke men were not singing. It was in *Le Roi de Lahore* that I heard her, with Lascelle. I never listened to anything more magnificently done than Lascelle's singing of the big baritone *aria*. Maurel followed him as a baritone. He was a great artist also, with possibly more intelligence in his singing than Lascelle. Lascelle relied entirely on his glorious voice; in consequence he never realised all in his career that might have been possible. In reality, if you have one great gift, you have to develop as many other gifts as possible in order to present and to protect that one properly! A little later I heard Maurel in *Iago*. (This reminds me of *Othello* in Munich, when Vogel, the tenor, sang out of tune and nearly spoiled Maurel's work). What an actor, and what an intelligence! One felt in Maurel a man who had studied his *rôles* from the original plots. He played a great part in costuming, but, curiously enough, he could never play parts of what I call elemental picturesqueness. His Amonasro in *Aïda* was good, but it was a bit too clean and tidy. He looked as if he were just out of a Turkish bath, immaculate, in spite of his uncivilised guise. He could, however, play a small part as if it were the finest *rôle* in the piece; and he had an inimitable elegance and art, even with a certain primitive romantic quality lacking. But what days those were—of what marvellous singing companies! I hear no such vocalism now, in spite of the elaborate and expensive opera that is put on each year.

In my mother's diary of this period I find:

Louise presented to Verdi and we had no idea she would appear in any newspaper in consequence. . . .

She went to hear the damnation of *Faust* last Sunday and says the orchestra was *very* fine. The singing is not so much. She went to hear *Aïda* last night at the Grau Opera House with Verdi to conduct and Krauss as Aïda. Chorus and orchestra fine artists. *Well*—she was *disappointed!* Krauss sings so false and has not as much power as Louise. She came home quite proud of herself. Took her opera and marked everything. Says her *tempo* was very nearly correct; but yet she was disappointed. Krauss changes her dress. Louise does not. . . .

We went to Miss Van Zandt's *début*. She made a veritable success. Has a very light tone. The *Théâtre Comique* is small. She is extremely slender and, if not worked too hard, will develop into a fine artist. Our box joined Patti's. I sat next to her and we lost no time in chatting over everything that was interesting to us both. She told me her whole story. I was very much interested; and had a most agreeable evening. Was glad I went.

In a letter written by my mother to my father I find another mention of my meeting Verdi:

"Louise was invited to breakfast with Verdi, the composer of *Aïda*. She said he was the most natural, unaffected, and the most amiable man (musical) she ever met."

CHAPTER XXIX

TEACHING AND THE HALF-TALENTED

I HAVE gone abroad nearly every summer and it was on one of these trips, in 1877, that I first met Lilian Nordica. It was at a garden party given by the Menier Chocolat people at their *usine* just outside Paris, after she had returned from making a tour of Europe with Patrick Gilmore's band. A few years later she and I sang together in Russia; and we have always been good friends. At the time of the Gilmore tour she was quite a girl, but she dressed her hair in a fashion that made her look much older than she really was and that threw into prominence her admirably determined chin. She always attributed her success in life to that chin. Before becoming an opera singer she had done about everything else. She had been a book-keeper, had worked at the sewing machine, and sung in obscure choirs. The chin enabled her to surmount such drudgery. A young person with a chin so expressive of determination and perseverence could not be downed. She told me at that early period that she always kept her eyes fixed on some goal so high and difficult that it seemed impossible, and worked toward it steadily, unceasingly, putting aside everything that stood in the path which led to it. In later years she spoke again of this, evidently having kept the idea throughout her career. "When I sang Elsa," she said,

"I thought of Brunhilde,—then Isolde,—" My admiration for Mme. Nordica is deep and abounding. Her breathing and tone production are about as nearly perfect as anyone's can be, and, if I wanted any young student to learn by imitation, I could say to her, "Go and hear Nordica and do as nearly like her as you can!" There are not many singers, nor have there ever been many, of whom one could say that. And one of the finest things about this splendid vocalism is that she has had nearly as much to do with it as had God Almighty in the first place. When I first knew her she had no dramatic quality above *G* sharp. She could reach the upper notes, but tentatively and without power. She had, in fact, a beautiful mezzo voice; but she could not hope for leading *rôles* in grand opera until she had perfect control of the upper notes needed to complete her vocal equipment. She went about it, moreover, "with so much judition," as an old man I know in the country says. But it was not until after the Russian engagement that she went to Sbriglia in Paris and worked with him until she could sing a high *C* that thrilled the soul. That *C* of hers in the Inflammatus in Rossini's *Stabat Mater* was something superb. Not many singers can do it as successfully as Nordica, although they can all accomplish a certain amount in "manufactured" notes. Fursch-Nadi, also a mezzo, had to acquire upper notes as a business proposition in order to enlarge her *répertoire.* She secured the notes and the requisite *rôles;* yet her voice lost greatly in quality. Nordica's never did. She gained all and lost nothing. Her voice, while increasing in register, never suffered the least detriment in tone nor *timbre.*

It was Nordica who first told me of Sbriglia, giving

him honest credit for the help he had been to her. Like all truly big natures she has always been ready to acknowledge assistance wherever she has received it. Some people—and among them artists to whom Sbriglia's teaching has been of incalculable value—maintain a discreet silence on the subject of their study with him, preferring, no doubt, to have the public think that they have arrived at vocal perfection by their own incomparable genius alone. All of my training had been in my native country and I had always been very proud of the fact that critics and experts on two continents cited me as a shining example of what American musical education could do. All the same, when I was in Paris during an off season, I took advantage of being near the great teacher, Sbriglia, to consult him. I really did not want him actually to do anything to my voice as much as I wanted him to tell me there was nothing that needed doing. At the time I went to him I had been singing for twenty years. Sbriglia tried my voice carefully and said:

"Mademoiselle, you have saved your voice by singing far *forward*."

"That's because I've been worked hard," I told him, "and have had to place it so in self-defence. Many a night I've been so tired it was like *pumping* to sing! Then I would sing 'way, '*way* in front and, by so doing, was able to get through."

"Ah, that's it!" said he. "You've sung against your teeth—the best thing in the world for the preservation of the voice. You get a *white*, flat sound that way."

"Then I don't sing wrong?" I asked, for I knew that the first thing great vocal masters usually have to do is to tell one how not to sing.

"Mademoiselle," said Sbriglia, "you breathe by the

grace of God! Breathing is all of singing and I can teach you nothing of either."

Sbriglia's method was the old Italian method known to teachers as *diaphragmatic*, of all forms of vocal training the one most productive of endurance and stability in a voice. I went several times to sing for him and, on one occasion, met Plançon who had been singing in Marseilles and, from a defective method, had begun to sing out of tune so badly that he resolved to come to Paris to see if he could find someone who might help him to overcome it. He was quite frank in saying that Sbriglia had "made him." I used to hear him practising in the Maestro's apartment and would listen from an adjoining room so that, when I met him, I was able to congratulate him on his improvement in tone production from day to day. Phrasing and expression are what make so many great French artists—that, and an inborn sense of the general effect. French actors and singers never forget to keep themselves picturesque and harmonious. They may get off the key musically but never *artistically*. Germans have not a particle of this sense. They are individualists, egoists, and are forever thinking of themselves and not of the whole. When I heard Slezak, I said to myself: "If only somebody would photograph that man and show him for once what he looks like!"

The worst thing Sbriglia had to contend with was the obtuseness of people. They did not know when they were doing well or ill, and would not believe him when he told them. I remember being there one day while a young Canadian girl was making tones for the master. She had a good voice and could have made a really fine effect if she could only have heard herself with her brain. After he had been working with her for a time, she sang a delightful note properly placed.

"Good!" exclaimed Sbriglia.

"That was lovely," I put in.

"*That?* I would n't sing like that for anything! It sounded like an old woman's voice!" cried the girl, quite amazed.

Sbriglia threw up his hands in a frenzy and ordered her out of the house. So that was an end of her as far as he was concerned.

Sbriglia really loved to teach. It was a genuine joy to him to put the finishing touches on a voice; to do those things for it that, apparently, the Creator had not had time to do. I know one singer who, when complimented upon his vast improvement, replied without the slightest intention of impiety:

"Yes, I am singing well now, thanks to Sbriglia,— and, of course, *le bon Dieu!*" he added as an afterthought.

Everyone knows what Sbriglia did for Jean de Reszke, turning him from an unsuccessful baritone into the foremost tenor of the world. Sbriglia first met the Polish singer at some Paris party, where de Reszke told him that he was discouraged, that his career as a baritone had not been a fortunate one, and that he had about made up his mind to give it all up and leave the stage. He was a rich man and did not sing for a living like most professionals. Sbriglia had heard him sing. Said he:

"M. de Reszke, you are not a baritone."

"I am coming to that conclusion myself," said Monsieur ruefully.

"No, you are not a baritone," repeated Sbriglia. "You are a tenor."

Jean de Reszke laughed. A tenor? He? But it was absurd!

Nevertheless Sbriglia was calmly assured; and he was the greatest master of singing in France, if not in the world. After a little conversation, he convinced M. de Reszke sufficiently, at least, to give the new theory a chance.

"You need not pay me anything," said the great teacher to the young man. "Not one franc will I take from you until I have satisfied you that my judgment is correct. Study with me for six months only and then I will leave it to you—and the world!"

That was the beginning of the course of study which launched Jean de Reszke upon his extraordinarily prosperous and brilliant career.

Speaking of Sbriglia leads my thoughts from the study of singing in general to the struggle of young singers, first, for education, and, second, for recognition. I would like to impress upon those who think of trying to make a career or who would like to make one the benefit to be derived from reading the twenty-third and twenty-fourth chapters of George Eliot's *Daniel Deronda*, in which she makes clear how much early environment counts. There must have been some musical atmosphere, even if not of an advanced or educated kind. Music must be absorbed with the air one breathes and the food one eats, so as to form part of the blood and tissue.

It is sad to see the number of girls with the idea that they are possessed of great gifts just ready to be developed by a short period of study, after which they will blossom out into successful singers. Injudicious friends—absolutely without judgment or musical discrimination—are responsible for the cruel disillusions that so frequently follow. I would like to cry out to them to reject the thought; or only to entertain it when encouraged by those capable by experience or training of truly judging their gifts. Many and many a girl comes out of a household where the highest musical knowledge has been the hand-organ in the street, and believes that she is going to take the world by storm. She is prepared to save and scrimp and struggle to go upon the stage when she really should be stopping at home, ironing the clothes and washing the dishes allotted her by a discriminating and judicious Providence. Said Klesner to Gwendolen who wants to go on the stage in *Daniel Deronda:*

You have exercised your talents—you recite—you sing— from the drawing-room *Standpunkt*. My dear *Fräulein*, you must unlearn all that. You have not yet conceived what excellence is. You must unlearn your mistaken admirations. You must know what you have to strive for, and then you must subdue your mind and body to unbroken discipline. Your *mind*, I say. For you must not be thinking of celebrity. Put that candle out of your eyes and look only at excellence. You would, of course, earn nothing. You could get no engagement for a long while. You would need money for yourself and your family. . . .

A mountebank's child who helps her father to earn shillings when she is six years old—a child that inherits a singing throat from a long line of choristers and learns to sing as it learns to talk—has a likelier beginning. Any great achievement in acting or in music grows with the growth. Whenever an artist has been able to say, "I came, I saw, I conquered," it has been at the end of patient practice. Genius at first is little more than a great capacity for receiving discipline. Singing and acting, like the fine dexterity of the juggler with his cups and balls, require a shaping of the organs toward a finer and finer certainty of effect. Your muscles—your whole frame—must go like a watch, true, true, true, to a hair. That is the work of springtime, before habits have been determined.

This demonstrates what I cannot emphasise too heartily—the impossibility of taking people out of their normal environment and making anything worth while of them. There is a place in the world for everybody and, if everybody would stay in that place, there would be less confusion and fewer melancholy misfits. Singing is not merely vocal. It is spiritual. One must be *in* music in some way; must hear it often, or, even, hear it talked about. Merely hearing it talked about gives one a chance to absorb some musical ideas while one's mental attitude is being moulded. Studying in classes supplies the musical atmosphere to a certain extent; and so does hearing other people sing, or reading biographies of musicians. All these are better than nothing—much better—and yet they can never take the place of really musical surroundings in childhood. Being brought up in a household where famous composers are known, loved, and discussed, where the best music is played on the piano and where certain critical standards are a part of the intellectual life of the inmates is a large musical education in itself. The young student will absorb thus more real musical feeling, and judgment, and knowledge, than in spending years at a conservatory.

I have often and often received letters asking for advice and begging me to hear the voices of girls who have been told they have talent. It is a heart-breaking business. About one in sixty has had something resembling a voice and then, ten chances to one, she has not been in a position to cultivate herself. It is difficult to tell a girl that a woman must have many things besides a voice to make a success on the stage. It seems so—well!—so *conceited*—to say to her:

"My poor child, you must have presence and personality; good teeth and a knowledge of how to dress; grace of manner, dramatic feeling, high intelligence, and an aptitude for foreign languages besides a great many other essentials that are too numerous to mention but that you will discover fast enough if you try to go ahead without them!"

An impulsive and warm-hearted friend was visiting me once when I received a letter from a young woman whom I will call "E. H.," asking permission to come and sing for me. I read the note in despair and threw it over to my friend.

"What are you going to do about it?" she asked, after she had glanced through it.

"Nothing. The girl has no talent."

"How do you know that?" protested my friend.

"By her letter. It is a crassly ignorant letter. I feel perfectly sure that she can't sing."

"You are very unkind!" my friend reproached me. "You ought at least to hear her. You may be discouraging a genuine genius——"

"Now see here," I interrupted, "'E. H.' is evidently ignorant and uneducated. She further admits that she is poor. These facts taken together make a terrible handicap. She'd have to be a miracle to make good in spite of them."

"I will pay her expenses to come here and see you," declared my dear friend, obstinate in well-doing, like many another mistaken philanthropist.

I told her that she might take that responsibility if she liked, but that I would have nothing to do with raising a girl's false hopes in any such way. "It's a little hard on her," I said, "to have to borrow money to take a journey simply to be told that she can't sing. However, have it your own way and bring her."

She came. I saw her approaching up the driveway and simply pointed her out to my misguided friend. Anyone would have known the minute he saw "E. H." that she could not sing. She slouched and dragged her feet and was hopelessly ordinary, every inch of her. It was not merely a matter of plainness, but something far worse. She was quite hopeless. It turned out, poor soul, that she was a chambermaid in a hotel. People had heard her singing at her work and had told her that she ought to have her voice cultivated. It was, as usual, a case of injudicious friends, and, by the way, the very fact of being carried away by such praise is in itself a mark of a certain lack of intelligence. This girl had no temperament, no ear, no equipment, no taste, no advantages in the way of having heard music. I had to say to her:

"You have a pretty voice but nothing else, and not a sign of a career. Dismiss it all, for you must have something more than a few sweet notes."

She cried, and I did, too. I hate to be obliged to tell girls such disagreeable truths.

Another girl came to me with her mother. She was full of herself and her mother equally wrapped up in her. She had taken part in small village affairs in the little Connecticut town where she lived. Her voice was not bad, but she produced her notes in a wrong manner. Her teacher had encouraged her and promised her success. But teachers do that, many of them! I do not know that they can altogether be blamed.

"You don't breathe right," I said to this Connecticut

girl. "You don't produce your tone right. You 've no experience and, of course, you believe your teacher. But you forget one thing. Your teacher has to live and you pay him for stimulating you, even if he does so without justification."

What I did not go on to say to her, although I longed to, was that she was not the *build* of which *prime donne* are made. A *prima donna* has to be compactly, sturdily made, with a strong backbone to support her hard work and a *lifted* chest to let the tones out freely. A niece of Bret Harte's, who appeared for a time in grand opera, drooped her chest as she exhausted her breath and, when I saw her do it, I said:

"She sings well; but she won't sing long!"

She did n't.

My Connecticut girl was big and sloppy, a long-drawn-out person, such as is never, never gifted with a big voice.

There is something else which is very necessary for every girl to consider in going on the operatic stage. Has she the means for experimenting, or does she have to earn her living in some way meanwhile? If the former is the case, it will do no harm for her to play about with her voice, burn her fingers if need be, and come home to her mother and father not much the worse for the experience. I sympathise somewhat with the teachers in not speaking altogether freely in cases like these. There is no reason why anyone should take from a girl even one remote chance if *she* can afford to take it. But poor girls should be told the truth. So I said to my young Connecticut friend:

"My dear, you are trying to support yourself and your mother, are n't you? Very well. Now, suppose you go on and find that you can't—what will you do

then? What are you fitted for? What can you turn
your hand to? What have you acquired? Look how
few singers ever arrive and, if you are not one of the
few, will you not merely have entirely unfitted yourself
for the life struggle along other lines?"

Herewith I say the same to four-fifths of all the girl
singers who, in villages, in shops, in schools, everywhere, are all yearning to be great. They came to me
in shoals in Paris and Milan, begging for just enough
money to get home with. I have shipped many a
failure back to America, and my soul has been sick
for their disappointment and disillusionment. But
they will *not* be guided by advice or warning. They
have got to learn actually and bitterly. Neither are
they ever grateful for discouragement nor yet for
encouragement. If you give them the former, they
think you are a selfish pessimist; and if you give them
the latter, they accept it as no more than their due. As
I have previously mentioned, I have known only one
grateful girl and she was of ordinary ability. Emma
Abbott, for whom I certainly did a great deal, was only
grateful because she knew it was expected of her by
the world at large. I believe she really thought that all
I did was to hasten her success a little and that she
really had not needed my assistance. Possibly, she had
not. But this other girl, to whom I gave a little,
unimportant advice, wrote me afterwards a most
appreciative letter, saying that my advice had been
invaluable to her. It was the only word of genuine
gratitude I ever received from a young singer; and I
kept her letter as a curiosity.

I believe there are, or were, more would-be *prime
donne* in Chicago than anywhere else on earth. I shall
never forget appointing a Thursday afternoon in the

Windy City to hear twelve aspirants to operatic fame—pretty, fresh, self-conscious, young girls for the most part. There was one of the number who was particularly pretty and particularly aggressive. She criticised the others lavishly, but hung back from singing herself. She talked a great deal about her voice, saying that she had sung for Theodore Thomas and that he had told her there was no hall big enough for it! Such colossal conceit prejudiced me in advance and I must confess I felt a little curiosity to hear this "phenomenal organ." It proved to be perfectly useless. She had neither power nor quality nor comprehension. She could, however, make a big noise, as I told her. On Sunday my friends began coming in to see me, full of an article that had appeared in one of the papers that morning. Everyone began with:

"Good morning, Louise. My dear! Have you seen,"—etc.

The article, that had quite openly been given the paper by the young lady whose voice had been so much admired by Theodore Thomas, described my unkindness to young singers, my jealous objection to praising aspirants, my discouragement of good voices!

As a matter of fact, I have always been the friend of young girls, especially of young singers. So far from wishing to hurt or discourage them, I have often gone out of my way to help them along. And I believe that every time I have been obliged to tell a young and eager girl that there was no professional triumph ahead of her, it has cut me almost, if not quite, as deeply as it has cut her. For I always feel that I am maiming, even killing some beautiful thing in discouraging her,—even when I know it to be necessary and beneficial.

Another thing that I wish young would-be artists

21

would remember is that, if it is worth while to sing the music of a song, it is equally worth while to sing the words, and that you cannot sing the words really, unless you are singing their meaning. Do I make myself understood, I wonder? Once a girl with a sweetly pretty voice sang to me Nevin's *Mighty Lak a Rose*, the little negro song which Madame Nordica gave so charmingly. When the girl had finished, I said:

"My dear, have you read those words?"

She looked at me blankly. I know she thought I was crazy.

"Because," I proceeded, "if you read the poetry over before you sing that song again, you'll find that it will help you."

She had, I presume, "read" the words or she could not have actually pronounced them; but she had not made the slightest attempt to read the spirit of the little song. No picture had come to her of a rosy baby dropping asleep and of a loving mammy crooning over him. She had not read the *feeling* of the song, even if she had memorised the syllables. Girls hate to work. They, even more than boys, want a short cut to efficiency and success. Labour and effort are cruel words to them. They want the glamour and the fun all at once. What would they say to the noble and inspiring example of old E. S. Jaffray, a merchant of sixty, whom I once knew, who, at that age, decided to learn Italian in order to read Dante in the original?

The best way—as I have said before and as I insist on saying—for anyone to learn to sing is by imitation and assimilation. My friend Franceschetti, a Roman gentleman, poor but of noble family, has classes that I always attend when I am in the Eternal City, and wherein the instruction is most advantageously given.

He criticises each student in the presence of the others and, if the others are listening at all intelligently, they must profit. But you must listen, and then listen, and then keep on listening, and finally begin to listen all over again. You must keep your ear ready, and your mind as well.

Just as Faure, when he heard the bad baritone, said to himself, "that 's my note! Now how does he do it?" so you must hold yourself ready to learn from the most humble as well as from the most unlikely sources. Never forget that Faure learned from the really poor singer what no good one had been able to teach him. Remember, too, that Patti learned one of her own flexible effects from listening to Faure himself: and that these great artists were not too proud to acknowledge it. I never went to hear Patti, myself, without studying the fine, forward placing of her voice and coming home immediately and trying to imitate it.

Yet, after all one's efforts to help, one can only let the young singers find out for themselves. If we could profit by each other's experience, there would be no need for the doctrine of reincarnation. But I wish—oh, how I wish—that I could save some foolish girls from embarking on the ocean of art as half of them do with neither chart or compass, nor even a seaworthy boat.

A better metaphor comes to me in my recollection of a famous lighthouse that I once visited. The rocks about were strewn with dead birds—pitiful, little, eager creatures that had broken their wings and beaten out their lives all night against the great revolving light. So the lighthouse of success lures the young, ambitious singers. And so they break their wings against it.

CHAPTER XXX

THE WANDERLUST AND WHERE IT LED ME

THAT season of 1879 in Paris was certainly a wonderful one; and yet, before it was over, I caught that strange fever of unrest that sends birds migrating and puts the Romany tribes on the move. With me it came as a result of over-fatigue and ill-health; an instinctive craving for the medicine of change. The preceding London season had been exacting and, in Paris, I had not had a moment in which to really rest. Although the days had been filled most pleasantly and interestingly, they had been filled to over-flowing, and I was very, very tired. So, in the grip of the wanderlust, we packed our trunks and went to Aix-les-Bains. We had not the slightest idea what we would do next. My mother was not very well, either, and my coloured maid, Eliza, had to be in attendance upon her a good deal of the time, so that I was forced to consider the detail of proper chaperonage. We were in a French settlement and I was a *prima donna*, fair game for gossip and comment. Therefore, I invited a friend of mine, a charming young Englishwoman, down from Paris to visit me. She was very curious about America, I remember. She was always asking me about "the States" and was especially interested in my accounts of the anti-negro riots. The fact that they had been almost entirely instigated by the Irish Catholics in

New York excited her so that she felt obliged to go and talk with a priest in Aix about it. It was she, also, who said something one day that I thought both amusing and significant.

"My dear," she exclaimed, "tell me what are 'buttered nuts'?"

"Never heard of them," I replied.

"Oh, yes, my dear Louise, you must have! They are in all American books!"

Of course she meant *butternuts*, as I laughingly explained. A moment later she observed meditatively, "you know, I never take up an American novel that I don't read some description of food!"

I think what she said was quite true. I have remarked it since. Although I do not consider that we are a greedy nation in practice when it comes to food, we do love reading and hearing about good things to eat.

Presently, as my mother felt better and had no real need of me, I decided to take a little trip, leaving her at Aix with Eliza. Not quite by myself, of course. I never reached such a degree of emancipation as that. But I asked my English friend to go with me, and one fine day she and I set out in search of whatever entertaining thing might come our way. I had been so held down to routine all my life, my comings and goings had been so ordered and so sensible, that I deeply desired to do a bit of real gypsy wandering without the handicap of a travelling schedule. No travelling is so delightful as this sort. Don Quixote it was, if I remember rightly, who let his horse wander whithersoever he pleased, "believing that in this consisted the very being of adventures."

We went first to Geneva and so over the Simplon

Pass into Italy. We dreamed among the lakes, reading guide-books to help us decide on our next stopping-point. So, on and on, until after a while we reached Vienna. Three hours after my arrival there Alfred Fischoff, the Austrian impresario, routed me out.

"Where are you bound for?" he wanted to know.

"Nowhere. That is just the beauty of it!"

"Ah!" he commented understandingly. And then he asked, "How would you like to sing?"

Even though I was on a pleasure trip the idea allured me, for I always like to sing.

"Sing where?" I questioned.

"Here, in Vienna."

"I could n't. I don't sing in German," I objected.

"You could sing *als Gast*" (as a guest), he said.

Finally it was so arranged and, I may add, I was the only *prima donna* except Nilsson who had ever been permitted to sing in Italian at the Imperial Opera House, while the other artists sang in German. A letter from my mother to my father at that time discloses a light upon her point of view.

"Louise telegraphed for Eliza and her costumes. I thought at first she was crazy, but it appears she was sane after all. A fine Vienna engagement. . . ."

It was an undertaking to travel in Germany in those days. The German railway officials spoke nothing but German and, furthermore, they are never adaptable and quick like the Italians. In France or Italy they understood you whether you spoke their language or not; but a Teuton has to have everything translated into his own untranslatable tongue. When my mother had finally gathered together my costumes, she wrote out a long document that she had translated into German, concerning all that Eliza was to do, and where she was to go, and gave it to her so that she could produce it along the way and be passed on to the next official without explanation or complication. And after this fashion Eliza and my costumes reached me safely. She was a good traveller and a good maid. She was also very popular in that part of the world. Negroes had no particular stigma attached to them on the Continent. Many of them were no darker of hue than the Hindu and Mohammedan royalties who journeyed there occasionally. So, wherever we went, my good, dark-skinned Eliza was a real belle.

There was much to interest me in Vienna, not only as a foreign capital of note, but also as a curiosity. In a long life, and after many and diverse experiences, I never had been in a city so entirely bound up in its own interests and traditions. The luckless sinner battering vainly upon the gates of Heaven has a better fighting chance, all told, than has the ambitious outsider who aspires to social recognition by the Viennese aristocracy. If an American is ever heard to say that he or she has been received by Viennese society, those hearing the speech may laugh in their sleeve and wonder what society it was. The thing cannot be done. A handle to one's name, an estate, all the little earmarks of "nobility" are not only required but insisted on. I believe it to be a safe statement to make that no one without a title, and a title recognised by the Austrians as one of distinction, can be received into the inner circle. Even diplomatic representatives of republics are not exempt from this ruling. They may have the wealth of the Indies, and their wives may possess the beauty of Helen herself, and yet they are not admitted. For this reason Austria is a most difficult post for republican legations. Republican representatives do not stay there long. Usually, the report is that they are recalled for diplomatic reasons, or their health has failed, or some other pride-saving excuse to satisfy a democratic populace. Vienna was, and I suppose is, the dullest Court in the whole world. The German Court at one time had the distinction of being the dullest, but that has looked up a bit during the reign of the present Kaiser. But Austria! The society of Vienna has absolutely no interest in anything or anybody outside its own sacred Inner Circle.

On one occasion I was guilty of a great breach of etiquette. Meyerbeer's son-in-law, a Baron of good lineage, was calling on me, and a correspondent from *The London Daily Telegraph*, whom I had met socially and not professionally, happened to be present. Although I knew from my foreign experiences that possibly it was hardly the correct thing to do, I, not unnaturally, presented them to each other. To my surprise the Baron became stiff and the young Englishman somewhat ill at ease. I must say, however, the Englishman carried it off better than the Baron did. When the Austrian had departed, my newspaper acquaintance told me that I had committed a social *faux pas* in making them known to each other. Introductions are absolutely *taboo* between titled persons and "commoners," as they are sternly called. A baron could not meet a newspaper man!

As a case in point, an Englishman of very distintinguished connections arrived in Vienna at the time of one of the Court balls. He applied at his Embassy for an invitation, but was told that such a thing would be quite impossible. Viennese etiquette was too rigid, etc. Therefore, he did not go to the ball. But it so chanced that, a little later, when he went to call on the

British Ambassador, he mentioned, casually enough,
that he had a courtesy title but never used it when
travelling.

"Why did n't you say so?" exclaimed the Ambassador. "I could have got you an invitation quite easily,
if you had only explained that!"

Even the opera was very official and imperial. The
Court Theatre was a government house, and the
manager of it an *Intendant* and a rather grand person.
In my time he was Baron Hoffman; and he and the
Baroness asked me often to their home and placed
boxes at the opera at my disposal, this last courtesy
being one that the regular artists at the opera are
never permitted to receive. The Imperial Opera House
of Vienna is perhaps the most complete operatic organi-
sation in existence and especially, at that time, was the
company rich in fine *prime donne*. Mme. Materna
was considered to be the greatest dramatic singer then
living. Mlle. Bianchi was a marvellous *chanteuse légère*,
the equal of Gerster. Mme. Ehn was the most
poetical of *prime donne* and not unlike Nilsson. Of
Lucca's fame it is needless to speak again.

I sang seven *rôles* in Vienna: *Lucia*, the *Ballo in Maschera*, *Mignon*, *Traviata*, *Trovatore*, *Marta*, and one act
of *Hamlet*,—the mad scene, of course. It was during
Marta that I had paid to me one of the most satisfying
compliments of my life. Dr. Hanslick was then the
greatest musical critic of Europe, a distinguished and
highly cultivated musical scholar, even if he did war
against Wagner and the new school. To the astonishment of the whole theatre, between the acts, he wandered in by himself behind the scenes to call upon me
and offer his congratulations. Only one other singer
had ever been thus honoured by him before. He was

graciousness itself and, in his paper, the *Neue Frei Presse*, he wrote these memorable words:

"Miss Kellogg is an artist of the first order—the only one to compare with Patti. It is the first time since Patti has gone that we have heard what one can call singing! I congratulate Vienna on having heard such a colossal artist!"

Later, I was asked to the Hoffmans' again to meet Herr Hanslick and his wife; and they were only two of the many distinguished and interesting people that I met at the *Intendant's* house. Sonnenthal was one of them, the great actor from the Hoftheatre. And Fanny Elssler was another. I wonder how many people to-day know even the name of Fanny Elssler, the dancer who captivated the young King of Rome and lived with him for so long? There is mention of her in *L'Aiglon*. When I met her she was seventy odd, and very quiet and dull. She was vastly respected in Austria and held an exceedingly dignified position.

I learned enough German to be able to sing in German for the *Intendant* and his friends, with I know not what sort of accent. They were very polite about it always, saying more than once to me, "what a gentle accent!" But my German was dealt with less kindly by my audience one night. The spoken dialogue in *Mignon* simply had to be made comprehensible and therefore I had mastered it, as I thought, quite acceptably enough. But somewhere in it I came what our English friends call a most awful "cropper." I do not know to this day what dreadful thing I could have said, but it afforded the house an ecstasy of amusement. The whole audience laughed loudly and heartily and long; and I confess I was considerably disconcerted. But, all things considered, the Viennese audiences were satisfactory to sing to. They have one little custom, or mannerism, that is decidedly encouraging. When they like anything very much, they do not break the action by applauding, but, instead, a little soft "Ah!" goes all over the house. It was an indescribably comforting sound and spurred a singer on to do her best to please them. I sang Felina in *Mignon*, and the Viennese, to my eternal gratitude, liked me in the part. I remembered Jarrett and the "wooden gestures" he had fixed upon me in the *rôle*, and it was most satisfactory to have people in the Austrian Capitol declare that I was "an exquisite creation after Watteau!" Of course the Germans and Austrians were so wedded to Materna's rather heroic style of singing that I suppose any less strenuous methods might well have struck them as unforceful, but—*à propos* of Materna and the inevitable comparison of my work with hers—the *Fremden Blatt* was kind enough to print:

"The grand voice, the powerful high tones, and the stupendously passionate accents were not heard. Yet she knows how to sing with a full, strong voice, with high tones, and with a graceful passionateness!"

That expression "graceful passionateness" has remained in my vocabulary ever since, for it is a triumph of clumsy phraseology, even for a German paper.

I want to quote Dr. Hanslick once more;—it is such a lovely and amazing thing to quote:

"From her lips," said this illustrious critic, speaking of your humble servant, "we have heard Verdi's hardest and harshest melodies come forth refined and softened."

Is this believable? Edward Hanslick did really apply the adjectives "hard" and "harsh" to Verdi's music! It has to be read to be believed, but what he said is on file.

Speaking of "gentle accent," I had, on one occasion, the full beauty of the Teutonic language borne in upon me in a peculiarly striking form. It was in *Robert der Teufel*, that I heard in Vienna. The instance that struck me was in the great scene during which he practises magic in the cave and makes the dead to rise so that they can dance a *ballet* later on. Alice is wandering around, and the devil is in a great state of mind lest she has seen or overheard something of his magic.

"*Was hast du gesehen?*" says he.

"*Nichts!*" she replies.

"*Nichts?*" he repeats.

"*Nichts,*" insists she.

That "*Nichts!*" was repeated over and over until the whole theatre echoed and resounded with "nichts-ts-ts ts!" like spitting cats. There never was anything less musical.

"Heavens, Alfred," said I to Fischoff, who was with me at the time, "can't they change it to '*Nein?*'"

But he regarded me in a shocked manner at the very idea of so sacrilegiously altering the text!

German scores are full of loud ringing passages, built on guttural, hissing, spitting consonants. But, then, we must remember that librettists the world over are apparently men of an inferior quality of intellect who know little about music or singing. I cannot help feeling that by nature and cultivation the German writers of the texts for opera suffer from an additional handicap of traditional density. Even one of the greatest of all operas, *Faust*, suffers from being built upon a German theme. At least, I should perhaps say, it suffers in sparkle, vivacity, dramatic glitter. In the deeper, poetic meanings it remains impervious alike to time, place, and individual view-point. I never fully appreciated the *rôle* of Marguerite until I met the German people at close range. Then I learned by personal observation why she was so dull, and limited, and unimaginative. Such traits are, as I suddenly realised, not only individual; they are racial. Any middle-class girl of sixteen might of course have been deceived by Faust with the aid of Mephisto, but that Gretchen was German made the whole thing a hundred times simpler.

CHAPTER XXXI

WHEN I received my engagement to sing at the Opera in Petersburg I was much pleased. The opera seasons in Russia had for years been notably fine. Since then they have, I understand, gone off, and fewer and fewer stars of the first magnitude go there to sing. In 1880, however, it was a criterion of artistic excellence and position to have sung in the Petersburg Opera. My mother and I, a manager to represent me, my coloured maid Eliza, and some seventeen or eighteen trunks set out from Vienna; and we looked forward with pleasurable anticipation to our winter in the mysterious White Kingdom, not knowing then that it was to be one of the dreariest in our lives.

Our troubles began just before we reached Warsaw, when we had to cross the frontier. We were, of course, stopped for the examination of passports and luggage and, although the former were all right, the latter was not, according to the views of the Russian officials. I had, personally, fifteen trunks, containing the costumes for my entire *répertoire* and to watch those Russians inspect these trunks was a veritable study in suspicion. It was late at night. Unpleasant travelling incidents always happen late at night it would seem, when everything is most inconvenient and one is most tired. The Russians appeared ten times more official than the

officials of any other nation ever did, and the lateness
of the hour added to this impression. Indeed they were
highly picturesque, with their high boots and the long
skirts of their coats. The lanterns threw queer shadows,
and the wind that swept the platform had in it already
the chill of the *steppes*. I have no idea what they
believed me to be smuggling, bombs or anarchistic
literature, but they were not satisfied until they had
gone through every trunk to its uttermost depths.
Even then, when they had found nothing more dangerous than wigs and cloaks and laces, they still seemed
doubtful. The trunks might look all right; but surely
there must be something wrong with a woman who
travelled with fifteen personal trunks! And I do not
know that I altogether blame them. At all events they
were not going to let me cross the frontier without
further investigation, and I was rapidly falling into
despair when, suddenly, I had a brilliant thought. I
gave an order to my maid, who proceeded to scatter
about the entire contents of one trunk and finally
found for me a large, thin, official-looking document,
with seals and signatures attached to it. The Russians
stood about, watchful and mystified. Then I presented
my talisman triumphantly.

"The Czar!" they exclaimed in awed whispers; "the
Czar's signature!"

Whereupon several of them began bowing, almost
genuflecting, to show their respect for anyone who
possessed a paper signed by the Czar. It was only my
contract. The singers at the Russian Opera are not
engaged by an impresario, but by the Czar, and that
document which served us so well on this occasion was a
personal contract with His Imperial Majesty himself.

So we succeeded in eventually crossing the frontier

and getting into Russia, and, after that, the *espionage* became a regular thing. The spy system in Russia is beyond belief. One is watched and tracked and followed and records are kept of one, and a species of censorship is maintained of everything that reaches one. At first, one hardly realises this, for the officials have had so much practice that it is done with the most consummate skill. Every letter was opened before it reached me and then sealed up again so cleverly that it was impossible to detect it except with the keenest and most suspicious eye. Every newspaper that I received, even those mailed to me by friends in England and France, had been gone over carefully, and every paragraph referring to Russia—the army, the government, the diplomacy policy, the Nihilistic agitations—had been stamped out in solid black.

We stopped at the Hotel d'Europe, and one might think one would be free from surveillance there. Not a bit of it. We soon saw that if we wanted to talk with any freedom or privacy we should have to hang thick towels over the keyholes. And this is precisely what we did!

As soon as we reached Petersburg, I was called for a rehearsal—merely a piano affair. I went to it garmented in a long fur cloak, some flannel-lined boots that I had once bought in America for a Canadian trip, and a little bonnet perched, in the awful fashion of the day, on the very top of my head. It was early in October at this time and not any colder than our normal winter climate in the United States of America. There is but little vibration of temperature in Russia, but there are days before November when the snow melts that are very trying. This was one of them. The first thing that happened to me at that rehearsal, to which I went in my flannel-lined shoes and my little bonnet, was that a stern doctor confronted me and called me to account for the manner in which I was dressed! A doctor at a rehearsal was new to me; but it seemed that the thoughtful Czar employed two for this purpose. So many singers pretended to be ill when they really were not that His Majesty kept medical men on the spot to prove or disprove any excuses. The doctor who descended upon me was named Thomaschewski. He was the doctor mentioned in Marie Bashkirtseff's *Journal*; and he remained my friend and physician all the time I was in the city. Said he, brusquely, on this first meeting:

"Never come out dressed like that again! Get some goloshes immediately, and a hat that comes over your forehead!"

I did not understand at the moment why he insisted so strongly on the hat. I soon learned, however, what so few Americans are aware of, that it is through the forehead that one generally catches cold. As for the goloshes, it was self-evident that I needed them, and, after that morning, I never set foot out of doors in Russia without the regular protection worn by everyone in that climate. A big fur cap, tied on with a white woollen scarf arranged as we now arrange motor veils, completed the necessary outfit.

Marcella Sembrich and Lillian Nordica were both in the opera company that year. Sembrich had a small, high, clear voice at that time; but she was always the musician and well up in the Italian vocal tricks. Scalchi was there, too, and Cotogni, the famous baritone. He was a masterful singer and an amusing man, with a quaint way of putting things. He is still living in Rome and has, I am sorry to say, fallen from his

22

great estate upon hard times. The tenors were Masini and a Russian named Petrovitch, with whom I sang the *Ballo in Maschera*. They were all very frankly curious about "the American *prima donna*" and about everything concerning her. The *Intendant* of the Imperial Opera was a man with the title of Baron Küster, the son of one of the Czar's gardeners. No one could understand why he had been made a Baron, but, for some reason, he was in high favour.

My *début* was in *Traviata*, as Violetta. There was an enormous audience and the American Minister was in a stage box. Throughout the performance I never lost a sense of isolation and of chill. The strangeness, the watchfulness, the sense of apprehension with which the air seemed charged, were all on my nerves. It was said that the Opera-House had been undermined by the Nihilists and was ready to explode if the Czar entered. This idea was hardly conducive to ease of mind or cheerfulness of manner. I was glad that it was not sufficiently a gala occasion for the Czar to be present. Never before had I ever sung without having friends in front, friends who could come behind the scenes between the acts and tell me how I was doing and, if need be, cheer me up a bit. I knew nobody in the audience that first night, which gave me a most forlorn feeling, as if the place were filled with unfriendliness as well as with strangers. At last I thought of the American Minister, Mr. Foster (our legation in Russia had not yet attained the dignity of an embassy). I sent my agent to the Fosters' box, asking them to call upon me in my *loge* at the end of the opera. When he delivered the message, he was met by blank astonishment.

"Of course we should be delighted—and it is very

kind of Miss Kellogg," said Mr. Foster, "but there is not a chance that we should be allowed to do so!"

And they were not.

The vigilance, even on the stage, was something appalling. Every scene shifter and stage carpenter had a big brass number fastened conspicuously on his arm, strapped on, in fact, over his flannel shirt so that he could be easily checked off and kept track of. Everything in Russia is numbered. There are no individuals there—only units. I used to feel as if I must have a number myself; as if I, too, must soon be absorbed into that grim Monster System, and my feeling of helplessness and oppression steadily increased.

I had over twenty curtain calls that evening—the largest number I ever had. But they did not entirely repay me for the heaviness of heart from which I suffered. Never before or since was I so unhappy during a performance. The house had been undoubtedly cold at first. As an American correspondent to one of the newspapers wrote home: "The house had small confidence in an operatic singer from America, for all history of that country is silent on the subject of *prime donne*, while there is no lack of account of such other persons as Indians, Aztecs, and emigrants from the lower orders of Europe!"

In Russia they still reserve the right of hissing a singer that they do not like. It is lucky that I did not know this then, for it would have made me even more nervous than I was. My curtain calls were a real triumph. Even the ladies of the audience arose and waved their handkerchiefs, calling out many times: "Kellogg, *sola!*" They wanted me to receive the honours alone; and the gentlemen joined in their calls, "Kellogg! Kellogg! Kellogg!" until they were hoarse.

The subscribers to the opera were divided into three classes in Petersburg; and, as a singer who was popular was demanded by all the subscribers for each of the three nights, it was a novel sensation to conquer an entirely new audience each night.

In the Opera-House, as in every other house in Petersburg, one had to go through innumerable doors, one after the other. This architectural peculiarity is what makes the buildings so warm. Russians build for the cold weather as Italians build for warm. The result is that one can be colder in an Italian house than anywhere else on earth, and more correspondingly comfortable in a Russian. Even the Petersburg public Post-Office had to be approached through eight separate doorways. There were a number of other unusual features about that theatre. One was the custom of permitting the *isvoshiks* (drivers) and *mujiks* (servants) to come inside to stay while the opera was going on. It struck me as most inconsistent with the general strictness and red tape; but it was entertaining to see them stowed away in layers on ledges along the walls, sleeping peacefully until the people who had engaged them were ready to go home. Another odd thing was the odour that permeated the house. It was not an unpleasant odour; it seemed to me a little like Russia leather. I could not imagine what it was at first. Afterwards I found that it *did* come from the sheepskins worn by the *isvoshiks*. The skins are cured in some peculiar way which leaves them with this faint smell.

The thing I particularly appreciated that first night was the honour and good fortune of making my *début* with Masini, who, according to my opinion, was without exception the best tenor of his time. He would have pleased the most exacting of modern critics, for he was the true *bel canto*. It is told of him that, in the early years of his career, he sang so badly out of tune that no impresario would bother with him. So he retired, and worked, until he had not only overcome it but had also made himself into a very great artist. The night before I sang with him, I went to hear him. At first I thought his voice a trifle husky, but, before the evening was over, I did not know if it were husky or not, he sang so beautifully, his method was so perfect, his breath-control was so wonderful. It was a naturally enchanting voice besides. I have never heard a length of breath like his. No phrase ever troubled him; he had the necessary wind for anything. In *L'Africaine* there is a passage in the big tenor solo needing very careful breathing. Masini did simply what he liked with it, swelling it out roundly and generously when it seemed as if his breath must be exhausted. When the breath of other tenors gave out, Masini only just began to draw on his. I am placing all this emphasis on his method because I know breathing to be the whole secret of singing—and of living, too! Masini was a grave, kind man, not a great actor, but with a stage presence of complete repose and dignity. His manner to me was charmingly thoughtful and considerate during our work together. Yet he was a man who never spoke. I mean this literally: I cannot recall the sound of his speaking voice, although I rehearsed with him for a whole season. His greatest *rôle* was the Duke in *Rigoletto* and there was no one I ever heard who could compare with him in it.

Nordica was a young singer doing minor *rôles* that season and, both being Americans, we saw a good deal of each other and exchanged sympathies, for we equally disliked Russia. Our Yankee independence was being constantly outraged by the Russian spy system, and we were always at odds with it. One night, when we were not singing ourselves, we had a box together to hear our fellow-artists, and invited Sir Frederick Hamilton to share it with us. As we knew there was sure to be a crowd after the opera, Nordica suggested that we should leave our wraps in an empty dressing-room behind the scenes and go out by that way when the performance was over. This we accordingly did, going behind through the house by the back door of the boxes, and as a matter of course we took Sir Frederick with us. We had momentarily forgotten that in Russia one never does what one wants to, or what seems the natural thing to do. When we were discovered bringing an Englishman behind the scenes, there was nearly a revolution in that theatre!

I sang in *Traviata* four or five times in Petersburg and in *Don Giovanni* and in *Semiramide*. This last was the forty-fifth *rôle* of my *répertoire*. The Russian Opera season was less brilliant than usual that year because the Czarina had recently died and the Court was in mourning. The situation was one that afforded me some amusement. The Czar, Alexander, who was killed that same winter, had for a long time lived with the Princess Dolgoruki, as is well known, and, when the Czarina died, he married the Dolgoruki within a few weeks. To be sure, the marriage did not really count, for she could never be a Czarina because she was not royal, but she was determined to establish her social position as his wife and insisted on keeping him in the country with her at one of the out-of-the-way places. And all the time the Czar went right on with his official mourning for the Czarina! There was something about this that strongly appealed to my American sense of humour. When the Czar did finally leave the country palace and come back to Petersburg, he was in such fear of the Nihilists that he did not dare come in state, but got off the train at a way-station and drove in. Fancy the Czar of all the Russias having to sneak into his own city like that! And the worst of it was that all that vigilance was proved soon after to have been justified. Because of the situation of affairs, the Royal Box at the Opera was never occupied. Even the Czarevitch and his wife (Dagmar of Denmark, sister of Alexandra of England) could not appear. I am inclined to believe that, on the whole, Petersburg society was rather glad of the dull season. As there were no Court functions, the individual social leaders did not have to keep up their end either, and it must have been a relief, for times were hard, owing to the recent Nihilistic panic, and Russians do not know how to entertain unless they can do it magnificently. As a result of the dull social season, I did not go out much in society. But I was much interested in such glimpses as I had of it, for "smart" Russia is most gorgeously picturesque. Many Americans visit Petersburg in summer when everyone is away and so never see the true Russian life. Indeed, it is a very stunning spectacle. The sleighs, the splendid liveries, the beautiful horses, the harnesses, the superb furs—it is all like a pageant. I loved to see the *troikas* drawn by three horses, with great gold ornaments on the harnesses; and the *drozhkis* in which the *isvoshiks* drive standing up. The third horse of the *troika* is one of the typically Russian features. He is attached to the pair that does the work, and his part is to play the fool.

I remember a famous sleigh ride I had in a very

smart *drozhki*, behind a horse belonging to one of the English Embassy secretaries. The horse was an extraordinarily fast one and the *drozhki* was exceptionally light and small. The seat was so narrow that the secretary and I had to be literally buttoned into it to keep us from falling out. The *isvoshik's* seat was so high that he was practically standing erect and nearly leaning back against it. Evidently the man's directions were to show off the horse's gait to the best advantage; and I know that the speed of that frail sleigh upon the icy snow crust became so terrific that I had to grip the sash of the *isvoshik* in front of me to stay in the sleigh at all.

And, oh, the flatness and mournfulness of those chill wastes of snow outside the city! It was of course bitterly cold, but one did not feel that so much on account of the fine dryness of the air. For me the light—or, rather, the lack of it,—was the most difficult thing to become accustomed to. But if I did not altogether realise the cold for myself, I certainly realised it for my poor horses. I had a splendid pair of blacks that winter and, when I was driven down to the theatre, they would be lathered with sweat. When I came out they would be covered with ice and as white as snow. There would be ice on the harness too, and the other horses we passed were in the same condition. I was much distressed at first, but it appeared that Russian horses were quite used to it and, so I was told, actually throve on it.

Petersburg is full of little squares and in every square were heaps of logs, laid one across another like a funeral pyre, which were frequently lighted as a place for the *isvoshiks* to warm themselves. The leaping flames and the men crowded about, in such contrast to the white snow, seemed so startling and theatrical in the heart of the city that nothing could have more sharply reminded us that we were in a strange and unknown land.

The fact that the days were so unbelievably, gloomily short (dawn and bright noonday and the afternoon were unknown) grew to be very depressing. Coasting on the great ice-hills is a favourite Russian amusement, and it is a fine winter sport. But that, too, is shadowed by the strange half-light, which, to anyone accustomed to the long, bright days of more temperate lands, is always conducive to melancholy. There was no sun to speak of. Such as there was moved around in almost one place and stopped shining at four in the afternoon. I never had the least idea of the time; hardly knowing, in fact, whether it was day or night.

CHAPTER XXXII

GOOD-BYE TO RUSSIA—AND THEN?

PRINCE OLDENBURG, the Czar's cousin, was the only member of the Royal Family who could be called a patron of music and had himself composed more or less. On his seventy-fifth birthday the Imperial Opera organised a concert in his honour, that took place at the Winter Palace; and we were really quite *intriguée*, having heard of the Winter Palace for years. I said to Nordica:

"If you 'll find out how we get there, I 'll send my carriage for you and we will go together."

She found out, and we arranged to have the hotel people instruct the coachman as to the particular entrance of the palace to which he was to drive us, for he was a Russian and did not understand any other language. Once started, he had to go according to instructions or else turn around and take me back to the hotel for new directions and a fresh start. More than once have I found myself in such a dilemma. However, on this occasion, he seemed to be fairly clear as to our destination and showed gleams of intelligence when reminded that he must make no mistake, since there were only certain doors by which we could enter. The others were open only to the Royal Family and the nobility.

Among the five *prime donne* who had been invited,

346

or, rather, commanded, to appear at this function, there had been some discussion as to our costumes. All of them except myself sent for special gowns, one to Paris, one to Vienna, one to Berlin, one to Dresden —for this concert was to be before members of the Imperial Family and extra preparations had to be made.

"What are you going to wear?" Nordica asked me.

"Well," said I, "I 'll never be in Russia again—God permitting—and I shall wear a gown that I have, a creation of Worth's, made some years ago, without period or date." It was really a gorgeous affair and quite good enough, of an odd, warm, rust colour that was always very becoming to me.

We arrived at the palace before anyone else and were driven to the door indicated. There we were not permitted to enter, but were directed to yet another entrance. Again we met with the same refusal and were sent on to another door. At last we drove in under a porte-cochère and an endless stream of lackeys came out and took charge of us. When they had escorted us inside, one took one golosh, and one took another, and then they took off our furs and wraps, and there was no escape for us except by mounting the beautiful red-carpeted marble staircase. At the top of it we were met by two very good-looking young men in uniform, who received us cordially and escorted us to the ballroom, leaving us only when the other artists arrived. The other artists looked cross, I thought. At any rate, they looked somewhat ill at ease and conscious of their elegant new clothes. It was the crackling, ample period, in which it was difficult to be graceful. About the middle of the evening Dr. Thomaschewski came up to me and said:

"The Grand Duchess Olga desires me to ask who made Mlle. Kellogg's gown. She finds it the handsomest she ever saw!"

So much for my old clothes! I was thankful to be able to say the gown was a creation of Worth's; and I did not add how many years before! The next day, after the affair of the concert was pleasantly over, Nordica came into my room like a whirlwind.

"There's the d—— to pay down in the theatre!" she exclaimed breathlessly. "All the other *prime donne* are threatening to resign! And, apparently, it is our fault!"

"What have we done?"

"It seems," she went on with an appreciative chuckle, "that we came up the Royal Staircase and were received as members of the Imperial Family, while they had to come in the back way as befitted poor dogs of artists!"

"Nordica," said I, "isn't that just plain American luck! Such a thing could never happen to anybody but an American!"

We learned in due course that our handsome young men, who had been so agreeable and courteous, were Grand Dukes! But the other *prime donne* recovered from their mortification and thought better of their project of resigning.

We began to be frightfully tired of Russian food. The Russian arrangement for cold storage was very primitive. They merely froze solid anything they wanted to keep and unfroze it when it was needed for use. The staple for every day, and all day, was *gelinotte*, some sort of game. We lived on it until we were ready to starve rather than ever taste it again. It was not so bad, really, in its way, if there had not been so much of it. Some of the Russian food was possible

enough, however. The famous sour milk soup, for
instance, made of curdled milk and cabbage and, I
think, a little fish, was rather nice; and they had a pretty
way of serving *bouchers* between the soup and fish
courses. But my mother and I began to feel that we
should die if we did not have some plain American
food. In fact, we both developed a vulgar craving for
corned-beef. And, wonder of wonders! by inquiring
at a little shop where garden tools were sold, we found
the thing we longed for. As it turned out, the shop was
kept by an American and his wife; so we got our
corned-beef and my mother made delicious hash of it
over our alcohol lamp. She was famous for getting up
all manner of dainty and delicious food with a minute
saucepan and a tiny spirit flame.

The water everywhere was horrid and we were
obliged to boil it always before we dared to take a
swallow. And all these things told on my poor mother,
whose health was becoming very wretched. She came
to hate Russia and pined to get away. So I tried to
break my contract and leave (considering my mother's
health a sufficiently valid reason), but, although money
was due me that I was willing to forfeit, I found I could
not go until I had sung out the full term of my engagement. I was so wrathful at this that I went to see
the American Minister about leaving in spite of everything; but even he was powerless to help us. Apparently
the Russians were accustomed to having their country
prove too much for foreign singers, for the Minister
remarked meditatively:

"Finland used to be open, but so many artists
escaped that way that it is now closed!"

It proved to be even harder to get out of Russia than
it had been to get in. One mother and daughter whom

I knew went to five hotels in twenty-four hours, trying to evade the officials, so as to leave without the usual red tape; but they were kept merciless track of everywhere and their passports sent for at every one of the five. Such proceedings must be rather expensive for the government. Some Russian friends of mine once came to Aix without notifying their governmental powers and were sent for to come back within twenty-four hours. Fancy being kept track of like that! I am devoutly thankful that I do not live under a *paternal* government. In time, however, we did succeed in obtaining permission to leave Russia; and profoundly glad were we of it. I had but one desire before we left that dark and frigid land forever, and that was to see the Czar just once. My friends of the English Embassy told me that my best chance would be on the route between the Winter Palace and the Military Riding Academy, where the Czar went every Sunday to stimulate horsemanship. So I started out the following Sunday, alone, in my brougham.

There were crowds of the faithful blocking the way everywhere—well interspersed with Nihilists, I have little doubt. Russian men are, on the whole, impressive in appearance; big and fierce and immensely virile. They are half-savage, anyway. The better class wear coats lined and trimmed with black or silver fur; while a crowd of soldiers and peasants make a most picturesque sight. On this occasion the cavalry and mounted police patrolled the route, and ranks of soldiers were drawn up on either side. Yet there was such a surging populace that, in spite of all the military surveillance, there was some confusion. I was driven up and down very slowly. Then I grew cold and got out of the carriage to walk for a short distance. I had gone but a little way and was turning back when I felt a hand on my shoulder. It was an official who informed me that I might drive but could not be permitted to walk! So I re-entered the brougham and was driven again, up and down, bowing sweetly each time to the officer who had halted me and dared to take me by the shoulder. And, finally, I caught only a glimpse of the Czar, through the hosts of guardians that surrounded him like a cloud. I could not believe that he cared for all that pomp and ceremony, for he was a weary-looking man and I felt sorry for him. I believe that he would have been as democratic as anyone could well be if he could only have had half a chance. The wife of the shop-keeper who sold garden tools told me that the Czar was perfectly accessible to them and very friendly. He liked new inventions and patents and ingenious farming implements and American machine inventions. A man I once knew had been trying for months to obtain an official introduction at Court in order to exploit a patent which he thought would interest His Majesty, and in vain. But, when he chanced to meet a friend of the Czar's in a picture gallery and told him about his idea, he had no further difficulty. His Minister, who had told him it was hopeless to try to get access to the Czar, was amazed to find him going about at the Court balls in the most intimate manner.

"How did you do it?" he demanded. "How did you manage to reach the Czar?"

"Just met him through a friend as I would any other fellow," was the reply.

We were in Petersburg at the Christmas and New Year's celebrations, which are held two weeks later than ours are. The customs were odd and interesting— notably the one of driving out in a sleigh to "meet the

New Year coming in." This pretty custom was always observed by Mme. Helena Modjeska and her husband, Count Bozenta, even in America. I went to services in several of the churches, where I heard divine singing, unaccompanied by any instrument. The vibrations were very slow and throbbed like the tones of an organ. Nothing can be more splendid than bass voices. The decorations of the churches were strange and barbaric to eyes accustomed to the Italian and French cathedrals. The savagery as well as the orientalism of the Russians comes out in a curious way in their ecclesiastical architecture. The walls were often inlaid with lapis and malachite, like the decorations of some Eastern temple, and the *ikons* were painted gaudily upon metals. There were no pews of any sort; the populace dropped upon its knees and stayed there.

The little wayside shrines erected over every spot where anything tragic had ever happened to a royal person are an interesting feature of worship in Russia. As the rulers of Russia have usually passed rather calamitous lives, there are plenty of these shrines, and loyal subjects always kneel and make them reverence. I could see one of these shrines from my window in the Hotel d' Europe and marvelled at the devout fervour of the kneeling men in their picturesque cloaks, praying for this or some other Emperor, with the thermometer far below zero. It was always the men who prayed. I do not remember ever seeing a woman on her knees in the snow.

Our experiences in the shops of Petersburg were sometimes interesting. Of course in the larger ones French was spoken, and also German, but in the small places where "notions" were sold, or writing materials, only Russian was understood. To facilitate the shopping of foreigners, little pictures of every conceivable thing for sale were hung outside the shops. All one had to do was to point to the reproduction of a spool, or a safety pin, or an egg, or a trunk, and produce a pocketbook. One day my mother wanted some shoe buttons and we wagered that she could not buy them unaided. I felt sure there would be no painting of a shoe button on the shop wall. But she came back victoriously with the buttons, quite proud of herself because she had thought of pointing to her own boots instead of wasting time hunting among the pictures.

It was the collection of Colonel Villiers that first awakened in me an interest in old silver, and the beginning I made in Russia that winter ended in my possessing a collection of value and beauty. Villiers was a member of the Duke of Buckingham's family and was a Queen's Messenger, a position of responsibility and trust. And I had several other friends at the British Embassy. Lord and Lady Dufferin I knew; and one of the secretaries, Mr. Alan, now Sir Alan Johnston, who married Miss Antoinette Pinchot, sister of Gifford Pinchot, I had first met in Vienna. The night that Villiers arrived in Petersburg (before I had met him) some of the English *attachés* had been invited to dine with us; but the First Secretary arrived at the last moment to explain that the Queen's Messenger was expected with private letters and that they had to be received in person and handed in at Court promptly.

"It's the only way they have of sending really private letters, you see," he explained. "Alexandra probably wants to tell Dagmar about the children's last attacks of indigestion, so we have to stay at home to receive the letters!"

Well—the glad day did finally come when my mother

23

and I turned our backs on Russia and its eternal twilight and repaired to Nice for a little amusement and recuperation after the Petersburg season. A number of our friends were there, and it was unusually gay. I was warmly welcomed and congratulated, for Petersburg had put the final *cachet* upon my success. Although I might win other honours, I could win none that the world appraised more highly than those that had come to me that year. In a letter to my father, from Nice, my mother says:

The Grand Duke Nicholas has been here in our hotel a month, and his two sons and suite, doctor, *Aide-de-camp*, and servants. There is an inside balcony running two sides of the hotel which is lovely; but the whole is square with other rooms—this width carpeted—sofa—chairs—table—a glass roof. We all assemble there after dinner, and sit around and talk, take *café* and tea on little tables. . . . We sat every day after dinner close to the Grand Duke (the Czar's brother) and his suite; knew his doctor and finally the Duke and his sons. I was sitting on the balcony, because I could see everybody who came in or who went out, and I was looking down and saw the Grand Duke receive the despatch of the assassination—and the commotion and emotion was the most exciting thing I ever witnessed. The Grand Duke is a most amiable gentleman, sweet and good as a man can be; his son, sixteen, was the loveliest and most gentle and affectionate of sons. I looked at the Duke all the time. I was almost upset myself by the excitement. Despatches came every twenty minutes. I looked on—sat there *seven hours*. As the Russians outside heard of it they would come in—I saw two women cry—the Duke stayed in his room—I heard that he had fainted—he is in somewhat delicate health. . . . It seemed as if the others were looking around for their friends and for sympathy, as was natural. I had not talked much with the Doctor because

I never felt equal to it in French—especially on ordinary subjects of conversation—but he looked up and saw me on the balcony and came directly to me. I took both his hands—the tears came into his eyes—and we *talked*—the words came to me, enough to show him we were his friends. I said America would sympathise with Russia. He seemed pleased and said, "Yes; but Angleterre, no!" I did not have much to say to that. But I did him good. He told Louise and me the particulars. We both knew the very spot near the bridge where the Czar had fallen. Our sympathy was mostly with the man whose brother had been murdered and his friends. There was a long book downstairs in which people who came in wrote their names from time to time. I do not understand it exactly, but Louise says it contains the names of those who feel an allegiance. Many Russians came in the day of the assassination and wrote their names. Our Consul wrote his, and a beautiful sentence of sympathy. He wanted to lower our flag, but dared not, quite. Louise and I went down and wrote ours—and, while standing, the Duke's physician said to us that there had not been one English name signed. The hotel is all English, nearly. It was an interesting, eventful day. The Duke was pleased when Louise told him his people had been very kind to her in Russia at Petersburg. They all left day before yesterday at 6 P.M.

The assassination of the Czar took place three weeks to the day from that Sunday when I had seen him. It all came back to me very clearly, of course—the troops, the crowding people, and the snow. No wonder they were watchful of him, poor man!

The bottom dropped out of the season at Nice and people began to flit away. The tragedy of the Czar's death spread a shadow over everything. Nobody felt much like merry-making or recreation, and, again, I was becoming restless—restless in a new way.

"Mother," I said, "let's go back to America. I have had enough of Nice and Petersburg and Paris and Vienna and London. I'm tired to death of foreign countries and foreign ways and foreign audiences and foreign honours. I want to go home!"

"Thank God!" said my mother.

CHAPTER XXXIII

THE LAST YEARS OF MY PROFESSIONAL CAREER

A T Villefranche, on our way to Nice, I had been given a formal reception by the officers of the flagship *Trenton*, that was then lying in the harbour. Admiral Dahlgren was in command, and the reception was more of a tribute to the *prima donna* than a personal tribute. It was arranged under the auspices of Lieutenant Emory and Lieutenant Clover; and I did not sing. Emory was a natural social leader and the whole affair was perfect in detail. A much more interesting reception, however, arranged by Lieutenant Emory, was the informal one given me by the same hosts not long after. Although informal, it was conducted on the same lines of elegance that marked every social function with which Emory was ever connected. As soon as we appeared on the gun deck, accompanied by Lieutenant-Commander Gridley, to be presented to Captain Ramsay, the orchestra greeted us with the familiar strains of *Hail, Columbia!* At the end of the *déjeuner* the whole crew contemplated us from afar as I conversed with our hosts, and, realising what might be expected of me, I sang, as soon as the orchestra had adjusted their instruments, the solo of Violetta from *Traviata: Ah force e lui che l'anima*. As an *encore* I sang *Down on the Suwanee River*. The orchestra not being able to accompany me, I accompanied myself

357

on a banjo that happened to be handy. I was told afterwards that "the one sweet, familiar plantation melody was better to us than a dozen Italian cavatinas." After the *Suwanee River*, I sang yet another negro melody, *The Yaller Gal Dressed in Blue*, which was received with much appreciative laughter.

On our way from Nice we went to Milan to visit the Exposition, which was an artistically interesting one, and at which we happened to see the father and mother of the present King of Italy. From Milan we went to Aix-les-Bains; and from there to Paris.

I returned to America without an engagement; but on October 5th the Kellogg Concert Company, under the management of Messrs. Pond and Bachert, gave the first concert of a series in Music Hall, Boston. I was supported by Brignoli, the "silver-voiced tenor," Signor Tagliapietra, and Miss Alta Pease, contralto. With us, also, were Timothie Adamowski, the Polish violinist; Liebling, the pianist, and the Weber Quartette. My reception in America, after nearly two years' absence abroad, was, really, almost an ovation. But I want to say that Boston has always been particularly gracious and cordial to me. By way of showing how appreciative was my reception, I cannot resist giving an extract from the *Boston Transcript* of the following morning:

Her singing of her opening number, Filina's *Polonaise* in *Mignon*, showed at once that she had brought back to us unimpaired both her voice and her exquisite art; that she is now, as formerly, the wonderfully finished singer with the absolutely beautiful and true soprano voice. Her stage experience during the past few years, singing taxing grand soprano parts, so different and more trying to the vocal physique than the light florid parts, the Aminas, Zerlinas, and Elviras, she began by singing, seems to have had no injurious effect upon the quality and trueness of her voice, which has ever been fine and delicate; just the sort of beautiful voice which one would fear to expose to much intense dramatic wear and tear. Its present perfect purity only proves how much may be dared by a singer who can trust to a thoroughly good method.

In the following May I sang with Max Strakosch's opera company in Providence to an exceptionally large audience. One of the daily newspapers of the city said, in reference to this occasion:

Miss Kellogg must take it as a compliment to herself personally, for the other artists were unknown here, and therefore it must have been her name that attracted so many. She has always been popular here, and has made many personal as well as professional friends. She must have added many more of the latter last night, for she never appeared to better advantage. She was well supported by Signor Giannini as Faust [we gave *Faust* and I was Marguerite] and Signor Mancini as Mephistopheles.

This same year, 1882, I went on a concert trip through the South. In New Orleans I had a peep into the wonderful pawnshops, large, spacious, all filled with beautiful things. I had long been a collector of pewter and silver and old furniture and, on this trip, took advantage of some of my opportunities. For instance, I bought the bureau that had belonged to Barbara Frietchie, and a milk jug and some spoons that had belonged to Henry Clay. Also, I visited Libby Prison and various other prisons, a battle-field, and several cemeteries. One cemetery was half filled with the graves of boys of seventeen, eighteen, and nineteen years of age, showing that in the Civil War the South could not have kept it up much longer. The sight was pitiful!

In 1884 I went on a concert tour with Major Pond in the West, making of it so far as we could, as Pond said, something of a picnic. We crossed by the Northern Pacific, seeing, I remember, the ranch of the Duc de Morney, son of the Duc de Morney who was one of Louis Philippe's creations, and who had married the daughter of a wealthy ranchman, Baron von Hoffman. The house of his ancestor in the Champs Élysées and the house next door that he built for his mistress were points of interest in Paris when I first went there. In Miles City, on the way to Helena, Montana, we visited some of the gambling dens, and were interested in learning that the wildest and worst one in the place was run by a Harvard graduate. The streets of the town were strangely deserted and this we did not understand until a woman said to me:

"Umph! they don't show themselves when respectable people come along!"

My memory of the trip and of the Yellowstone Park consists of a series of strangely beautiful and primitive pictures. We passed through a prairie fire, when the atmosphere was so hot and dense that extra pressure of steam was put on our locomotive to rush our train through it. Never before had I seen Indian women carrying their papooses. I particularly recall one settlement of wigwams on a still, wonderful evening, the chiefs gorgeous in their blankets, when the fires were being lighted and the spirals of smoke were ascending straight up into the clear atmosphere. One day a couple of Indians ran after the train. They looked very fine as they ran and finally succeeded in getting on to the rear platform, where they rode for some distance. At Deer Lodge I sang all of one evening to two fine specimens of Indian manhood. We went down the Columbia River in a boat, greatly enjoying the impressive scenery. One of my most vivid mental impressions was that of an Indian fisherman, standing high out over the rushing waters, at least forty feet up, on a projection of some kind that had been built for the purpose of salmon fishing, his graceful, vigorous bronze form clearly silhouetted against the background of rock and foliage and sky. On the banks of the river farther along we saw a circus troupe boiling their supper in a huge caldron and smoking the *kalama* or peace pipe. I was so hungry I wanted to eat of the caldron's contents but, on second thoughts, refrained. And we stopped at Astoria where the canning of salmon was done, a town built out over the river on piles. The forest fires had caused some confusion and, for one while, we could hardly breathe because of the smoke. Indeed we travelled days and days through that smoke. The first cowboy I ever saw drove me from the station of Livingston through Yellowstone Park. In Butte City my company went down into the Clarke Copper Mine, but I did not care to join them in the undertaking. Our first sight of Puget Sound was very beautiful. And it was at Puget Sound that I first saw half-, or, rather, quarter-breeds. I remember Pond saying how quickly the half-breeds die of consumption.

Later, that same year, I went South again on another concert tour. All through the State of Mississippi there was a strange, horrible flavour to the food, I recall, and, so all-pervading was this flavour that finally I could hardly eat anything. The contralto and I were talking about it one day on the train and saying how glad we should be to get away from it. There being no parlour-cars, we were in an ordinary coach, and a woman who sat in front of me and overheard us, turned around and said:

"*I* know what you mean! *I* can tell you what it is. It's cotton seed. Everything tastes of cotton seed in this country. They feed their cows on it, and their chickens. *Everything* tastes of it; eggs, butter, biscuits, milk!"

This was true. The only thing, it seems, that could not be raised on cotton seed was fruit; and unfortunately it was not a fruit season when I was there.

The recollection of this trip necessitates my saying a little something of Southern hospitality. I was not satisfied with any of the arrangements that had been made for me. I had also taken a severe cold, and, when we reached Charlottesville, where we were to give a concert, I said I would not go on. This brought matters to a climax. I simply would not and could not sing in the condition I was; and declared I would not be subjected to any such treatment as the insistence of the management. The end of it was that I took my maid and started for New York.

The trip at first promised to be a very uncomfortable one. Travelling accommodations were poor; food was difficult to obtain, and I was nearly ill. At one point, where the opening of a new bridge had just taken place, we stopped, and I noticed a private car attached to our train, which I coveted. Imagine my gratitude and pleasure, therefore, when the porter presently came to me and said courteously that "Colonel Cawyter" sent his compliments and invited me into his private car. I accepted, of course. But this was not all. As I was making inquiries about train connections and facilities for food, of one of the gentlemen in the car, he realised what was before me, and said that I could go to his home where his wife would care for me. I protested, but he insisted and gave me his card. When we reached the station, I took a carriage and drove to the house, where I was received very courteously. It was a simple household of a mother, grandmother, and children, and they had already lunched when I got there. But they piled on more coal, and in a very short time made me a lunch that was simply delicious—all so easily, simply, and naturally, in spite of the haphazard fashion in which they seemed to live, as to quite win my admiration. And this incident of Southern hospitality enabled me to proceed on my way nourished and restored.

Another incident that I recall was of a similar nature in its fundamental kindness. I had no money with which to pay for my berth, and was asking the conductor if there was anyone who would cash a check for me, when a perfect stranger offered me the amount I needed. At first I refused, but finally consented to accept the loan in the same spirit in which it had been offered.

On the reorganised version of this trip we went down into Texas, giving concerts in Waco, Dallas, Cheyenne, San Antonio, and Galveston, among other places. This was before the wonderful railroad had been built that runs for miles through the water; and before the tidal wave that wiped the old Galveston out of existence. At Cheyenne, I remember, we had to ford a river to keep our engagement. At Waco a negro was found under the bed of one of the company; a bridge was burning; and a *posse* of men, with bloodhounds, was starting out to track the incendiaries. I remember speaking there with a negro woman who had a white child in her charge. The child was busily chewing gum and the woman told me that often the child would put her hand on her jaw saying, "Oh, I 'm *so* tired!" But she could not be induced to stop chewing! At Dallas we sang in a hall that had a tin roof, and, during the concert, a terrific thunderstorm came on, so that I had to stop singing. This is the only time, I believe, that the elements ever succeeded in drowning me out. I never before had seen adobe houses, and I found San Antonio very interesting, and drove as far as I could along the road of the old Spanish Missions that maintain the traditions and aspects of the Spanish in the New World. The Southern theatres are the dirtiest places that can be imagined; and I recall eating opossum that was served to us with great pride by my waiter.

From this time on I did not contemplate any long engagements. I did not care for them, although I sometimes went to places to sing—and to collect pewter!

I never formally retired from public life, but quietly stopped when it seemed to me the time had come. It was a Kansas City newspaper reporter who incidentally brought home to me the fact that I was no longer very young. I had a few grey hairs, and, after an interview granted to this representative of the press—a woman, by the way—I found, on reading the interview in print the next day, that my grey hairs had been mentioned.

"They 'll find that my voice is getting grey next," I said to myself.

I really wanted to stop before everybody would be saying, "You ought to have heard her sing ten years ago!"

Carl Strakosch
From a photograph by H. W. Barnett

The last time I saw Patti I said to her:

"Adelina, have you got through singing?"

"Oh, I still sing for *mes pauvres* in London," she replied; but she did n't explain who were her poor.

On my last western concert tour I sang at Oshkosh. A special train of three cars on the Central brought down a large delegation for the occasion from Fond du Lac, Ripon, Neenah and Menasha, Appleton and other neighbouring towns. The audience was in the best of humour and a particularly sympathetic one. At the close of the concert I remarked that it was one of the finest audiences I ever sang to. And I added, by way of pleasantry, that, having sung at Oshkosh, I was now indeed ready to leave the stage!

But there were even more serious reasons that influenced me in my decision, one of which was that my mother had for some time past been in a poor state of health. More than once, when I went to the theatre, I had the feeling that she might not be alive when I returned home; and this was a nervous strain to me that, combined with a severe attack of bronchitis, brought about a physical condition which might have had seriously lasting results if I had not taken care of myself in time.

It was not easy to stop. When each autumn came around, it was very difficult not to go back to the public. I had an empty feeling. There is no sensation in the world like singing to an audience and knowing that you have it with you. I would not change my experience for that of any crowned head. The singer and the actor have, at least, the advantage over all other artists of a personal recognition of their success; although, of course, the painter and writer live in their work while the singer and the actor become only traditions. But such traditions! On the subject of the actor's traditions Edwin Booth has written:

> In the main, tradition to the actor is as true as that which the sculptor perceives in Angelo, the painter in Raphael, and the musician in Beethoven. . . . Tradition, if it be traced through pure channels and to the fountain-head, leads one as near to Nature as can be followed by her servant, Art. Whatever Quinn, Barton Booth, Garrick, and Cooke gave to stagecraft, or as we now term it, "business," they received from their predecessors; from Betterton and perhaps from Shakespeare himself, who, though not distinguished as an actor, well knew what acting should be; and what they inherited in this way they bequeathed in turn to their art and we should not despise it. Kean knew without seeing Cooke, who in turn knew from Macklin, and so back to Betterton, just what to do and how to do it. Their great Mother Nature, who reiterates her teachings and preserves her monotone in motion, form, and sound, taught them. There must be some similitude in all things that are True!

The traditions of singing are not what they used to be, however, for the new school of opera does not require great finish, although it does demand greater dramatic art. It used to be that Tetrazzinis could make successes through coloratura singing alone; but to-day coloratura singing has no great hold on the public after the novelty has worn off. But it does very well in combination with heavier music, as in Mozart's *Magic Flute* or *The Huguenots*, and so modern singers have to be both coloraturists and dramaticists. *A propos* of singing and methods, I append a newspaper interview that a reporter had with me in Paris, 1887. He had been shown a new dinner dress of white *moire* with ivy leaves woven into the tissue, and writes:

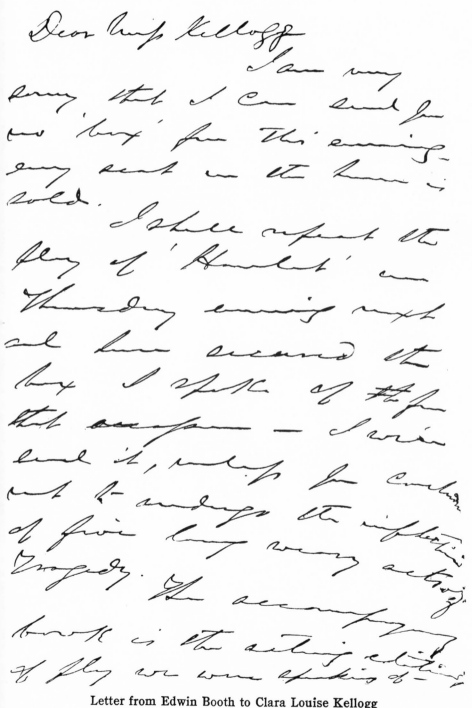

Thursday

Dear Miss Kellogg

I am very sorry, that I can send you no 'box' for This evening, — every seat in the house is sold.

I shall repeat the play of 'Hamlet' on Thursday evening next and have secured the box I spoke of for you that occasion — I will send it, unless you conclude not to undergo the infliction of five long weary acts of Tragedy. The accompanying book is the acting edition of play we were speaking of —

Letter from Edwin Booth to Clara Louise Kellogg

I examined the rustling treasure critically and decided it was a complete success. The train was long, the stuff rich, the taste perfect, and yet—the great essential was wanting. I could not but reflect on the transformation which would come over that regal robe were it once hung on the shapely shoulders of the famous *prima donna*.

"You see, there is nothing like singing to fill out dresses where they should be filled out, and conversely," said Sbriglia, who happened to be present as we came back into the *salon*; "consequently my advice to all ladies who wish to improve their figure is to take vocal lessons."

"Yes," agreed Miss Kellogg, "if they can only find right instruction. But, unfortunately good teachers nowadays are rarer than good voices. Even the famous Paris Conservatory does n't contain good vocal instruction. If there be any teaching in the world which is thoroughly worthless, it is precisely that given in the Rue Bergère. But I cannot do justice to the subject. Do give us your ideas, Professor, about the Paris Conservatory and the French School of voice culture."

"As to any French vocal school," replied Sbriglia, "there is none. Each professor has a system of his own that is only less bad than the system of some rival professor. One man tells you to breathe up and down and another in and out. One claims that the musical tones are formed in the head, while another locates them in the throat. And when these gentlemen receive a fresh, untrained voice, their first care is to split it up into three distinct parts which they call registers, and for the arrangement of which they lay down three distinct sets of rules.

"As to the Conservatory, it is a national disgrace; and I have no hesitation in saying that it not only does no good, but is actually the means of ruining hundreds of fine voices. Look at the results. It is from the Conservatory that the Grand Opera chooses its French singers, and the simple fact is that in the entire *personnel* there are no great French artists. There are artists from Russia, Italy, Germany, and America, but there are none from France. And yet the most talented students of the Conservatory make their *débuts* there every year with fine voices and brilliant prospects; but, as a famous critic has well said, 'after singing for three years under the system which they have been taught, they acquire a perfect "style" and lose their voice.'

"You ask me what I consider to be the correct method. I dislike very much the use of the word 'method,' because it seems to imply something artificial; whereas in all the vocal processes, there is only a single logical method and that is the one taught us all by nature at our birth. Watch a baby crying. How does he breathe? Simply by pushing the abdomen forward, thus drawing air into the lungs, to fill the vacuum produced, and then bringing it back again, which expels the air. And every one breathes that way, except certain advocates of theoretical nonsense, who have learned with great difficulty to exactly reverse this operation. Such singers make a bellows of the chest, instead of the abdomen, and, as the strain to produce long sounds is evidently greater in forcing the air out than in simply drawing it in, their inevitable tendency is to unduly contract the chest and to distend the abdomen."

"Let me give you an illustration of the truth of M. Sbriglia's argument," said Miss Kellogg, rising from her seat. "Now watch me as I utter a musical note." And immediately the rich voice that has charmed so many thousands filled the apartment with a clear "a-a-a-a" as the note grew in volume.

"You see Miss Kellogg has little to fear from consumption!" exclaimed Sbriglia. "And I am convinced that invalids with disorders of the chest would do well to stop taking drugs and study the art of breathing and singing."

"And even those who have no voice," said Miss Kellogg, "would by this means not only improve in health and looks, but would also learn to read and speak correctly, for the same principles apply to all the vocal processes. It is astonishing how few people use the voice properly. For instance I could read in this tone all the afternoon without fatigue, but if I were to do this" (making a perceptible change in the position of her head), "I should begin to cough before finishing a column. Don't you notice the difference? In the one case the sounds come from here" (touching her chest) "and are free and musical; but in the other, I seem to speak in my throat, and soon feel an irritation there which makes me want the traditional glass of sugar and water."

"The irritation which accompanies what you call 'speaking in the throat,'" explained Sbriglia, "is caused by pressing too hard upon the vocal cords, that become, in consequence, congested with blood, instead of remaining white as they should be. Persons who have this habit grow hoarse after very brief vocal exertion, and it is largely for that reason that American men rarely make fine singers. On the other hand, look at Salvini, who, by simply knowing how to place his voice, is able to play a tremendous part like Othello without the slightest sense of fatigue.

"About the American 'twang'? Oh, no, it does not injure the voice. On the contrary, this nasal peculiarity, especially common among your women, is of positive value in a proper production of certain tones."

24

CODA

THE Coda in music is, literally, the tail of the composition, the finishing off of the piece. The influence of Wagner did away with the Coda: yet, as my place in the history of opera is that of an exponent of the Italian rather than the German form, I feel that a Coda, or a last few words of farewell, is admissible.

In some ways the Italian opera of my day seems banal. Yet Italian opera is not altogether the thing of the past that it is sometimes supposed to be. More and more, I believe, is it coming back into public favour as people experience a renewed realisation that melody is the perfect thing, in art as in life. I believe that *Mignon* would draw at the present time, if a good cast could be found. But it would be difficult to find a good cast.

Italian opera did what it was intended to do:—it showed the art of singing. It was never supposed to be but an accompaniment to the orchestra as German opera often is; an idea not very gratifying to a singer, and sometimes not to the public. Yet we can hardly make comparisons. Personally, I like German opera and many forms of music beside the Italian very much, even while convinced of the fact that German critics are not the whole audience. At least, the opera could not long be preserved on them alone.

It seems to me as I look back over the preceding pages that I have put into them all the irrelevant

" Elpstone "
New Hartford, Connecticut

matter of my life and left out much that was important. Many of my dearest *rôles* I have forgotten to
mention, and many of my most illustrious acquaintances I have omitted to honour. But when one has
lived a great many years, the past becomes a good deal
like an attic: one goes there to hunt for some particular
thing, but the chances are that one finds anything and
everything except what one went to find. So, out of my
attic, I have unearthed ever so many unimportant
heirlooms of the past, leaving others, perhaps more
valuable and more interesting, to be eaten by moths
and corrupted by rust for all time.

There is very little more for me to say. I do not
want to write of my last appearances in public. Even
though I did leave the operatic stage at the height of
my success, there is yet something melancholy in the
end of anything. As Richard Hovey says:

> There is a sadness in all things that pass;
> We love the moonlight better for the sun,
> And the day better when the night is near.
> The last look on a place where we have dwelt
> Reveals more beauty than we dreamed before,
> When it was daily . . .

In our big, young country of America there are the
possibilities of many another singer greater than I have
been. I shall be proud and grateful if the story of my
high ambitions, hard work, and kindly treatment should
chance to encourage one of these. For, while it is true
that there is nothing that should be chosen less lightly
than an artistic career, it is also true that, having
chosen it, there is nothing too great to be given up for
it. I have no other message to give; no further lesson
to teach. I have lived and sung, and, in these memories,

have tried to tell something of the living and the singing: but when I seek for a salient and moving word as a last one, I find that I am dumb. Yet I feel as I used to feel when I sang before a large audience. Somewhere out in the audience of the world there must be those who are in instinctive sympathy with me. My thoughts go wandering toward them as, long ago, my thoughts would wander toward the unknown friends sitting before me in the theatre and listening. So poignant is this sense within me that, halting as my message may have been, I feel quite sure that somehow, here and there, some one will hear it, responsive in the heart.

INDEX